John Petherick

Travels in Central Africa, and Explorations of the Western Nile Tributaries

Vol. II

John Petherick

Travels in Central Africa, and Explorations of the Western Nile Tributaries
Vol. II

ISBN/EAN: 9783337083892

Printed in Europe, USA, Canada, Australia, Japan

Cover: Foto ©Andreas Hilbeck / pixelio.de

More available books at **www.hansebooks.com**

TRAVELS IN CENTRAL AFRICA,

AND

EXPLORATIONS

OF THE

WESTERN NILE TRIBUTARIES.

BY

MR. AND MRS. PETHERICK.

WITH APPENDICES ON FRESH-WATER TURTLE, FISHES OF THE NILE, ETC.
BY DRS. GRAY AND GÜNTHER.

IN TWO VOLUMES.

VOL. II.

LONDON:
TINSLEY BROTHERS,
18 CATHERINE STREET, STRAND.
1869.

CONTENTS.

FROM PETHERICK'S NOTE-BOOK.

	Page
My wife attacked by typhus fever—She is delirious—Once more on the Nile .	1
The men's careful tendance of *Sitta Madame*—We enter the Sobât—Depth and width of river, and rate of current	2
The Shillooks of the White Nile—Their habits and customs	3
The Sultan and his Council—A singular custom	4
The Djibba, their weapons and ornaments	5
A warlike negro race	6
The Nuba race, comprising the Bonjack and Shillook—"Civilizing effects of Egyptian sway"—The policy of "amity and commerce"	7
Moosa Pasha enforces the payment of an impost from Melik, Nassur of Tekkela—A refusal, and desperate encounter	8
Moosa Pasha's inhuman treatment of prisoners—Negro adoption of Mahommedanism	9
The Nuba population—Ignorance and superstition—Description of an idol .	10
The Dinka, their habits and customs	11

MRS. PETHERICK RESUMES HER JOURNAL.

The comfort of returning health—Ruins of the village of Mahommed Cheir—Defeat of the oppressor	12
Birket il Djebelein mountains—We meet boat-loads of slaves—A piteous sight—Arrive at Donagla—Meet Monsieur de Pryssenaere	13
A present of birds	14

EXTRACTS FROM LETTERS.
(From June, 1863, to April, 1865.)

Return to Khartoum	15
Wearying for news from home—Intelligence of the death of Dean Littler .	16
Petherick is troubled—The guinea-worm	17

CONTENTS.

	Page
A post arrives—Extract from a letter from Madame Tinné	18
False friends—Treachery working against Petherick.	19
We dine with Speke and Baker—Conversation respecting the "succour dodge"	20
The "Kathleen" leaves Khartoum—The Pasha's impost upon soldiers, sailors, &c.—Petherick objects to the same	21
The Pasha threatens to seize the *dahabyeh* of the Dutch lady travellers—Miss Capellan overwhelmed with grief	22
How we spent Christmas Day—New Year's Day—Injustice towards Petherick	23
Dispatch a messenger to the Sultan of Darfour—Petherick's anxiety to ascertain the fate of Dr. Vogel—Consul Cameron's position—Petherick's offer to proceed to Abyssinia to negotiate for release of captives—Abolition of the British Consulate at Khartoum	24
Petherick's trade summarily stopped—The aggressive policy of the Viceroy	25
A touching incident—"We are going home"	26
Christmas tree—Thoughts of dear old England	27
Our sale of goods—Meet Mr. Joyce	28
Missionaries from Abyssinia—Kallakla on the White Nile	29
Intense heat, a trying journey in view—An *al fresco* dinner	30
Consul Cameron a prisoner—Death of Madame Tinné	31
Miss Capellan returns to Khartoum—Meet Baron d'Ablaing and Baron Heuglin	32
Miss Tinné's boat arrives with its melancholy freight—Great lamentation	33
Hot winds of Kallakla—We return to Khartoum	34
Arrival of De Bono's boats from Gondokoro—News of Baker—Result of the message to the Sultan of Darfour	35
Petherick's communication with Dr. Petermann, Secretary of the Geographical Society of Gotha, respecting the fate of Dr. Vogel and Herr Beurmann	36
Letter to Dr. Petermann—Particulars of the death of Dr. Vogel	37—40
Translation of the seal and letter from the Sultan of Darfour	41
Note to MS. on Vogel and Beurmann, published by Dr. Petermann	42
Extracts of letters resumed—Death of Adrienne, Baronne de Capellan	43
Moosa Pasha's conduct towards Petherick—My last letter from Khartoum—A painful parting from our servants	44

FROM PETHERICK'S NOTE-BOOK.

The commencement of our homeward journey	45
The Blue Nile—Miss Tinné and Von Heuglin accompany us—Our *reis's* present	46
Arab hospitality—Reach Damir—Substantial presents from the chief	47
Arrive at Berber—Difficulty of procuring camels for the desert journey—More of Moosa Pasha's base conduct	48
Biography of Moosa Pasha	49
The Pasha's hatred of mankind	50
Moosa Pasha's conduct as Governor of Keneh in Upper Egypt	51

CONTENTS.

	Page
Miss Tinné and suite proceed overland to Sonakim—The Djebel Mezzum	52
An old hag's superstitions—A Pagan stronghold	53
Cataract of Aboo Simoon—Bewitching little islands	54
Lovely scenery—Hard rowing	55
Our boat caught in a whirlpool, my wife in a fainting condition—The Chor Koodi—Presents from the Sheikh	56
An obliging schoolmaster—The date-palm and its cultivation	57

EXTRACTS FROM LETTERS RESUMED.

The "Kathleen" dispatched to Korosko with our pet birds . . . 58
A singular ceremony—Aboo Hamed—Petherick's anxiety for my journey across the desert 59
Kindness of Miss Tinné—I have a severe attack of erysipelas—Monsieur Lefargue's remedy for the same 60
Albanian soldiers—On board the "Kathleen" sailing down the Nile . 61
Petherick constructs a swinging palanquin for my desert journey—Wild donkeys 62
Sufferings in the desert—I fall off the dromedary—Petherick's alarm . 63
I experience a slight sunstroke—The fate of my pet birds . . 64
Assouan—Mr. Ewing's *dahabyeh* casts anchor near ours—A fair-haired child . 65
We visit Edfoo—Luxor, and the residence of Lady Duff Gordon—The luxury of an English newspaper 66
I read an account of the sudden death of Captain Speke—Prostrated by fever —A ministering angel 67
Extract from letter sent to my sister 68
The "Kathleen" at Roda Island—Myrtles and roses—We land, and receive a visit from Dr. Paterson and Dr. Ogilvie 69
Boulac—We discover that our servants have been systematically robbing us— They desert us 70
Polly's disasters—Visit to the palace and gardens of Shoobra—The wife of His Highness Dhuleep Singh 71
The sale of the "Kathleen"—Lady Duff Gordon—Cairo—Visit from Consul Reade and his wife 72
Affectionate farewells—Alexandria—The sea once more . . . 73

APPENDICES.

APPENDIX A. By J. PETHERICK.

The object of my visit to England in 1859—I call upon Sir R. Murchison— Proposed and elected a member of the Royal Geographical Society . 77
Introduction to Captain Speke—Write a paper for the British Association at Aberdeen—Speke induces me to give a rough-hand sketch of my travels . 78

CONTENTS.

	Page
Correspondence with Captain Speke	79
He proposes to join with me in an expedition to discover the Nile's source	80
Captain Speke's invitation to visit him at "Jordans"—His letter to the Secretary of the Royal Geographical Society concerning his proposition—I agree to assist him in his undertaking under certain conditions	81
The reading of my paper on the Nile before the members of the Royal Geographical Society—The President's remarks thereon	82
Our proposed expedition freely discussed—Letter to Sir R. Murchison	83
My former experience in the Soudan provinces	84
The Council of the Royal Geographical Society apply to the Foreign Office for a grant to enable me to afford assistance to Captain Speke—Their refusal—An extract from the Society's "Proceedings," showing how I became connected with the Speke expedition	85
I accompany Captains Speke and Grant to "Jordans"—Amicable relations—Their departure from England	86
Speke writes for "instructions"—Letter from Mr. Francis Galton apprising me of the same	87
My reply, containing directions for Captain Speke	88
A meeting of the Royal Geographical Society—The President heads a subscription towards defraying my expenses	89
Amount subscribed for my intended expedition	90
My letter to the President and Council of the Royal Geographical Society concerning my intentions	91
Agreement between Consul Petherick and the Royal Geographical Society	92
Instructions for Consul Petherick's Expedition up the White Nile in aid of Captains Speke and Grant	93, 94
Letter from Sir Samuel Baker at Constantinople to me, asking information concerning the route between Cairo and Khartoum	95
More letters from Baker—Expresses a wish to meet and travel with me	96
The preliminaries for my departure to aid the Speke Expedition completed—Embarkation from Liverpool	97
Meet Miani at the Cataracts of Assouan—Letter from Sir S. Baker at Cassala	98
Arrival at Khartoum—Issue a notice prohibiting the traffic in slaves by ivory traders	99
Affrays between negro aborigines and the Arabs	100
I have a double duty to perform—Letter from the Secretary of the Royal Geographical Society, conveying some news from Speke—I dispatch two boats under my agent, with instructions and a letter to Captain Speke	101
I convey to Speke my reasons for not accompanying Abd il Majid	102
I dispatch a third boat to support Abd il Majid—Wicked insinuations	103
My endeavour to raise means to meet the additional expense	104
The "Sources of the Nile"—I receive a letter from Baker at Sofi	105

CONTENTS.

	Page
List of things to be forwarded to Baker at Sofi	106
A *pont-volant*—The post from Katariff to Khartoum	107
Another letter from Baker	108
Reply to Baker's letter, urging him to give up the project of travelling southwest	109
Dr. Brownell calls upon me with a letter of introduction from the Bey of Cairo—He joins our party as botanist	110
Our departure for the interior—We pass the confluence of the Bahar il Gazal .	111
We are joined by some boats from Gondokoro—An unprecedented rainy season	112
I order the arrest of Amabile on the charge of slave traffic—I become anxious to effect a meeting with Abd il Majid	113
We meet Abd il Majid—A history of his movements	114
The "Albert Nyanza"—I endeavour to fulfil my promise to Speke . .	115
Speke's letter from Karagwé—Invitation from the King of Uganda .	116
A splendid Court—The effect of the rainy season upon our men—Death of Dr. Brownell	117
Abd il Majid and Hhurshid sent under arrest to Khartoum—We reach Lolnun under adverse circumstances	118
Further progress by water impossible—I determine to proceed overland to Gondokoro	119
We arrive at the trading station of the Brothers Poncet, at Adôr—The men become discontented	120
My wife's courage and endurance—Arrive at Adael in the Bhol . .	121
Our reception at Neangara—Extract from Captain Speke's "Journal of the Discovery of the Source of the Nile"	122
A false accusation—What transpired at a meeting of the Royal Geographical Society during my absence	123
"The Nile and its Western Affluence"—On the road to Gondokoro . .	124
Stores for Speke at Gondokoro—We meet with reinforcements of our men from Khartoum	125
I am accused by the Consul-General of slave trading—Our arrival at Gondokoro—A weary journey of four hundred miles	126
We meet Baker, and Captains Speke and Grant—A very cool reception .	127
Who prompted the "succour dodge?"—Extract from Captain Grant's work, "A Walk across Africa"	128
Emphatic denial of the truth of Captain Grant's statements . . .	129
An idea of the manner in which I provided for the travellers—Extract from "Geographical Notes of Expeditions in Central Africa" . . .	130
The excess of expenditure over the sum subscribed—Injustice of Captain Grant's assertion	131
Facts to prove how I kept my appointment—The cause of Mr. Baker supplanting me in the Speke Expedition	132

CONTENTS.

	Page
Captain Speke writes me from Khartoum—A report of our death	133
Animosity of the Arab traders—Great commotion—The breaking open of my stores—The rioters joined by my own men	134
Good feeling of some of my men—The men of Mr. Baker's escort mutiny—He applies to me as Consul for assistance	135
Mr. Baker's claim upon the Egyptian authorities for the mutiny of his escort.	136
My proposal to Baker—My last hope for further explorations receives its death-blow	137
Speke and Grant's departure for Khartoum—A collection of plants for Kew Gardens	138
The desert Flora of Aboo Hamed—A succession of fevers and illnesses—My experience of Speke at Gondokoro	139
Slander and calumny—I decide upon entering proceedings against Capt. Speke	140
The Austrian Consular Agent, Dr. Natterer's, report upon the horrors of the slave trade on the White Nile—The report partially refers to myself—I demand an explanation from Dr. Natterer—His reply	141
Letter from Theodore Von Heuglin exonerating me from all participation in slave trading	142
I receive letters in vindication of my character from G. Thibaut, Administrator of the Imperial Vice-Consulate of France, and M. L. Hansal, Austrian Consul	143
The "hue and cry" vanishes on my return to Khartoum—The *Werko*	144
My trade summarily stopped—Moosa Pasha's unmitigated rage for my ruin	145
My opposition to the *Werko*—Translation of a French document, showing how Moosa Pasha set about accomplishing my ruin	146—148
Old Cairo—I report myself to Mr. Reade, our acting Consul-General—I learn that His Highness the Viceroy verbally accused me of slave trading	149
I request that Her Majesty's Government grant me the closest investigation into these charges—Reply from the Foreign Office	150
I receive the first intelligence of Consul Cameron's imprisonment—Offer my services to the British Government to execute any mission to the Court of Abyssinia	151
Treacherous behaviour of a *friend*—My offer rejected—Abolition of the Consulate—Earl Russell's letter	152
My suggestions to Lord Stanley respecting the relief of the captives in Abyssinia	153
Lord Stanley's reply	154
My treatment by Egyptian officers—An extract from the "Athenæum:" "Official England on the White Nile"	155
The protection of a Consul especially indispensable at Khartoum	156
The Khartoumers' support of slave traffic	157
Disclosures by Consul Reade of Cairo—The hotbed of Egyptian slave trade	158

CONTENTS.

xi

	Page
Slavery a domestic necessity to the Mahommedan—Baker receives the Society's gold medal	159
The Royal Geographical Society supports Baker	160
Sir Roderick Murchison assigns to Baker all the charge he had confided to me—My protest to the President and Council of the Royal Geographical Society	161
I demand justice at the hands of the President of the Royal Geographical Society	162
His reply	163
My last appeal to the Council of the Royal Geographical Society	164
A reply from the Assistant Secretary	165
A memorandum submitted for my revision by the Royal Geographical Society	166—167
Continuation of my correspondence with the Royal Geographical Society	168
"Minute of Council" of the Royal Geographical Society	169, 172
Appendix to same, containing my agreement with the Royal Geographical Society	172, 173
The reverses I experienced in my undertaking	174
Extract of letter from Sir R. Murchison	175
Facts to prove that I endeavoured to carry out my instructions	176
Letter from Dr. Shaw	177
Mussaad's journey *not* a trading one—Captain Grant's statement	178
Extract from Captain Speke's work	179—180
How the council of the society acted upon the report of my death—The society virtually and morally my debtor	181
Extract of account rendered to the Royal Geographical Society	182—183
Dr. Petermann's opinion of my journey, an extract from the "*Mittheilungen*" of Gotha	184
My last communication to the President and Council of the Royal Geographical Society before starting on my expedition	185
The justice of the Royal Geographical Society as shown towards me	186

APPENDIX B.

DESCRIPTIONS OF A NEW SPECIES OF FRESH-WATER TURTLE AND CHAMÆLEON. BY J. E. GRAY, F.R.S.

Tyrsa Nilotica—Trionichidæ	189
Aspidonectes aspilus—Fordia Africana	190
Nilotic *trionyx*	191
Chamaeleo Senegalensis—C. affinis—C. lucrigatus	192, 193

APPENDIX C.

THE FISHES OF THE NILE, by Dr. ALBERT GÜNTHER, F.R.S., F.Z.S., &c.

	Page
Mr. Petherick's collection of the fishes of the Nile	197
Dr. Friedrich Hasselquist's "Reise nach Palæstina"—Peter Forskal's "Descriptiones Animalium"—Sonnini's "Voyage dans la Haute et Basse Egypt"	198
The ichthyological labours of Geoffroy St. Hilaire (father and son)—Dr. Eduard Rüppell's discoveries—De Joannis' collections	199
J. J. Rifaud's "Voyage en Egypte depuis 1805 jusqu' en 1827"—Cuvier and Valenciennes—Russegger's "Reisen"—Sir Samuel Baker's notes	200
List of Fishes of the Nile	201—204
Differences of the Faunæ of the Upper and Lower Nile, and their affinity to the West and East African Faunæ	205
PERCIDÆ (PERCHES)—LATES—*L. niloticus*	206, 207
LABYRINTHICI—CTENOPOMA—*C. petherici*	207, 208
MUGILIDÆ—MUGIL—*M. cephalus*—*M. capito*—*M. petherici*—*M. saliens*—*M. cryptochilus*	209—214
OPHIOCEPHALIDÆ—OPHIOCEPHALUS—*O. obscurus*	214, 215
CHROMIDES—CHROMIS—*C. niloticus*	216
SILURIDÆ—CLARIAS—*C. anguillaris*—*C. parrimanus*—*C. lazera*—*C. macracanthus*—*C. hasselquistii*	217—219
HETEROBRANCHUS—*H. bidorsalis*—*H. intermedius*—*H. longifilis*	219—221
SCHILBE—*S. uranoscopus*—*S. mystus*—*S. dispila*—*S. hasselquistii*	221—224
EUTROPIUS—*E. niloticus*	225
SILURANODON—*S. auritus*	226
BAGRUS—*B. bayad*—*B. docmac*	227, 228
CHRYSICHTHYS—*C. auratus*—*C. macrops*	228—230
CLAROTES—*C. laticeps*	230—232
AUCHENASPIS—*A. biscutatus*	232, 233
SYNODONTIS—*S. sorex*—*S. macrodon*—*S. serratus*—*S. schal*—*S. humeratus*—*S. membranaceus*	233—236
RHINOGLANIS—*R. typus*	236—238
MOCHOCUS—*M. niloticus*	238, 239
MALAPTERURUS—*M. electricus*	239, 240
CHARACINIDÆ—CITHARINUS—*C. geoffroyi*—*C. latus*	240, 241
ALESTES—*A. dentex*—*A. kotschyi*—*A. macrolepidotus*—*A. nurse*—*A. rüppellii*	241, 243
HYDROCYON—*H. forskalii*—*H. brevis*	244, 245
DISTICHODUS—*D. niloticus*—*D. rostratus*—*D. engycephalus*—*D. brevipinnis*	245—248
ICHTHYBORUS—*I. microlepis*—*I. besse*	248—250

CONTENTS.

	Page
COREGONUS—*niloticus*	250—252
MORMYRIDÆ—MORMYRUS—*M. caschive*—*M. oxyrhynchus*—*M. geoffroyi*—*M. hasselquistii*—*M. cyprinoides*—*M. bane*—*M. discorhynens*—*M. borci*—*M. isidori*—*M. dorsalis*—*M. petersii*—*M. anguilloides*	252—257
GYMNARCHUS—*G. niloticus*	257
CYPRINODONTIDÆ—HAPLOCHILUS—*H. fasciolatus*	258
CYPRINIDÆ—LABEO—*L. niloticus*—*L. coubie*—*L. forskalii*	259—261
BARBUS—*B. bynni*—*P. perince*	261—263
BARILIUS—*B. niloticus*—*B. thebensis*—*B. bibie*	263, 264
CLUPEIDÆ—CLUPEA—*C. finta*	264, 265
OSTEOGLOSSIDÆ—HETEROTIS—*H. niloticus*	265, 266
ANGUILLIDÆ—ANGUILLA—*A. vulgaris*—*A. latirostris*	266, 267
GYMNODONTIDÆ—TETRODON—*T. lineatus*	267
GANOIDEI—POLYPTERUS—*P. bichir*—*P. senegalensis*	267, 268
DIPNOI—LEPIDOSIREN—*L. annectens*	268
Explanation of the plates	268
Mr. Consul Petherick's Observations, from the Journal of the Royal Geographical Society of London	270, 271
Final Result of Mr. Consul Petherick's Observations	272

LIST OF ILLUSTRATIONS.

	Page
LETTER FROM THE SULTAN OF DARFOUR TO CONSUL PETHERICK,	Frontispiece.
A SHILLOOK STOOL .	4
DJIBBA WARRIOR	6
KHARTOUM	30
MUGIL CAPITO .	210
RHINOGLANIS TYPUS .	237
COREGONUS NILOTICUS	251
BARILIUS NILOTICUS—BARILIUS THEBENSIS .	263
BARILIÚS BIBIE .	264
NEW SPECIES OF FISHES (THREE PLATES) .	268
MAPS .	End of Vol.

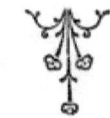

TRAVELS IN CENTRAL AFRICA,

AND

EXPLORATION OF WESTERN NILE TRIBUTARIES.

FROM PETHERICK'S NOTE-BOOK.

May 25th.—Yesterday my wife, though far from well, accompanied me to the shore, to be as usual my time-keeper, and a double set of observations were taken. Addressing her and receiving no reply, I found she was insensible. Carrying her first into the shade, and conveying her from thence to the "Kathleen," she remained apparently lifeless. When, at last, she opened her eyes, she knew me not. Carefully noticing the symptoms of the attack, I found it was typhus fever: already delirium had seized her.

Soon after my wife's illness commenced, I moved from the fetid marsh, in which we had remained too long, and on the *2nd* of this month were out of the Bahar il Gazal, and once more on the Nile; but it was only this morning (the *4th*) that I indulged myself in the hope she was really recovering.

On the 5*th* the invalid still better. We had her on deck—all on board feel happy. It quite unmans me to see how tender to her the men are; some with lines out fishing, others with guns on the look-out for shots at wild fowl as they skim along the surface of the water; and the cook has so thoroughly scoured his copper pans, that he can see his face reflected as he places them in readiness for the food which is to tempt the "*Sitta Madame*" to eat.

June 6th.—Entered the Sobât. Took depth and width of river, and rate of current; and it resulted that the discharge of waters per second amounted to eight thousand six hundred and fifteen cubic feet, being three hundred and thirty-five feet more than the volume of the White Nile before its junction with the Bahar il Gazal.

The idea of navigating the Sobât, even for a short distance, was abandoned, as our grain was rapidly diminishing, and could not, contrary to our expectation, be replaced. How different to what I had known it! The frequent raids upon them by the slave traders, Mahommed Kheir and his wild nomad Arab coadjutors, had so scared the negroes, who had been so often deceived and preyed upon, that they would trust no one, and fled on the approach of our boat.

Proceeding downwards on the *7th June*. The wind is dead against us; we can make no way, and for hours are compelled to make fast to the shore. Last year these northern winds at the same date would have been our salvation; but it was not to be.

One of my interpreters, employed at my station, at the Bahar il Gazal, wishing to return to Khartoum, I exchanged him for another from my boat. He was a Shillook, who in his infancy had been captured by the Bagara nomad Arabs, and had served twenty years in the Egyptian army of the Soudan. Since his discharge he had intermarried with the Dinka at the Kytch and Rohl. He spoke the Dinka and Shillook dialects and Arabic fluently, besides being an intelligent man and excellent servant. From him I gleaned most of the following particulars respecting the Shillook, Dinka, and Djour tribes.

The Shillooks of the White Nile inhabit a narrow district bordering on the western shore of the river between 9° 30′ to 13° of north latitude. Their chief, or Sultan as he is called, from the circumstance of his really exerting an authority over his fellow-countrymen—who literally are his subjects, and from whom he exacts a revenue—resides at his capital, called Daenab; nothing more nor less than a poor collection of some two or three hundred conical reed huts; and, indeed, were it not for some exceedingly fine delaeb palm trees, gracefully interspersed here and there amongst the dwellings, the capital of the Shillook would not be worth looking at. These people are governed with an iron hand. They are obliged to deliver all the elephants' tusks they may become possessed of, all skins of animals, wild or domestic, and all the fat of the animals slaughtered, to the Sultan. In addition an annual tax, consisting of one-tenth of the yearly produce of grain and cattle, is scrupulously imposed and levied.

Murder is punished with death to the criminal and the forfeiture of wives and children to the Sultan, who retains them in bondage. Robbery amongst themselves is of rare occurrence. If practised on strangers, it is praiseworthy; but if followed by detection, it is punished by confiscation of the property stolen, and the condemnation of the culprit and his children to the service of the Sultan, who may at his option sell them to slave traders.

His Majesty declares peace and war. The latter may be described as the general state in which they live, the Dinka being their most inveterate enemy. If victorious, after the deduction of one-tenth for the Sultan, the booty is divided amongst the combatants, in proportion to the number of spearsmen each individual took into the field. Although admitting to his council the most wealthy of his subjects, the power of this potentate with regard to them is unlimited. No person is allowed to approach his Majesty in an erect position;

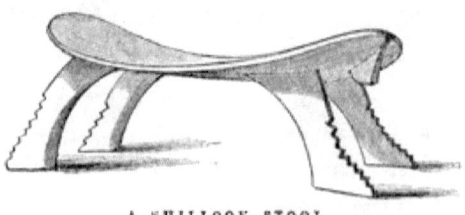

A SHILLOOK STOOL.

but the moment any one seeking an audience is ushered into the royal presence, the attendants compel him to crawl on hands and knees. When sitting in state on a stool, on judgment or reception days, surrounded by his council squatting on the ground, his guard, consisting of a score or more of his most favoured slaves armed with lance and shield, would be the only persons permitted to stand erect. Such is the devotion of his subjects that, to prevent its being trodden on and polluted, even his ministers will vie with one another to catch upon their hands, head, or shoulders the saliva which is squirted from the royal mouth.

Notwithstanding his might, state, and the circumstance of his office being hereditary in his family, he acknowledges his fealty to Jockdeng, Sultan of the Bonjack, by the payment of an annual tribute, amounting to the one-tenth part of his revenue.

The Bonjack are a powerful tribe in possession of a considerable district on the north side of the Sobât in about 9° north latitude and 33° east longitude, at that point of the river where it receives its principal tributaries from the north and east. They border on the Dinka negroes to the west, the Shookryeh nomad Arabs to the north, the Gallas on the east, and the Djibba negroes to the south. The latter, apparently with a mixture of Galla in them, speak a different dialect, and vary in colour from the jet-black of the Dinka and Shillook to a dark copper-colour. Their manners and customs also differ. Although they do not scalp their fallen enemies, they cut off the hair of their heads, and interweave it with their own to form ear-lappels, or sometimes a long tail reaching to the ankles. This they ornament with a thick coating of cowrie-shells, and add a few ostrich feathers to its extremity. Unlike the former, they are not absolutely naked, but wear a hide suspended from the shoulder, falling round the loins; and their faces show a stronger growth of beard, which the black negro, except in rare instances, is almost without.

My having been possessed of some of the weapons and ornaments of the Djibba, the annexed sketch, which illustrated an article I had the honour to read in 1860 at the United Service Institution, and was printed in their journal, will give a better idea of a native of this tribe than any description I can convey. The ornament on the arm is of massive ivory, and the sharp-edged missile in his right hand is of hard wood, and to preserve it from being blunted it is covered with a leather case.

The Dinka proper inhabit the eastern Nile-bank from the Egyptian territory to the Sobât; and are bounded eastwards by the Shookryeh nomad Arabs and the Bonjack.

This is the parent stock from which are descended a vast number of minor tribes, known under various designations, but preserving

DJIBBA WARRIOR.

the original habits and language. They stretch on the East Nile-bank to the confines of the Barri, to the territories of the Djour on the Bahar il Gazal westwards, and terminate with the Madar, bordering on the Moro, in Ncambara, to the south. The most powerful are the Dinka proper and the Nouaer. The latter inhabit both sides of the Nile 8° to 9° 20, latitude, and a portion of the lower part of the Bahar il Gazal, and are the most warlike, noble, and courageous negro race that I know of.

The Nuba race comprises the Bonjack and the Shillook; and stretching away inland, they inhabit the mountains and more sterile districts of the limits of the great Zachara Desert bordering on Kordofan to the north, and Darfour to the west. Some of these mountains—such as the group of Tekkela and Djibboon—yield, in small quantities, gold of a superior ductility, and consequently the district has excited the cupidity of the Egyptian Government and its Governors; the inhabitants, unfortunately, have to a great extent experienced what in England has been misnamed the "civilizing effects of Egyptian sway." The inhabitants of the Nuba mountains are merely subject to the casual marauding military expeditions of that Government, and after being robbed of as much grain, cattle, and slaves as can be obtained, they are left to the tender mercies of the Bagara Arabs who infest the plains. Tekkela, however, has been subjugated, and although not invested with a garrison, is tributary to Egypt by the payment of an annual tax of slaves and gold. Owing to the idea having been started (at a later date than the events recorded in this journal) by a scientific society in London, that her Majesty's Government should encourage the Viceroy of Egypt to enter into relations of amity and commerce with the tribes adjoining the Equator, I will cite, for the information of my readers, a few instances of the means employed in these out-of-the-way regions by the Egyptian officials for carrying out that policy of " amity and commerce."

The following, out of many instances that have occurred, came to my knowledge during my residence in the tropics of Central Africa. My informant was a cavalry officer employed on the *razzia* in question, and an eye-witness to the following occurrence. In consequence of the failure of the Egyptian Governor of Kodofan to levy several years' arrears of impost, consisting of ninety adult slaves and three hundred and eighty ounces of gold per annum, from Melik, Nassur of Tekkela, and the defeat and subsequent retreat of the former in endeavouring to enforce the same, Moosa Pasha, the late Governor-General of the Soudan, in his then capacity of Sub-Governor-General, was sent to retrieve the fortunes of the day. By reason of a disagreement with the unsuccessful Governor, Moosa Pasha turned his attention not so much against Tekkela, as to other smaller negro communities and nomad Arabs, who also had been guilty of withholding their tribute. For the purpose of better locomotion, he discarded the use of regular infantry, and chose in preference one thousand two hundred irregular Arab cavalry, under their several Melik chieftains, and three hundred mounted nomad Arab allies. When in the vicinity of that portion of the revolted Arabs who were under the command of Hamsa and Sheik Hassab Allah, surnamed " Il Tôr " (" the bull "), Moosa Pasha, in the act of reconnoitering, was hotly pursued, and all but taken prisoner. From the execrations that were launched against him, he concluded that, if captured, certain death would be his fate, and no sooner was he within the precincts of his own camp and in safety, than he vowed he would inflict a dire revenge, and make his name in future a dread and horror in the land.

In his turn, with the whole of his force, he so persistently followed upon the track of the Arabs, that coming up to them, hampered as they were with their numerous herds and flocks, he killed a large number, took fifty females and a host of children into slavery, besides capturing thousands of cattle. A brother of Sheik Hamsa was killed whilst defending the chief's family from ignominy and slavery; and amongst eighteen notable prisoners were sons of the latter and the veteran sheik, Hassab Allah (Il Tôr). By a drum-head court-martial, held on the spot, a sentence of death was awarded to all, with the exception of a feeble old man. But now, to the astonishment of his followers, Moosa Pasha waived the sentence, and, to their disgust, insisted on their witnessing the infliction of the most abhorrent and inhuman punishment that one man can inflict upon another, and then turned the poor victims adrift as emblems of his revenge.

I could follow up this subject with accounts of wholesale robbery, treachery, and villany of the darkest dye, which are inflicted upon the negro race by these supposed "civilizers;" but, rather than shock the reader, I will return to my subject of the habits and customs of the Nuba and Dinkas.

In the districts of the White Nile bordering on the Egyptian territory, from the frequent *razzias* committed on them by that Government and its subjects, considerable portions of the inhabitants are periodically carried off into slavery and entire herds of cattle are lifted. The miseries thus entailed upon whole communities are beyond description; and it may easily be imagined with what feelings of hatred and revenge the Shillook and Dinka negroes look upon their despoilers.

In common with a great portion of the aborigines that border on Mahommedanism, beyond the influence of the Egyptian Government, as far west as the Atlantic, many communities of the Nuba, without the expenditure of a piastre or the efforts of missionaries, have adopted the faith of Mahomet solely from the force of contact and example. Although young converts to that faith, the negro Mussulmans are, perhaps, its most bigoted supporters, and devote half a lifetime to crossing and re-crossing a great portion of the African continent in the seven-times-repeated homage to their prophet's shrine at Mecca.

The whole of the Nuba population that have not become converts to Islamism, and the inhabitants skirting that portion of the White Nile and its tributaries that I have followed up, I can safely vouch for, know not God. They believe in neither future reward nor punishment, but have faith in a supernatural power exerted over the elements, as professed by the common rain-maker; and, as it strikes me, if not this, another superstition, the veneration for a bull, practised by them, may be a corrupted relic of a portion of the creed or habits and customs of the ancient Egyptians. The animal thus chosen and eventually worshipped is generally the finest piebald beast that can be procured. He is petted and caressed to such an extent that he soon comes to understand his position, and always leads the other cattle. When that object is attained to the satisfaction of his happy owner, his legs and ankles are decorated with the most choice of iron and copper rings, and from the tips of his long horns the tails of cows and giraffes are suspended. Songs are composed and sung in his praise, and, believed to be invested with supernatural powers, he is idolized, and his aid is invoked to divert from them every evil that may threaten any portion of or the entire community with which his master may be connected. When it is remembered that, with some rare exceptions in those districts where tsetse flies prevent the rearing of cattle, the negroes are exclusively herdsmen, this kind of worship extends to a vast portion of Central Africa. When dead, the sacred piebald is buried with great ceremony; and on the death of his master, he is slaughtered, and his horns fixed on a post denote his owner's grave.

Some tribes inter the heads of families within the hut they inhabited when alive; but the Dinka generally is buried in a sitting posture outside the entrance.

From my knowledge of the form of government in vogue among the Shillooks, I may state that most of the communities of the

Nuba are similarly ruled, and that their chiefs are styled *meks* or *mellicks,* viz., kings.

The Dinka and the whole of the tribes that derive their origin from them may be said to have no form of regular government; and, freed from restraint and taxation of every kind, their habits differ considerably from the Shillook. Instead of living in closely packed communities dependent on each other, they reside in far-distant, isolated, stockaded enclosures. These comprise the dwellings and cattle-huts;—each of the latter during tempestuous weather will afford shelter to a hundred head of cattle. A small plot of tobacco is frequently cultivated within these high barricaded enclosures, and every man's house may truly be said to be his castle.

Every district is more or less independent of its nearest neighbour, although of the same tribe and under the same chief or *benj*. The latter's position is denoted by the term of "*dit*," meaning "excellency," that is affixed to his name by all who address him. The chieftainship is considered hereditary in families; but as the qualification is that of being the richest, bravest, and wisest of the community, frequent squabbles and internal feuds arise. This probably is the main cause of so many tribes of different appellations that spring from the same source and speak a similar language, and yet are quite independent of each other.

The *benj*, although powerless to levy a tax, or by the exercise of his authority to punish a crime, is followed and implicitly obeyed during war, and is looked up to, as it is he who decides the choice of pasturage. Aided by his council of wealthy elders, disputes and grievances, whether internal or with members of an adjoining tribe, are submitted to him for adjustment; but in cases where loss of life is concerned, club law is the highest authority. Cases of aggression by individuals of one tribe upon another are most difficult of adjustment; and during my annual visits in this direction, being a powerful neutral, my good offices have often been called into requisition as an arbitrator. I am happy to say that upon several occasions when "war to the knife" would have otherwise resulted, my decision of a fine of cattle, ornaments, or agricultural implements was willingly submitted to on the part of the culprit, individual or community, and the *amende* has invariably been gladly and thankfully accepted by the party aggressed.

MRS. PETHERICK
RESUMES HER
JOURNAL.

June 8th.—How grateful am I to feel that health is returning, and how thankful to all who have so patiently and tenderly nursed me through a distressing illness!

We are sailing quietly, dreamily on. At noon passed the village of Mahommed Cheir: it was in ruins. The Shillooks, whom he had so hunted and oppressed, rose at last, and defeated him; then Mahommed Cheir fled to the Nuba mountains.

June 9th.—Whilst pleasantly sailing in the Pond, as it is called, between the two mountains Birket il Djebelein, we remarked five boats, the Ottoman flag floating from their masts, moored to the bank; and on the shore a multitude of slaves, many of whom, as seen aided by glasses, we fancied had encircling the neck that terrible fork of wood before described. To convince ourselves, Petherick ordered sail to be taken in, and we went on shore; as we did so these unfortunates were driven off to the adjacent woods, women, children, and the sick who were powerless to move, alone remaining, and these were stricken with *small pox* and all its attendant horrors!

Mere skeletons of boys and girls, with sad entreating eyes and uplifted hands, mutely, but with power more eloquent than speech, implored for help—which we could not give. Oh, the pain of that scene! The Bagara Arabs with their horses, these hired hunters of human beings, with some of their flesh-trading employers, were there. They almost impeded our return to the "Kathleen," for they had seen that pencil notes were taken of the number of their victims then on the spot. As we reached our boat, there, in the sweet waters of the Nile, was a dying, emaciated, aged negro; his agony would soon be over. Never can I forget the piteous sight: deaf ears were turned to my entreaties to rescue him; he had *gone there to die.*

June 11th.—Arrived at the arsenal of Donagla, where we remained a few hours to purchase some fine sont timber, that my husband wanted to remove to Khartoum, for repairing some old boats, and the construction of a contemplated new one. Monsieur de Pryssenacre, having noticed our boats from a distance, hastened on his dromedary to greet us. He had been six months travelling in the

Sennaer country, and he bore traces of having experienced hardships; but our appearance shocked him inexpressibly.

When here last year, a pair of pretty green paroquets had been given to me, and I now accepted a similar offering.

If all goes well, in a few days more we shall reach Khartoum.

July, 1869.

I entreat the indulgence of our readers. Only now preparing this work for the press, I felt conscious, our journal, ending as it does, upon our return to Khartoum from Gondokoro, in 1863, that subsequent interesting events, in connection with our travels, would of necessity be unrecorded. Knowing that my beloved sister, Mrs. Mc Quie, carefully retained our African correspondence, I obtained her permission to quote from the letters in her possession, though never intended for publication; from them I give the following extracts.

EXTRACTS.

From JUNE, 1863, to APRIL, 1865.

———◆———

"BRITISH CONSULATE,
"KHARTOUM,
"*June* 25*th*, 1863.

"SISTER DEAR,

"I thought that it would be with joyous feelings I should again write to you from our home, but, alas! I am very ill; fever has kept me in bed now a week from the time of our arrival. We were both so ill when the 'Kathleen' reached Khartoum that we were unable to land until the following day. No letters were here for us; and we have too much reason to fear that you still believe us no more. Your touching letter of inquiry to Madame Peney respecting us, which she brought to me, confirms this belief.

"All credits having been stopped, our home is a wreck, and I have seen but a trifling part of the ruin around us. Petherick has once been out, and it was then to visit the Governor, Moussa Pasha, officially.

"Ill as I have been, my thoughts were diverted from our troubles by a little home incident. Confined as I was to bed, I noticed that a pair of martins, or swift swallows, had built a nest, attached to the heavy beams which supported the roof of my chamber. The ways of these little birds were an attraction irresistible to me. The parent birds were constantly flying to and fro through the windows, which were always open, to feed their young. A few days elapsed, and then the wee heads appeared above the edge of the beautifully constructed nest, and such chirps were uttered that my heart became glad once more. At last the time came when the fledgelings might try their wings, and how proud seemed the parent birds when the little ones, encouraged, took their first flight—a whirl in the lofty room! then a dart was made through a window, when all but one shot safely through, the weak one falling to the ground. I, who deemed myself helpless, was out of bed quickly, and finding that the tiny bird was alive, placed it in a basket, and I put it on a table near to me. The mother flew back, noticed where the weak nestling was, and for a week she regularly brought to it insects, and once a large beetle. The bird was soon strong on the wing, and, to my regret, flitted; but a lesson I had learned, I threw off the desire to 'drift away,' and was once again enabled to help my suffering husband."

"July 17th.

"Still are we wearying for news from home: you cannot imagine how the yearning for letters from the loved ones retards my recovery. Petherick is in a more miserable state of health than myself.

"Oh, the bitter grief we feel for the loss of the good Dean Littler! a few days ago only were we aware of it. Mademoiselle von Capellan had received a few English papers: she sent them to us; in one I read the death of that worthy man. . . . . . Mademoiselle Capellan remains at Khartoum until the return of her sister, Madame Tinné. She passed a long day with us yesterday: we three were invalids: there was no effort to make amusement, but each, in our way, read, slept, or softly chatted as the hours passed."

"*August 23rd.*

"Still without a line from any of you: it pains me so. I drive off the thoughts at times, and am then a cheerful, happy wife; but when I hear of the arrival of a post, and there are no letters for us, the sorrow comes again. Peth. has been able to go to his divan the last two days: he is troubled; all our ivory on its way to England was sold at Alexandria, as he was believed dead; it was bought much under value, and the loss is heavy. The piano—purchased from Holdernesse, of Oxford Street—made in two parts for the convenience of transport, we have found heart to unpack; and notwithstanding the neglect it experienced upon arrival here months ago, its tone is perfect."

"*September 9th.*

" . . . . . The wounds on Petherick's legs, which I wrote to you about, have now been recognized as caused by the horrible guinea-worm: one is partially drawn out. The head, when it first protruded from the flesh, was turned on a straw, and gradually, as you would wind silk on a reel. When resistance is offered, the straw is placed on the leg, there to remain a few hours, we waiting the opportunity to wind up perhaps an inch or more. To extract the worm entire may take days; if broken, it burrows again, and months may elapse ere it protrudes, and always in a different place. I need not tell you how much pain my good husband is compelled to endure, and *he is so changed!* no longer has he energy or hope. Our affairs, which might be made smooth again, are growing worse. Peth. is unable to attend to business of any kind."

"*September 12th.*

"I have been again seriously ill (ague fever). Petherick is *much* worse. . . . . I will, if I am able, give you a passage or two from a letter sent to me by Madame Tinné: quote what you like, the proceedings of those adventurous ladies must prove of interest."

"*October 2nd.*

"Mona dear,

"I begin a letter to you, hoping that I may have the strength to write so that you may understand me. . . . We are both very ill, but dear Petherick has been well-nigh death. . .

"Last Saturday, towards sundown, Foxcroft (accompanied by Ibrahim) rushed into the saloon, crying, '*Backsheesh!*' Thinking he came for the reward promised if my gazelle, which had been missing three days, was brought, I gave the few dollars. Foxcroft, very pale, said, 'I bring you news of a post; it has arrived, and there is a bag for you!' Sister, dear, I had weeks ago made a vow that when a post for us was brought, even ere the bag was opened, an order should be given to slaughter a bullock for our people. Whilst this was issued, in my trembling hands I held the bag. At last the cloth was cut, when paper after paper fell out for Baker, Baker! then came letters for Baker, until Petherick said, 'Be a brave old girl, this is Baker's post!' but I could not be brave, and fell fainting to the ground.

"They tell me I remained all night unconscious, and when morning broke I was still in my day dress, and noon had long past ere I was made to comprehend that *there were* letters for us—they had covered me with them, trying thus to restore me. The first which I opened was in the fair handwriting of our mother, and at the top of the page was a golden bit of hair, attached by a thread to the paper, and I knew that my Frances, of whose marriage I received tidings at Gondokoro, was a mother. . . . . Oh, Mona, what anguish have we caused you! . . . .

"It was not until the eve of the second day that all the letters were read, then came the reaction for Petherick: all thought that he was dying; some one came and cut off his hair, and then they cupped the back of his head. . . . . Is it possible that Speke can so have acted? It seems incredible that he should impugn the honour and integrity of Petherick: my heart is filled with bitterness.

"Speke, thus to treat Petherick, must surely appear to the public as most ungrateful conduct—he not to say a word that everything we had was placed at his disposal.

"When at Gondokoro, I felt convinced that some treachery was working against Petherick, so I went to Baker's boat, and implored him (as we also purposed going in search of the unexplored lake, though Speke gave no directions or encouragement for Peth. to do so) not to offer his boats to Captain Speke, as he, Mr. Baker, well knew the peculiar position Petherick held, and that he was also aware that our boats had arrived prior to his. Mr. Baker replied, 'Oh, Mrs. Petherick, it will be a positive service to me if he goes to Khartoum in my boats, as the men are paid in advance, and his will serve as escort and guard.' Reluctantly waiving that request, I tearfully entreated, 'At least, then, Petherick will find grain and stores?' To this he assented, and I hastened back to tell Petherick (who had a touch of fever), and to give the necessary orders."

"In a short time everything that it was possible they could require was packed in baskets, including wine, aracki, but no brandy

—ours had been stolen or broken, as there were but five bottles in the stores, and one of these had been opened for the travellers. As we thought of going to the lake, that small quantity would be required; Speke was proceeding to Khartoum, where plenty could be obtained; and besides, a trader here had presented him with a case of cognac upon his arrival."

"I sent to Speke the list of things packed, and begged that if he thought of anything else, if possible, it should be provided. All were returned, with a note in which he said, 'all the articles enumerated had been packed up by friend Baker.'

"I cannot tell you my feelings: Petherick, so honest and true himself, believes every one the same, and would not listen to my fears that Speke and Baker wished us not well.

"They dined with us; and a tremendous ham which we brought out from England was cooked: this we always said was to be done when we met Speke. During dinner, I endeavoured to prevail upon Speke to accept our aid, but he drawlingly replied, 'I do not wish to recognize the succour dodge;' the rest of the conversation I am not well enough to repeat. I grow heart-sick now, as I did then, after all our toil. Never mind, it will recoil upon him yet, his heartless conduct. I soon left the table, and never dined with them again; I became ill, and did not hold up my head for weeks, though the morning they left I managed to go to their boat to bid them 'God speed,' and to impress upon Speke how obliged I should be if he would as soon as possible convey the intelligence of our well-being to our friends at home: how kindly he did so!!!

"You will be glad to hear that our *dahabyeh*, the 'Kathleen,' left Khartoum on December 14th, but did not clearly get away until the 16th, as the men *will* have their spell on shore: she goes to bring down Mr. Baker from Gondokoro, and is well laden with grain and stores of every description; as she is the swiftest boat on the river, in all probability will arrive at her destination in twenty-seven days. I fear that Mr. Baker and Captain Speke, by their expressed doubts as to Petherick keeping his promise with regard to sending a boat, &c., have inflicted needless pain upon the family of the former.

"There was a great difficulty getting the 'Kathleen' off; she was ready a week before she sailed. Upon the Pasha's return from Alexandria the end of last November, the first step he took was to lay an impost of two months' pay on all the soldiers, sailors, &c., who were going up the White River, deducting this from their wages; last year he put on one month, it now amounts to three, and as the sailors have work only for about half the year, it is impossible that they can pay, thus it falls upon their employers. All Khartoum is in an uproar, and the men of the boats have been scattering themselves over the country. Mr. Baker, when he left last year, refused to pay the one month's impost; it remains to be seen how that question will be settled.

"Petherick asserts that the Pasha should have given timely notice ere a new tax was levied, as all the traders' boats were on the point of starting when the order so unexpected was issued.

"Petherick wrote to the Pasha to that effect, and requested that, at least, travellers might be exempt from the tax; but *no*—he refused, so Petherick paid for Baker, but under protest.

"The most iniquitous act has been in the case of the Dutch ladies. Three of their boats had sailed ere the arrival of the Pasha, their *dahabyeh* remaining, as it was hoped that the steamer might be hired to tow her through the lake, as the ladies are in some trouble; but the Pasha would not let her go; moreover, he insisted upon the tax being paid on the boats which had previously sailed with their papers duly attested under the new regulation of last year.

"Monsieur Thibaut, the French Consular Agent (under whose protection the ladies are) demurred; it was useless, as the Pasha threatened to seize the *dahabyeh* and bring back the other boats; therefore Thibaut paid, under protest.

"This is a horrible place! When the ladies' boats returned from the Bahar il Gazal, they were filled with slaves, and the Dutch flag was the protection. An invalid servant of Von Heuglin's, returned in the boats for change of air, denounced the proceedings of the *reises* and their men. Mademoiselle von Capellan pleads in vain through her Consul for redress,—it is a hopeless task: the servant is dead, and no one will bear witness. In the meantime, the slave traders composedly say, 'All the Europeans traffic in slaves, even the Dutch ladies.' This fills poor Miss Capellan with grief.

Your darlings ask if our gazelle is alive? Yes, but no longer here. When their uncle was so ill and unable to walk, the gazelle became impatient, and, to induce him to get up from the sofa, would charge him, once giving a very serious thrust (the gazelle had grown greatly, and its horns were long and handsome); therefore I gave our favourite to the Austrian Consul, who is sending a fine collection of animals to the Zoological Gardens at Vienna.

"And now for the last topic: Petherick's report to the Royal Geographical Society, with accounts, will, I think, be dispatched this day week. His Arab scribes have bolted, as he protests against the measures of the Pasha, and therefore they are afraid to serve him. May the coming new year prove a happier one to us all! Petherick must be in his place again: there has been nothing to conceal, no action to blush for, no wrong done to any one, and right will come right. Though some months may elapse ere we hear of a reaction in Petherick's favour, it will come at last, and with a clear conscience one can afford to wait."

"BRITISH CONSULATE,
"KHARTOUM,
"*New Year's Day*, 1864.

" SISTER DEAR,

" A happy new year to all ! . . . .

" Mademoiselle von Capellan has just left us; she came to an early breakfast, and on Christmas Day was with us until quite a late hour. Her clever little negress, Rose, accompanies her always, to the infinite delight of our Zitella; we usually keep the children in the saloon, to encourage them in their sewing tasks, when such a spirit of emulation is evinced; afterwards they are at liberty to amuse themselves in the garden."

"*January 8th.*

" Perhaps you are aware that this Consulate is to be abolished on February 1st, but you cannot imagine how the right and honest-minded people take its suppression to heart. Petherick is naturally indignant; for now that Khartoum is becoming better known, and about, it is said, to be connected with Egypt by rail, surely a British Consulate ought to be deemed of greater service than ever.

" I cannot, dare not trust myself to dwell upon the injustice done to Petherick, but will tell you of some proceedings he put afloat last month, the result of which we must await.

" The renewed uncertainty concerning the fate of Dr. Vogel in 1856, who, you will remember, was a member of that unfortunate expedition into Central Africa from Tripoli under Richardson, has induced Petherick, upon his own responsibility, to do his best to unravel, so that the hopes and fears of Vogel's relatives and the public may be set at rest.

"On the 18th of last month Petherick sent a trustworthy servant to Tendelti, the residence of the Sultan of Darfour. This messenger, mounted on a fleet dromedary, had in his charge valuable presents for, and a letter to, the Sultan Mahommed il Hussein, requesting permission for ourselves and a few attendants to pass through his country to the Sultan of Wadai, in order to ascertain the fate of Abd il Wahád ("Son of the Only One"): this name Dr. Vogel had assumed. Another circumstance induces us also to linger yet awhile. Mr. Hausmann, one of the missionaries who visited us here when on their way to Abyssinia, early in 1862, came to Khartoum a few days since. He gave lamentable accounts of the position in which Consul Cameron and the missionaries were placed, in consequence of the displeasure the Emperor Theodore evinced towards them. Theodore is incensed because our Queen has not answered his letter or letters, which were sent through Her Majesty's Envoy Cameron. Petherick is known to the Emperor Theodore by repute, and Mr. Hausmann believes that if Petherick, in his official capacity, visits Theodore, bearing suitable presents, the little difficulty which at present embarrasses may easily be surmounted.

"To Mr. Hausmann's judgment was left the selection of articles which, in his opinion, were best calculated to please Theodore. Rifles, guns, pistols, a gold watch, and my rare Bohemian glass were approved of. You will know how freely all was offered. I forget if you met poor Cameron when we were living at Russell Place. Petherick has communicated to the Government his willingness to go to the relief of Consul Cameron."

"*February 4th*, 1864.

"This Consulate was abolished by order of Earl Russell last Monday. . . . You cannot imagine the atrocities which take place here; whole batches of negroes are marched to the Government quarters, and even the dead and dying are thither dragged, that the captured may be duly accounted for.

"You will grieve to learn that Petherick's trade, which for so many years he has with industry and integrity persevered in, has been summarily stopped by order of the Governor-General, who, on behalf of the Viceroy, is following up an aggressive policy as far as Gondokoro on the populations of the White Nile, by the attempted monopoly of the entire trade of that river. With a view to forego the opposition of our Government to this vast extension of his southern frontier, his measures, forwarded to the Consulates, are headed by the announcement that they have for their object 'the better suppression of *the slave trade.*' Will this be believed in England, and can any one trust in the good faith of the Egyptian Government to put down a traffic to which its army, agriculture, and the domestic habits of its subjects are so greatly dependent for their support?

"I am uneasy about dear Miss Von Capellan: this is no place for her; she is in my opinion a greater heroine than any woman I ever knew, her sacrifice is self, her long and solitary residence in Khartoum, without kindred, waiting only the return of those so dear to her. She has the good word of all, and the love of many. If at the end of this month, when we hope to leave for Cairo, tidings from Madame Tinné (or that which is most to hoped for—her arrival) are received, and the ladies remain in that wild land still longer, Miss Capellan will travel with us; I beg you to tell this to her relatives, who must be anxious. To Mr. Tinné, for his kind sympathy, repeat, sister mine, our expressions of gratitude: they spring from the heart. Such a touching incident took place a day or two ago. When on our voyage to Gondokoro, one of our best men, Faki Mahommed, was seized by a crocodile, and we saw him no more. Dear Peth. gave orders that the wages he paid Faki should be continued to his infant son, who, with his mother, lived a long way off at Dongola. The uncle of this boy has travelled here from thence to tender his thanks, and to say no longer was the money required for the child, as he was dead. The fine old patriarch, with his grey beard, grand face, and turbaned head, was a picture to behold. I wept: he thought it was for the child I had never seen, and he stooped to kiss my hand; but my emotion arose from his noble act, thus to apprise Petherick of a circumstance which might never have been known to us—he to come so far for the sole purpose of giving up the pay which regularly had been received. He brought with him a quantity of delicate golded-tinted dates for Petherick's acceptance. With us the old man rested a night and day, and then returned to Dongola, bearing, as you may be sure, a gift or two to Faki's widow."

"KHARTOUM,
"*March 14th.*

"SISTER DEAR,

"I hardly know how to write, I am so glad, and yet so sad. The joy predominates, 'for we are going home!' We expect news of Madame Tinné. Last Saturday at an early hour, Mademoiselle Capellan came to give us tidings that boats from the Bahar il Gazal were seen at Wallad Shallai, a short distance from this, some four days, perhaps; but the north wind blows so strong against them that their progress must be very slow, indeed at times impossible. Ah! those treacherous winds, how they failed us! Poor Miss Capellan wept, and Peth. and myself were not without fears, because, what might the news be? if bad for her, we will try to console; and if the fair travellers are well and continue their inland journey, why, we will bring her with us to Alexandria: she is so sad and lonely. Petherick sent at once my dromedary with servant to Walld Shalli. I greatly enjoyed the packing of baskets with home-made bread, vegetables, limes, papers, and letters for the looked-for ladies.

"Miss Capellan remained with us, and in the evening the long-expected post arrived; but I was so agitated that very little was read: the Christmas cards and perfumed sachets from your Christmas-tree brought dear old England vividly to me."

"*March* 15th.

"So many letters, sister mine, from you, dating from the 27th of November, 1863, to the 24th of January, 1864, with all enclosures, papers, extracts relative to that cruel Speke, &c., that I only finished perusing them this morning; and you cannot be surprised that little fits of fever come. I am now working to send off a post to-day, if only to convey our thanks to you and dear Peter, and to his friends for their sympathy. In a few days I will go more into our troubles; but, oh! Mona dear, what consolation found I when reading to Petherick yesterday 'Unto the upright there ariseth light in the darkness'! the day will dawn. I do assure you, sister, that the shocking things said of us hardly pain me, because I feel that all will be made clear. The evening of the day you receive this ask your children to read the CVII. and

CXII. Psalms. I thank God He has restored to us strength; I daily go with Peth. to the river-side for a blow, and in the afternoon we ride out to the desert.

"Our sale is over. I am copying you a list of the *lares*, that you may judge how my good husband had surrounded me with comforts. And now, Mona, you must 'blow the fifes and beat the drums,' for we are going home. I believe and hope that in August at the latest you will find 'somebody knocking at your door:' may there not one dear face be absent, I pray. Give love the fondest to your children: their loving letters fall like dew upon my heart.

"The lilies of the valley dear Constance sent are fragrant as herself. Your little almanack is a treasure: it gives me the dates; I always know when it is Sunday, but am never quite sure about the week-days. Miss Capellan, like myself, forgets: she too had no almanack for last year. The Comtesse de Bisson, whom I think I mentioned to you resided a short time at Khartoum, on her way to Abyssinia, with her husband and a large suite, has lost her father; he was a fine, hale old man. Several of their party have also died. An Englishman, Mr Joyce, has arrived here; he is a manager of the trading company from Egypt: we see him frequently, he has been reading to us extracts from his New Year's letters from England, written by his little relatives. I so thank you, Mona, for the description of your dear ones dressed for the childrens' balls; every rosette I seem to see, and their flowing hair. You never weary giving me those details, but of yourself you say so little."

Give your Geraldine our tender love. You write to us, "she ran with a penny to a black man who was on the sand-hills, saying, 'tell your brothers in Africa to be kind to my Auntie Kate and Uncle John, and send them home.'"

"*March* 17th.

"I devote myself to a very revel, writing to thee and thine. I am so well! . . . . . Since my letter of Monday last, no further tidings have been heard of the travellers from the Bahar il Gazal, and our man has not returned from Wallad Shallai; we expect him to arrive every moment. Poor Miss Capellan is full of anxiety; I make her pass all the time with us she possibly can. Petherick is well and getting about again.

"Think what a change, sister! at five in the morning I rise—at that time the bed-room is almost dark; the windows face north and west.

"I hear, being a light sleeper, the mission bell: it rings now at that hour. Dressing rapidly, I go to my cages to let out the fowls, giving them grain and water, the little pet birds and the parrot I also feed. At six a.m. we partake of an early light breakfast, and then visit the animals as in the old days. The weather is no longer cold, and we shall soon again sleep out at nights. The missionaries from Abyssinia give us on Sundays the benefit of their prayers and preachings. At nine a.m. we assemble here: Mademoiselle von Capellan, also Mr. Joyce, attend regularly; when service is over we converse for a time, and then breakfast. I forgot to mention that another European traveller is amongst us, Herr von Diependael: he too attends, and is frequently a welcome guest."

"KALLAKLA,
"SEVEN MILES FROM KHARTOUM, WHITE NILE,
"*Easter Sunday*.

"We have removed from Khartoum, and I believe we start for Cairo in ten days. We are now in tents, with the traps about, we are to carry with us. It was thought advisable that I should rough it a little before the journey was commenced; and indeed I am enjoying it. Our encampment is close to the river; the air delicious, but at midday the heat is intense. As we have no boats at our command, we must travel on dromedaries across the Bayooda Desert to Wadi Halfa, the second cataract a little above Korosko. It will be a trying journey, even if we start at once; if delayed, the heat will be unbearable. Mr. Joyce has sent his tent out here; he and Petherick, after a couple of hours' shooting or fishing, each morning ride into Khartoum, and at six o'clock return to an *al fresco* dinner. A crocodile, a pair of turtles, loads of their eggs, and a number of fish, have been captured, and prepared to add to our collection. Mademoiselle von Capellan sends her tent to-morrow, and she will become a welcome guest. The report of Madame Tinné's boats coming down proved false; and I fear that Miss Capellan will not have the heart to leave without tidings. We left Khartoum in a great hurry, as the small pox was raging amongst our people. One fine little boy was the first to die: I had him in my arms a few hours before, not knowing what was the matter with the child.

"On Thursday I received your letter of January 31st, also cuttings from several newspapers. Do not grieve, dear sister, all will end well; Petherick will see Speke upon our return. Wait the result patiently: we have no fear.

"I can hardly realize that so soon we may meet: how my heart leaps when I think of it! how much have we to thank you for! what a pain have we been to you! but we will *talk* about that by-and-bye. We hope to arrive in England the end of August: this you will doubtless receive the close of May. The missionary who gave us sad accounts of the treatment Consul Cameron and the

KHARTOUM.

little band of Europeans received from the hands of Theodore, has written to say the Consul is now a prisoner in Theodore's camp. Petherick waits with impatience the reply to his request for authority from our Government to proceed to their aid. Perhaps, as Petherick is no longer Consul, and as Earl Russel says one is no longer required for those latitudes, red tape will tie the hands of the officials, and the captives may linger 'in durance vile.'"

"KALLAKLA,
"WHITE NILE,
"*March* 31*st*.

"SISTER DEAR,

"I enclose a letter to Mr. Tinné: it contains sad news. Peter will give it to him, I know full well, with every tender consideration. Poor Madame Tinné *is dead*. I have a few hours in which to write, and by degrees, perhaps, shall gather strength to give you particulars. I am ill to-day, the reaction of yesterday's tax.

"Mona, Miss Capellan is an angel upon earth, and there are so few that I trust God will let her remain yet awhile; but much I fear that she will join those, too soon, whom she saw in dreams so vividly the last few nights. It was but the day before yesterday (and yet it seems a year) that she came out to pass some little time with us. Petherick and Mr. Joyce rode to Khartoum, and then she and I had our chat. Talking always of those so dear to her, she said, 'I must tell you my dreams: last night I saw my lovely mother and my dead sister—the one next to me; they held out their arms from the bright clouds to take me there, and I was so happy. Then I awoke, but to sleep again and to dream of

Harriet (Madame Tinné) that she was dead.' I cheered her, and the smiles came back: she had wept as she recounted the dreams. We turned to the books lent us by Mr. Joyce, Miss Capellan selecting 'Money Lent,' and I, 'Sword and Gown.' Towards evening news was brought that Madame Tinné's boats were within a few hours of Kallakla. Petherick also had heard the same good news, and that '*all*' were well.' He hastened to us, and we three talked gaily of what we were to do to give pleasure to the travellers. When the moon rose, Miss Capellan determined to return to Khartoum to make her festive preparations, and, respecting her happy eagerness, she was permitted to depart, well attended. Such a lovely flush had enlivened her usually pale face that she looked beautiful. Ah, Mona! never more will that youthful expression light up her features. (Forgive me, dear, thus wandering.)

"We were strangely restless, though believing in the good news, and could not sleep. The moon was high when we heard the man on the look out for the expected boats hail one to stop. The *dahabyeh* was pulled to the shore and made fast—it proved to be the one occupied by Baron d'Ablaing and the Baron Heuglin. Petherick, hastily dressing, had no ears for the dialogue between the *reis* and our watchman, but I heard (listening intently) that some one was dead, and so told him. Peth , always anxious to keep a sorrow from me, made me give my word that I would not rise until he returned with certain tidings. When he did so, and said, 'let us say our prayers,' I knew that Death had struck his dart. Mona, dear! Madame Tinné died last July, her faithful maid in August, and Miss Tinné's maid in August (both Europeans).

"At sunrise Von Heuglin landed, and we three rode at once into Khartoum, I to break the news to poor Miss Capellan. (I trust myself not to speak of it now, I have too much fever.) Whilst with her Miss Tinné's boat passed onwards with its melancholy freight; with her she brought the body of her beloved mother, and that of her faithful attendant, Hanna. Miss Tinné, seeking retirement, goes to the Island of Tooti, a short distance from Khartoum. Miss Capellan proceeds at once there. Von Heuglin has accepted our Khartoum house during his stay, and the Baron d'Ablaing finds quarters in the town."

"KALLAKLA,
"WHITE NILE,
"April 17th.

"This will be a lamentation, I fear; I am sick at heart. Ready for the start, it was yesterday postponed, I am sure for good reasons; but here we remain—that is all I comprehend. Mona, I can hardly stand up against this fresh trial, it is such a crush to the hope I had allowed to grow (I can hardly think it will ever spring again) of seeing thee and all the dear ones once more."

"*Wednesday.*

"I am striving my very best to be patient; here, in tents, the thermometer shows 112°, and the chamseen wind comes with such hot blasts. For fifty days it generally continues—a few of these have, however, passed.

"The night gives one fresh life; we sleep out now—or ought to do; but at the lovely stars I gaze and gaze, and cannot close my eyes.

"My little servant, Zitella, has been very naughty, so she has been sent back to Khartoum.

"Foxcroft, poor boy! is very ill; since Christmas he has been an invalid; we often fear that he is *going*. He rallied when we first came here, but the last three days he cannot leave his tent. I visit him frequently: he is fretful and will not fancy to partake of any but the most unwholesome food for him.

"I write now when the sun is going down, and must, while there is light, say good night."

"KHARTOUM,
"*May 8th*, 1861.

"SISTER DEAR,

"I have so much to say I know not how to begin; but of my health I am sure you would first hear, and so I tell thee of it. The hot winds were almost death to me at Kallakla, and I for some time—a long time, days are as years in this land—kept up, but I broke down at last; so they made me come back to Khartoum. The rooms are, in comparison, cool—thermometer shows a difference of 15°—and there are more comforts: Fatma is such a kind nurse. When stronger I will tell you something very interesting about her.

"Foxcroft is seriously ill: on our way here he was obliged to rest twice in the villages, and once he fell fainting off his donkey. I rode a dromedary bravely, but at a tax too great, for upon entering our desolated saloon I could only reach the divan, where I fell powerless and unconscious. There is little hope of our starting for a month; the rains are then expected."

"KHARTOUM,
"*May 12th*, 1861.

"I hasten to give you news of Baker, that Peter may in some way make it known to his friends.

"Boats have arrived from Gondokoro belonging to De Bono. The corpse of his nephew, Amabili, was brought down—alas! for his young wife, who is here. Hurshid Aga (with whose men Baker sojourned) received a letter from his agent at Gondokoro, stating that from a negro he heard that Baker was then but a few hours' march from Gondokoro. The 'Kathleen' is the fastest boat on the river, so Baker may be looked for soon. We have been anxious for his safety, though he has proved no friend. The English heart clings to its kind, and we hope and trust he will turn up all right."

"KHARTOUM,
"*May* 14th.

"I told you Petherick had sent a messenger to Tendelti, the residence of the Sultan of Darfour, with presents and a request that we might traverse through his dominions to Wadai, to endeavour to ascertain the fate of Abd il Wahad, otherwise Dr. Vogel. Sadly interesting tidings have just been received, which Petherick will quickly communicate to the Royal Geographical Society."

I claim now the indulgence of the reader to pause in my correspondence with my sister, in order to insert my husband's subsequent communication with Dr. Petermann, the Secretary of the Geographical Society at Gotha, respecting the fate of Dr. Vogel and his friend Herr Beurmann.

"Dr. A. PETERMANN,
"Redaction der Mittheilungen,
"GOTHA. "October, 1866.

"MY DEAR SIR,

"In obedience to the instructions of Her Majesty's Government, dated September 24th, 1857, I offered, through the Governors of the Provinces of Khartoum and Kordofan, a reward of one hundred dollars (Maria Theresa) for a letter from the lost traveller, Dr. Vogel; and, if detained a prisoner, one thousand dollars for his ransom. From various sources I obtained what I considered trustworthy information of his death, and for which I was honoured with the approval of Lord Clarendon, Her Majesty's Secretary of State for Foreign Affairs, dated February 25th, 1858.

"But, in the latter end of 1863, my having learned that some fresh doubts had arisen with regard to the fate of Dr. Vogel, I determined, upon my own responsibility, to attempt an indisputable solution of the question. With this view, on December 18th, 1863 (corresponding to Regeb, 1280, of the Hægira), I dispatched a messenger, per dromedary, from Khartoum to Tendelti, the residence of the Sultan of Darfour. He had charge of different kinds of presents, and a letter to Sultan Mahommed il Hussein, requesting permission for my wife and self to traverse his country, for the purpose of proceeding to the Sultan of Wadai, in order to ascertain the fate of "my brother" Abd il Wahad.

"On the following 14th of May, 1864, Hadji Dries and two companions sought and obtained my hospitality during their sojourn at Khartoum. They were on a pilgrimage to Mecca, and the eldest of them, Hadji Dries, had already performed six pilgrimages, and being now advanced in years, if he lived to accomplish this his seventh duty, he purposed to devote the remainder of his life to the service of the shrine of his prophet. With reference to white men who some years ago were travelling in his country, the old man said he had known most of them intimately. Abdelkerim (Dr. Barth) had returned to his country, but Jacoub (Richardson), on his way to Kuka, died at Ungurutua; and Tabib (Overweg) had been taken ill at Kuka, and died soon afterwards at Maduari. Abdelkerim (Dr. Barth), prior to his setting out from Kuka for Zanzibar, had deposited four boxes and a large telescope with Hadji Beshir, the Vizier, but the former having been slain by Sultan Abderahman, they were seized by him. His brother, Omar, subsequently deposed and slew him, and then took possession of the boxes and their diminished contents. On the arrival, some four or five years afterwards, of Abd il Wahad (Dr. Vogel), the boxes, in a dilapidated state, were consigned to him, and he, Dr. Vogel, gave them to Hadji Dries. The lock had been forced, and most of the contents had vanished. Hadji Dries found therein several bottles, some empty, and others full of unknown medicines; one containing Epsom salts he partially used, and the remainder were then in his possession. Hadji Dries produced from his wallet a large pocket-book, whence, carefully folded in paper, he disclosed a green-lined envelope containing a sheet of note paper, or rather half a sheet of letter paper doubled in form of note paper on which were written the following recommendations, copies of which, on May 22nd, 1864, I forwarded to the Royal Geographical Society, viz.:

"'KOUKA,
"'*December 31st, 1855.*

"'I beg to recommend to the good-will of all my friends the bearer of this, El Hadge-a-Dris, from Kouka, who has shown me, during my stay here, always the greatest kindness, done everything in his power to oblige me, and proved always an honest and very useful friend.

"'(Signed) EDWARD VOGEL,
"'*African Expedition.*'

"'The soussigned has riden this recommendation, and has found that all was Mr. Vogel has said is very true, so that also he can recommend the Hadji-il-Dries to all his friends who will read this verbs.

"'*Kuka, September 3rd*, 1862.   "'(Signed) BEURMANN.'

"With the permission of Hadji Dries, I retained the original documents, and in lieu thereof, on the eve of his departure, May 27th, 1864, I gave him copies, and adding a few lines from myself in testimony of my high estimation of him, I earnestly solicited in his behalf the attention and good services of Her Majesty's Consul at Djedda, or whomsoever he may have occasion to apply to for assistance.

The servants who arrived at Kuka with Abd il Wahad (Dr. Vogel), were dismissed from his employ, and returned to Tripoli, with the exception of an European, who was called Milad (Corporal Maguire). He was left at Kuka in charge of several boxes and a quantity of baggage, with which, after the death of Vogel, he left for Tripoli; but on the way he was robbed and murdered in the desert by the Touarig. Hadji Dries was at Zinder on the departure of Milad, and at that place some of the stolen property was brought to Sheikh Baba, and Hadji Dries recognized a sextant and a watch that had belonged to Vogel. Hadji Dries was on intimate terms and in daily intercourse with Vogel during his stay at Kuka. He sought for and engaged four liberated slaves as servants to accompany Dr. Vogel on the journey to and from Wadai at the fixed sum of ten dollars each.

"The day after he had received the above document, viz., January 1st, 1865, poor Vogel departed from Kuka on his unfortunate journey to Wadai. Hadji Dries accompanied him for about two hours on the road, and then took leave of him. Vogel rode a grey horse that had been given to him by Sheikh Omar, Sultan of Burnou; the servants walked, and one camel carried the whole of his baggage. About three months afterwards, it became known that Vogel had been received, entertained, and treacherously murdered at Abusha or Abesta, the residence of Sultan Sherif of Wadai, about one day's journey south of Wara, the capital. This statement was shortly afterwards corroborated by two of the servants, who, after a narrow escape from a similar fate and subsequent death from thirst during their flight from Wadai, had returned to Kuka. They told Hadji Dries that their master had been unexpectedly fallen on and murdered by the attendant slaves of Sultan Sherif because he would not adopt Islamism, and acknowledge that Mahomet was God's prophet. Their two comrades were also speared to death for serving a Christian, but they owed their lives to the darkness of the night that covered their retreat. They avoided all habitable localities during the day-time, and at night they watched their opportunity of stealthily obtaining water from wells, wherewith to quench their thirst, until they were out of the district, and they did not consider themselves safe until their arrival in Kanem.

"Hadji Dries did not believe that any of the effects of Vogel would have been preserved. He had seen some small bottles of medicine and one of quicksilver in the possession of an Arab smith originally from Tunis, and then in the employ of Sultan Sherif.

"Beurmann, under the name of Ibrahim Bey, was hospitably received by Sheikh Omar at Kuka during four or five months. He then left for Jacuba or Bauchi (twenty days' journey south-west from Kuka), where his horse died. After his return to Kuka, he remained there a month to rest himself and prepare for a journey to Wadai. On the eve of his departure, with four free negroes, Sheikh Omar presented Beurmann with a fine black horse. He left a box, full of books, papers, and instruments, in the care of Mahommed Ben el Sag, of the Walled Suliman, and a chief of Arab horsemen in the service of Sheikh Omar, Sultan of Burnou. Beurmann met with no obstacle until he arrived at Maw or Mayo, in Kanem, where, with signs of friendship, he was detained and hospitably supported by the Khalifa Betshimi, or Mousa. This chief sent to inform Sultan Sherif of the character of his guest, who, after taking leave of Betshimi, was waylaid and murdered by negro horsemen, the slaves of Sultan Sherif. The whole of his effects and arms—comprising several double fowling-pieces, percussions, double pistols, and a breech-loading rifle—were conveyed to the Sultan.

"Thus ended the account of Hadji Dries, who left my house, in continuation of his pilgrimage, on May 28th, 1864.

"In common with the generality of Africans and Orientals, Hadji Dries knew not his own age, and attaching little or no importance thereto, his recollection of dates was not trustworthy; but his statements leave no doubt on my mind with regard to the certainty of the disastrous and melancholy fate of the unfortunate travellers, who, in the ardour of their zeal, fell victims to the stern and uncompromising fanaticism that stamps the character of the ignorant and barbarous Mahommedans who inhabit these regions. In the course of the month following the departure of Hadji Dries,

June, 1864, my messenger returned from Darfour, with the Sultan's answer to my letter—of which I annex a photograph, three-fourths the size of the original. The following is a translation of the seal:

"'FROM THE CHIEF OF THE BELIEVERS,
AND THE DESCENDANT OF THE GENEROUS MAHOMMED IL MUSCHDI,
SON OF THE SULTAN MAHOMMED IL FADE, SON OF SULTAN ABD IL RAHMAN
IL RASHID, SON OF SULTAN AHMED BEHR, SON OF SULTAN
MOUSA, SON OF SULTAN SULIMAN.
PEACE BE UNTO THEM.—1250.'

"The letter is translated thus:

"'Praise be to God alone, and may Mahomet's glory be honoured by God!

"'From His Highness the great Sultan and the venerable Successor, Head of the Believers, and the Maintainer of the Flag of Equity over the heads of the people. Generous by descent, whose trust is in Almighty God, our Master and Ruler, the Sultan Mahommed il Hussein il Machdi, victorious by the will of God, Amen, to his Excellency Her Britannic Majesty's Consul.

"'We have to inform you that your letter reached us with your messenger, Mahommed il Shaygi, and we have understood the contents to be that you desire to come to see us, and you asked our permission, and we do not dislike your arrival; but to abstain from examining and other matters, because many learned Christians came to our country and embraced the Mahommedan religion, and are living with us, rearing families, and you are one of them. We grant you leave to come to us, and as soon as your messenger reaches you, arise and come with him to us before the rainy season. Do not delay to journey at once, and to return direct; but to inspect the whole country you have no permission, but only to see us, and to return if you like. Come quick, before the rains, or you will be overtaken by them, and in our country the rain is heavy. But with regard to your brother (respecting whom you stated to be at Dar Wadai), we have heard of him, but during the reign of Sultan Sherif; but if he is the same that you allude to, God knows!

"'This is all we have to say to you, and God preserve you.

"'*Written on Monday, the 28th of the months of God, Ramadan, one of the months of the year 1280 from the Hegira of the most noble Prophet. God greet him, and peace be unto him.*

"'IN THE YEAR OF THE HÆGIRA 1280.'

NOTE TO MS. ON VOGEL AND BEURMANN,
PUBLISHED BY DR. PETERMANN.

"The information respecting the melancholy fate of Edward Vogel and M. V. Beurmann, so kindly conveyed to us by Mr. Petherick, and gleaned from a trustworthy person of Kuka, corresponds in general, and, indeed, especially so completely with the heretofore known data as to dispel all doubts of the lamentable death of both of the unfortunate travellers."

"Some hitherto unknown details are now communicated, particularly that V. Beurmann remained some time unmolested at Mayo on the confines of Wadai, the presumed scene of his death; and it was after he had left that place, in the continuation of his journey, that he was attacked and murdered. This new report asserts most positively, that Besche or Abeschr, the present residence of the Sultan of Wadai, lying south of Wara, is the place where Vogel met his death, just like . . . . informant. (See 'Geog. Mitt.': 1862, page 346). On the other hand, Vogel's servant Mahomed ben Suliman, states Wara, the old residence, to have been that locality (see 'Geog. Mitt.': 1863, page 225), and his having been an eye-witness, we must accord preference to his version. The man from Kuka could but relate what had been said in Burnou."

"To Mr. John Petherick, that highly meritorious Briton, for his explorations of the Upper Nile countries, we Germans must acknowledge our hearty thanks for the interest he has taken in the fate of our unfortunate countrymen, and for the zeal which he manifested in unravelling it.—A. P."

"*May 28th.*

"DEAR SISTER,

"I sometimes think that I shall never write another letter, I am so weak. I have now been eight days almost helpless;

no voice, no strength, unable to eat; sighs not to be controlled; and such home-yearnings! Petherick acquainted you with the death of dear Miss Capellan. It seems a dream. One morning I received a tiny note from her wishing to see me; I went at once, she was in bed, and knew me not for a few minutes; I saw that she was very ill. I dispatched a messenger to Miss Tinné; sent for the Doctor, and apprised Monsieur Thibaut.

"The Doctor soon came, and laughed at my fears: he said it was only a little fever; but in three hours she was dead—the following day was buried. All the Europeans attended the funeral of Miss von Capellan, which took place the following day. I send you the sermon that was preached here in her presence the day before her death, also the oration which was read at her grave."

* * * * * * * * *

"Poor Miss Tinné's grief is bitter.

* * * * * * * * *

"The 'Kathleen' has arrived, but not Baker; he has proceeded farther south, and will not return, so the traders say, until next season. We shall now proceed in the 'Kathleen' to Berber, and thus escape a long land journey, which would kill me. How from that place we travel I can give you no idea; it depends upon my health. Petherick talks of the Souakim route to the Red Sea, thence steamer to Suez: this is a quick journey, and water through the desert every second day. Foxcroft gets about a little now: he is pale and wan."

"*June 5th.*

"Our men who came down with the 'Kathleen' tell us that my former handmaiden, the wife of Wód Ali, gave birth to twin children, and then died. Petherick keeps up wonderfully, though Moosa Pasha does all in his power to crush him; such are his menaces and vengeance, that Petherick cannot secure the services of an Arab scribe. The European agent also, who had agreed to watch over our interest, and who was to receive liberal pay, has declined at the last moment. The British Consulate exists no longer."

June 6th.

"The post leaves to-day; I hasten to finish this. I believe that this day week we start. . . . . I shall not write again from Khartoum. Poor Fatma, who is broken-hearted, packs up our things, and makes delicate bread for our use in the desert; she is a noble creature. Foxcroft, Rechan, the boy Bine, and little Zitella are to accompany us: also the Janissary Shagir Mahommed.

"Miss Tinné will leave about the same time we do; and our boats will, as far as it is practicable, proceed together. No more then, Mona dear, perhaps for weeks, from your fond sister."

My next letter, I find, is not until September 26th, and too ill to make any notes; to fill up the interval I must again refer to my husband's memoranda.

FROM PETHERICK'S NOTE-BOOK.

July 2nd.—Saturday was looked upon as a lucky day by all connected with us, to commence our homeward journey. The Mission waggon, one built at the abandoned station of Santa Croce, had been borrowed and was on our premises at an early hour. Servants and sailors, under the superintendence of our old and tried servant Ibrahim (for many years my factotum), commenced conveying our traps on board. The willing fellows, in the absence of trained cattle to draw it, pulled and pushed the waggon, with a will, to and from the boat, situate from our house about three hundred and fifty yards. Before sunset everything was on board, and, although under the influence of a hurricane of wind and dust, we persisted to embark before the sun was on the horizon, in order not to lose the prestige of the day. Our moorings were shifted about a boat's length, and every one on board expressed satisfaction that our journey had commenced.

July 4th.—As usual, several trifles had been forgotten, and to wait for them we quietly dropped down stream, to enjoy the quiet and shade of a grove of date-palm trees, half a mile distant from the town.

In answer to a note from Miss Tinné, wrote a few lines to say my poor wife was very weak and feverish, but, knowing she was on the way home, she tried to be cheerful.

The Blue River, now a month on the increase, is swollen to about half its rise at high Nile, and its waters, during the summer so clear, had now, being charged with fertilizing mud, become brown in colour.

July 5th.—After a hard day's work with Arab secretaries, respecting my affairs, and wishing good bye to Joyce and others, at five p.m. we bade adieu to Khartoum, and from our hearts hoped we may never see it more. An hour before us, Miss Tinné, in a *dahabyeh*, her luggage in another, and Von Heuglin in a third boat, had passed by. At 6.30 p.m. they were moored under the village of Halfaya, and we continued a mile or two farther down, to the island of Om Hossân, where Bilal our *reis's* home was.

July 6th.—Bilal, according to the generous practice of the people of the Soudan, came on board, bringing dates, vegetables, fowls, and a sheep, to present to us. Driving before a strong south wind, we, in company with Miss Tinné, moored at Tamaniat, a large property, that is but indifferently cultivated for the heirs of Ahmed Pasha, a late Governor-General of the Soudan. But a couple of miles farther down, the river winds through a short range of basalt hills, called Djebel Raweeân, and the passage, owing to a sudden turn of the river in the midst of them, with a rock in the centre of the stream, is difficult to navigate, and many are the disasters, during high Nile, that occur here.

No one will attempt to navigate this portion of the river at night, so, to allow the sailors to cook their supper on shore, at five p.m. we make fast at the island of Wallad Hossoona.

Poor Kate continues in a sad state, and to tempt her to partake of some food I shot a few doves; but although the cook prepared them with all the care he was capable of, she would not look at them.

July 7th.—The night had been cool; and my suffering wife felt refreshed in the morning, and partook of some *medida* boiled flour, seasoned with salt. At six p.m., before a sharp breeze from the south, we passed the islands of Burnât, Guraeshâb, and Nassuri, whereon a few temporary hamlets existed. Sheep and goats were feeding off the remains of stubble. We neither tarried at Matemma or Shendy, but, anxious to get on, we, at sunset, made fast near a large grove of date-palms, that on the bank hid the village of Magaweer from view. This place is celebrated for the growth of onions, an important item in Arab cookery. We laid in a sufficient supply for the requirements of our servants, to last them until we hoped to arrive in Egypt.

July 8th.—Off at sunrise, and passed many islands, some prettily skirted with mimosa.

The general appearance of the surface, at this time of the year, is barren, as the crops had all long since been reaped, and they are not generally cultivated until after high Nile.

July 9th.—At ten a.m. reached Damir, an important mart for salt, that is obtained by artificial evaporation from the soil, with which it is highly impregnated. The chief was absent, but his brother, Il Lemin Wallad Hassan, overloaded us with attentions, and would insist upon making us presents of a sack of wheat, a couple of sheep, and a bushel of salt, as provender for our journey.

The day following we arrived at Berber, where we hoped to obtain the necessary camels to carry us across the desert of Aboo Hamed, to Korosko. Miss Tinné, intending to cross with the Bishari Arabs to the shore of the Red Sea at Souekim, disembarked, and occupied a neat house situated in a pleasant garden, on the outskirts of the town, and on the river-side. Von Heuglin occupied another house in the town; but we preferred remaining in our boat, that was replete with every comfort.

The Governor of the place, a Turk and an old acquaintance, received me with a show of cordiality that excited my suspicion, when he endeavoured to explain the difficulties that existed with reference to my procuring camels for the desert journey. There were many camels then in and around the town, but he assured me they had all been engaged, but he would *do his best* to cause me but as little detention as possible. The continuance of a daily journal would but contain a tiresome repetition of our frustrated hopes, and the daily procrastinations and false promises that were made to us by the Governor, the camel purveyor, and the guides that were sent to us, with endless tales, to explain the reason why other pleople were being supplied with camels in preference to ourselves.

A month had thus passed away, when I became aware that the Governor-General, Moosa Pasha, had issued private instructions that I was not to be provided with camels until he himself, on the opposite side of the river, should be far on his way to Dongola. The Pasha evidently wanted to forestall me in Egypt, to be the first to convey verbally, to His Highness, the difference that existed between us relative to the new regulations for the guidance of the White River trade. It was even rumoured that, now that I no longer held an official position as H.M. Consul, my life was in danger; but the Pasha, who had not yet left Khartoum, under no circumstances would permit me to reach Cairo before him.

Of the atrocity of this man's character I had many experiences, but of his biography, imparted to me from an unimpeachable quarter, I was unaware. My informant and the Pasha, in the enjoyment of social intercourse, were one hot noonday smoking their chibouks, when their privacy was intruded on by a poor woman, who begged for relief. The Pasha threw a cracked small gold coin, a *cheryeh*, to her, and the woman, handing it back as worthless, was doubly hurt to find the Pasha pocket it, and with an imprecation order her out of his presence.

"Why, Pasha, why so severe and penurious, you that are so rich?" rejoined the friend.

"Why? yes, you shall hear," said the Pasha, and he told the following:

"I need not tell you I am a Circassian, and in early youth was kidnapped and sold, a slave, to a Turkish grandee, in the Cairo market. Sent to be a soldier in the Egyptian army, I soon became a lieutenant, and in 1839, during the Syrian War under Ibrahim Pasha, for personal bravery I was made captain. In the Hills, three days' march from St. Jean d'Acre, my regiment was surrounded and destroyed by a kabila of Druses. In the *mêlée*, in conjunction with the remains of another company, the major in command, and myself, attempted to cut our way through the enemy, but overpowered in the attempt, we were compelled to surrender. In the division of the few prisoners that took place, the major and myself fell to the lot of an Arab chief. Secured each to a stirrup-leather, we were ignominiously conducted to his home, where for months we were subjected to the vilest treatment that one man can inflict on another—with no covering and but scanty clothing, our bed was on a poor mat in an open shed, whilst, hard-worked, beaten, and ill fed, we were treated with contempt. Another hardship was a total privation of tobacco, that we pined for more than bread; and but for the good heart of the *sheikh's* wife, who secretly afforded us scanty nourishment, we must have died of starvation. Life became intolerable; and barefooted we fled, but after two days' wanderings and sufferings we were re-taken. Thrashed within an inch of our lives, we were dragged back to our den, and our lot was, if possible, worse than before. We again determined to fly, but this time separately. What became of my companion I know not, but I, one night, arrived before Java. It was occupied by Egyptian troops; and not able to give the password when challenged, I was fired at, taken by the patrol, and consigned to prison. On the following day, when asked to account for myself, my appearance was so haggard and wretched, that my story was disbelieved: a suit of clothes was given to me, and on the receipt of a subsequent small sum of money, with three other prisoners I was ordered, under escort, to proceed to St. Jean d'Acre.

On the way, surprised by Druses, I was again made prisoner and taken into the Hills, in the expectation of a ransom; but nothing forthcoming, in a fortnight I escaped, and succeeded in gaining St. Jean d'Acre a few days before the bombardment. On the retreat to Egypt I again suffered intensely from hunger and distress, —no one cared for me, and, sick of life, can you wonder at my having taken a hatred to mankind, and vowed on oath that, whenever in my power, I would ill-treat, punish, yes, and torture every individual that with impunity I can? It is some satisfaction for the wrongs that have been inflicted on me, and the pains and indignities that I have suffered. Yes, I repeat, I hate mankind, and I will be revenged."

The following brief summary will show the subsequent career of the man whose vengeance, whilst in the pursuit of my duties as British Consul, for the protection of commerce and my individual interests as a trader, I had drawn down upon myself.

After the disastrous retreat of the Egyptian army from Syria, by way of recompense for his sufferings, Moosa Effendi was made a major and sent to the Soudan. In 1842, the then Governor-General, Ahmed Pasha, appointed him colonel in a regiment of infantry, and subsequently Governor of Khartoum. The subsequent Governor-General, Ahmed Pasha Menekli, appointed him his aide-de-camp, a commander of irregular horse, and at different periods created him Governor of the provinces of Dongola, Berber, and Kordofan. The next Governor-General, Hhalid Pasha, removed him from Kordofan, and made him his aide-de-camp, and in this capacity he commanded the troops that were sent against the Selaem Bagara Arabs. In an engagement that took place, Moosa Bey took an active part, and singling out an Arab chief, Sheikh Ahmed, he encountered and compelled him to fly. Both were well mounted, and the *sheikh* although he could not be overtaken, was forced to drive his horse into the Nile. Moosa would not follow, but swore, and discharged his pistols at him, but missing, he pardoned him.

The result of a second *razzia*, and the abominable treatment of his prisoners, I have before, in the course of these pages, recounted.

Notwithstanding his dismissal from the service that followed the above inhuman act, he was re-employed in 1853 as Governor of Keneh, in Upper Egypt, and the next act we find him distinguishing himself in, is, with the aid of a battalion of infantry, supported by artillery, in cold blood murdering three hundred Megribbin prisoners, who, during a revolt of the Arabs, had, under the offer of a free pardon, been induced to lay down their arms.

Subsequent to the above he became Chief of Police at Cairo, and President of the Council until 1859. His next important step was his appointment by the present Viceroy to the Governor Generalship of the Soudan, and in 1862 he was created Mushir, and General of Division, to take charge of the army that was then accumulating in the Soudan, and believed to take the field against the late Emperor of Abyssinia, and, although last not least, the occupation of the White Nile, and the conquest of its people.

August 27th.—Miss Tinné and her suite had obtained camels, and left for Souakim, and as there were none forthcoming for us, and furnished with letters to a *sheikh*, near Aboo Hamed, by the Governor, we determined to proceed thither by boat, in the hope, by the exercise of my own exertions in addition to the letters in question, to obtain a sufficient number of cattle wherewith to cross the desert.

With this view I sent on our own dromedaries and donkeys, and left our moorings with indifferent hopes of success. In two hours we arrived under Djebel Mezzum, a bleak sandstone rock, with the ruin of a *kiosk* on its summit, that had been constructed by an Egyptian Governor named Mochow Bey, not many years after the conquest of the Soudan, under the ill-fated Ismail Pasha. Before night we made fast opposite an island called Abydych.

The day following, *August 28th*, both sides of the river were marked by numerous groves of the bifurcated palm, intermingled with plantations of date-palms that were laden with clusters of ripening fruit. In the fields Indian-corn and millet were in blossom. At sunset we reached and made fast under the village of Aboo Beshr.

Before starting on the morning of *August 29th*, an old hag brought and threw over us dust from the grave of the saint Aboo Beshr, saying that if we retained it on our clothes we should pass without injury the cataract of Wadi 'l Homâr. We found it to consist of a series of very tame rapids and whirlpools, caused by dangerously immersed rocks of granite. The dust of the good *sheikh's* grave did not prevent us striking, harder than was pleasant, against some submerged rocks, much to the fear of my poor suffering wife, and the displacement of our rudder.

The banks, that had heretofore borne signs of cultivation, by Sakyeh, now became narrow and sterile. A low range of bare trap-rock permitted no shrub or blade of grass to grow, but at their base, within a few feet of the river-edge, some coarse grass, with occasional stunted and ill-conditioned dôm-palms, contributed to increase rather than diminish the wildness of the scenery. On the shelving side of the eastern range of hills appeared apparently an old Pagan stronghold, called Kâb-il-Marra : it was constructed of dry stonework, and leading from it down to the river-side, apparently for the purpose of securing water to its once inhabitants, is a pathway protected by a double row of strong wall, built of the same material, and twelve feet high. At about the distance of a mile farther down stream, and on the summit of the range, are the crumbling remains of what struck me to have been a watch-tower. I should have liked to have examined these old ruins, but the stream is very powerful, and being now near high Nile, and the channel encumbered with numerous bluff rocks, some visible and others under water, our *reis* opposed the attempt. After an hour and a half's hard rowing with a dozen sweeps, we got into a long tranquil reach; not a ripple on the water, over a mile in breadth.

At four p.m. we entered a western branch of the Nile, called Chor Aboo Simoon; between it and the main channel is the island of Bagaer, several miles in length. The object was to avoid a dangerous cataract, named Aboo Simoon, that obstructs the navigation of the principal stream. The island is beautifully wooded with mimosa and palm trees; and the passage we were gliding along, divided as it was with islands, bearing the most charming varieties of foliage and rich in pretty rocky and secluded nooks, where ever and anon a creaking Sakyeh, suspended one knew not how, formed a most pleasing change from the bleak and stern scenery we had just left. At five p.m. made fast alongside one of the most bewitching little islands I ever saw: the sides of the banks, high above the flooded water, were covered with the richest of grass, then such a host of entangled and voluptuous shrubs and evergreens clothed the surface, that it appeared a wonder how the tall date-palms could have won their way through the thicket that surrounded them; a little zig-zag pathway led up the bank, through the thicket, and on to a piece of cultivated land of one hundred acres in extent. In the centre of it were a few huts, and the kind old Arab proprietor bid us a cheerful welcome. Hadji Ahmed bade his healthful boys, that issued from the Indian corn and cotton-fields, get mats, *angeribs*, and I know not what, to make the most of us: the "fatted calf" was killed in the form of a kid, and the men were bid to climb the tall trees, and pick as much fruit as they chose. For all this kindness to utter strangers in all but name, it was with difficulty, when we left in the morning, that I could induce him to accept of a *matemma*, red bordered scarf.

Two hours' stiff pulling to evade many rocks that lay studded in our course, and on to which the strong current violently endeavoured to propel us, we gained the main stream, that in its wild and lovely beauty vied with the beautiful Chor we had left. The vegetation looked its best; but, on the other hand, the low murmuring sound of the deep and broad current, as it swept past innumerable bold and forbidding bare granite rocks, that started in all manner of grotesque forms to some fifty feet above its surface, sometimes rushing impetuously past, and then courting their vicinity in large and treacherous whirlpools, that seemed loth to leave them, inspired awe and loathing for the dangerous locality.

In parts more calm, rich groves of mimosa in full leaf, and now and then in bloom, stood out of the water with apparently no more solid footing to support them, whilst, peeping through the branches, sharp points of rocks seemed to steal a look, and dare our comparatively frail boat's approach. Another few hours of hard rowing to keep way on the boat, and make her feel the helm to steer us clear of danger, brought us to an awkward rocky ridge, hardly deserving the name of cataract, called Tarfaya. A quarter-of-a-mile-broad ridge of granite crossed the bed of the river, and although the fall was but trifling, the waters roared and lashed with anger, as they leapt over or passed between the immovable impediments.

A mile beyond is the village of the same name, and there we made fast for the night. It is on the east bank, but separated from the river by so extensive a grove of date-palms as to merit the name of a forest. Behind this village are extensive fields, that, with the aid of the Sakyeh, are made to produce Indian corn, cotton, tobacco, onions, and wheat.

August 31*st*.—A storm of wind from the north prevented us leaving until noon, and soon afterwards we sped through another passage of partly sunken rocks, called Neddi. A whirlpool catching hold of our boat, against the best efforts of our men, brought her in contact with the rocks, and some alarming shocks were sustained ere we could get off. My poor wife, in her weak state, could not control herself, and at last fell fainting into my arms. However, on we sped, and serious were my fears that in her high state of exhaustion, after all the illness and trials she had gallantly vanquished, she must succumb under the inevitable great fatigue that awaited her in crossing the desert.

At four p.m. passed through Chor Koodi, west of a large island of the same name, and made fast at the end of it for the night. Prior to reaching the island, the west Nile-bank presents a long continuous forest of date-palms, and behind it several villages; on the other side the country seemed deserted: the soil is poor and sandy, and the few and far-between stunted trees were dôm-palms and nebbac bushes.

September 1st.—The *Sheikh Bellad* (chief of the country), Wa'd Aboo Higl, lived some miles farther down, and to his whereabouts we proceeded, navigating an easy channel through quiet and interesting scenery. As usual the *skeikh* received us with a hearty welcome, and heaps of fruit, vegetables, and a sheep for presents. In return I repaired the lock of his gun, and gave him some powder and shot. While this was going on the crew had been busy in unshipping and landing our rudder. It had been cobbled up after the first injury it had received, but the second bumping had so shaken it that it was deemed prudent, if possible, to exchange the sternpost for a new one.

A search of several hours along the banks, for an appropriate tree proved ineffectual, but ten piastres (about two shillings) overcame the scruples of the village schoolmaster to give me a rafter from the roof of his house, that answered the purpose. Our crew and carpenter—for every boat proceeding down the cataracts is provided with one—worked with a will, and on September 2nd, the required repairs completed and our rudder shipped, away we sped at noon, and at three p.m. again joined the main stream. Another channel, Chor Kurgus, bordered profusely with date-palms, was shortly entered, and making fast at sunset, we spent the night on the island. Around its edges the date-palm throve superbly, and the fruit partly harvested. Numbers of dealers had already made considerable purchases. The fruit was packed in large bags made from the fibre of the tree that bore it, and on donkeys and camels it was to be conveyed southward, to supply the wants of thousands.

A rudely-constructed ferry-boat of thick planks staunched with rags, was there to convey these bags to the opposite shore on the mainland; but the population required no such vehicle to convey them across. Both men and women inflate a goat's skin, and thereon with impunity brave the swift current, that is a couple of hundred yards wide. Their clothes are, turban fashion, wound round their heads, to keep them dry. On the shoulder of a man we witnessed, nestled a child, and near him swam his wife. Although both struck out well with their arms and legs, the current bore them down fully a quarter of a mile, and with the aid of our glasses we gladly witnessed them scramble up the opposite bank.

September 3rd.—From this to Aboo Hamed, the left bank of the river being the most favoured. It supports, with fruit and serials, the populations of a few distant villages. On the right, the desert by degrees encroaches on to the edge of the river, and

Bishari Arabs, who exist on their flocks of goats and the services of a camel or two, form its sparse inhabitants.

EXTRACTS FROM LETTERS

RESUMED.

"IN A SHED ON THE CONFINES OF THE
ABOO HAMED DESERT.

"*September 26th*, 1864.

"We have been here some time waiting for camels, and now can *only* muster thirteen; so the half of our traps must be left in this miserable place until they can be forwarded. The 'Kathleen' has gone to Korosko with a light cargo and our pet birds (we hope to get them to England, when they will be presented to the London Zoological Gardens). I could not attempt the passing of the cataracts from this to Korosko; had I the courage to have done so, we should have been spared the desert journey."

"I did not know, or had forgotten, that there was a difficult one between Berber and this place, and not being prepared, the shock was very great to me. I noticed, the morning of that trying day, some of the crew sprinkling the blood of a newly-slaughtered sheep on the bow of the 'Kathleen,' whilst others were praying. I could get no explanation of this ceremony, for such it appeared to me. The crew then took to their oars, pulling and singing lustily; suddenly the boat touched a rock. This gave me no uneasiness—I had nerved myself for an occasional shock; but when bump after bump was repeated, and I looked from the windows and saw the 'Kathleen' in the midst of rocks, and rushing water swerving her round at times, her timbers crashing, the dreadful grating as she was pulled over, the shouting of the men to Mahomet, bird-cages flung in all directions about the cabins, the loud lamentations of the boy Bine, and even Petherick's look of alarm, all filled me with terror, and I was a veritable coward, losing, they tell me, my mind, for two or three days. You cannot picture the wretched quarters we are now in: the heat is intolerable during the day, and we are compelled to remain in this shed; light there is none, but that which creeps in through the low open portal; at night we sleep in the square or public streets, where do all the travellers. It is a weird sight to open one's eyes and see the tall camels with their noiseless step march past, bearing their loads and riders, then, a few paces beyond, sink on their knees and haunches to be unladen; here there is always a brief halt before entering the desert, to examine or acquire water-skins, and to make good deficiencies for the tedious journey to Korosko. How many have we seen come and depart, whilst we, from the tyranny of Moosa Pasha, have been forced to remain so long! Petherick has occupied himself making a kind of couch for me, which is to be swung between two camels, one going in advance, the other behind: I feel timid about it, as the last camel will be always looking over me. However, it is the only way I can cross the desert, for I am weak as a child.

"I think I wrote to you when we were so long a time at Berber, if I did not, I must tell you how very kind Miss Tinné was to me, visiting me often, and always consoling; I was ill all the time there, I believe chiefly from fright. One day, a hundred or more of Albanian soldiers in the Pasha's employ came on board the 'Kathleen' when Petherick was on shore, and there were only two of our servants on board. Their remonstances were unheeded, and the soldiers *would* come into the cabins and stare at me. I could not be divested of the belief that Petherick had been cruelly treated, and was regarded as powerless, or these men would not have thus behaved. I again became delirious, and when he returned I begged him show me his feet—I thought he had been bastinadoed. And up to this time even, the old horror returns, and he has again and again to assure me that such an outrage was never committed upon him. I had so mixed up an atrocity which Moosa Pasha had inflicted upon an old servant who arrived at Khartoum after we left, and who fled from thence, joining us at Berber, where he recounted his wrongs; therefore if Petherick absented himself even for a short time, I imagined he had been in the Pasha's power. You can judge, sister dear, how changed I must be. I had too a severe attack of erysipelas at that place, brought on by constantly having cans of water poured over my head whenever it was becoming confused. I am indebted to the French Consul at Berber, Monsieur Lafargue, for an infallible cure for that distressing complaint, which cannot be too widely known.

"After seeing me, he sent an elderly, genial Arab woman to be my doctor: she simply clarified a little fresh butter, adding to it as much fine salt as the butter would absorb, this was rubbed gently into the parts affected for ten minutes, repeated every hour or two, and in three days the cure was complete.

"Foxcroft left us at Berber; he liked not the idea of returning to England. Miss Tinné kindly took him into her service. Zitella, who had promised to be a good girl if she might accompany us, was a very naughty one; we therefore sent her back to Khartoum, protected by people whom Petherick knew.

"We have the hope of being off in a few days. Petherick expects that on the desert the temperature will be lower than it is here; I must, however, make up my mind to endure an inevitably trying journey; for a week we must travel at the rate of eighteen hours out of the twenty-four. We have so few camels, that to carry any quantity of water is out of the question; and there is but one place about the centre of the desert where it may be found, so the marches must be forced, and our poor servants must walk.

"I regret to tell you that the Albanian soldiers who so frightened me at Berber destroyed the tablet to the memory of Mr. Melly, which Petherick had assisted to place on his tomb at Gagee. They broke the marble, hoping to convert it into mouth-pieces for pipes. The people of Gagee were highly incensed, as the tomb was universally respected, and they were pleased to point it out to travellers. These Albanians were supported by the Viceroy; large numbers were on their way to the Soudan to strengthen the Egyptian army, who were then supposed to be preparing to invade Abyssinia. These lawless soldiers pillaged some villages *en route* to Khartoum. And now farewell. I hope to write to thee from Korosko."

"ON BOARD THE 'KATHLEEN,'
"SAILING DOWN THE NILE TO ASSOUAN.
"*October*, 1864.

"How we crossed the desert I know not; it had been all the time one long troubled dream, and as such I recount it.

"The morning we left our home in the shed at Aboo Hamed, they lifted me into the swinging palanquin which dear Petherick made for me. It was suspended between two camels. In it was placed a mattress with pillows; above, an awning with sliding curtains.

"Petherick mounted one of our dromedaries, the Shaygi Mahommed the other; these had travelled by land from Khartoum; also my donkey, and a magnificent wild donkey purchased by Petherick at Berber. This animal, with two others, had been caught at the mouth of the Atbara; a herd of them having come there to drink, were surprised by Arabs, who threw lassoes over them. The live stock consisted of two fine goats, two sheep, and sundry fowls; the latter were placed in a large cage on a camel. The start was happily effected, and Petherick's face became radiant as I declared myself so comfortably ensconced that it was impossible I could experience fatigue. All went well until late in the afternoon, when I noticed that the cage in which the fowls were had been turned carelessly end upwards, and the poultry were all in a heap on each other. Calling attention to this circumstance, the fowls were one after another thrown on to the sand: they had been suffocated. There they remained, as the Mahommedans will not eat anything which has not been slaughtered. At sunset a brief halt was allowed, when I was told that my palanquin impeded the march, as the camels carrying it travelled so slowly: Shaygi also said that the few water-skins had leaked considerably, and we might suffer from thirst. I assented to any proposition they made which could benefit others; so the palanquin was stripped of its cover, and in its crude state as an *angerib* was placed on a camel's back. The motion was dreadful: the couch was too long, and swayed so much, that with my best endeavours it was difficult to endure. Had a small one been made, such a one as Mr. Baker crossed the desert in, with a slight roof which he covered with leaves, it would have been feasible; two of these cages (as it were) belonging to him were at the Consulate on our return from the White River. For hours I thus travelled, moaning piteously, Petherick says; towards morning I remember entreating that they would let me ride my dromedary, which I did. Then for days memory became a blank, and I was always under the impression that we were approaching a high black wall through which there was no outlet.

"I took an unconquerable hatred to Shaygi Mahommed: to him I unjustly attributed my troubles. My hearing was so painfully intense, that at a great distance I could distinguish voices and sounds which others heard not, and sometimes long afterwards we would overtake a slowly-moving caravan of slaves. Once where we bivouacked I traced the imprint of many childrens' tiny feet: this filled my heart with grief; the tears I shed for the sufferings of those little ones relieved mine own, and I became more rational.

"We hardly ever rested, as the water quickly diminished: one skin burst and the contents were instantly lost. The night before we reached the wells all were pushing on for them, and no halt had been made for hours. I cried out, 'Let me remain behind! I am dying.' Petherick tells me some of the men caught me as I was falling off the dromedary, and that for hours I remained on the sand, the moonlight increasing the pallor of my countenance; with difficulty he overcame the belief, which he had shared with those around, that peace had come at last. He with two or three remained with me, whilst all the others went on to the wells, some soon to return with water, and with milk from kind Bedouins who were there with their cattle. Thus refreshed, I was enabled to continue the journey, and to find at the wells our tents up, a couch ready, and there, for hours, I slept. I believe we remained a few days at that place, I know that I gained strength, and when we again started I was quite gay, for every step taken was one nearer home. However, I soon relapsed into the old moaning and delirious state; the same black wall was ever before me. How many dead and dying camels we passed! a solitary one would sometimes stagger to its feet, and proceed with ours a short distance, then fall, and we abandon it to its fate. One of these poor animals I never can forget: I thought it was a skeleton, but the luminous beseeching eyes gazed at us from the spectral head, and yet no one gave it a drink, which I beseeched them to do. We were within a few hours of the river, when I experienced a slight sunstroke. Petherick would not allow me to move for some hours, therefore we remained with two of the servants; another, who went on, returned with sweet Nile-water and refreshing limes. As we approached Korosko, the *reis* of the 'Kathleen' and some of the crew advanced to greet us. After receiving their salutations, I asked how were the birds? the smiles of the men disappeared, and they held down their heads. We were soon on board, and there in their cages were my birds, but, with two or three exceptions, all dead. They had been neglected and starved; parrot Polly was alive, though reduced to a skeleton: she remembered us, gave a feeble cry, and was soon nestling in Petherick's hands. A pair of small and exquisite long-tailed doves were also alive. The men could not recover their spirits; Petherick's silence, and my tears, were a reproach more bitter than expressed anger.

"And now, darling, I must do my very best to get strong and well. Peth. grieves to see the weak state I am in; at times I am very petulant, and he is so patient and forbearing."

"'THE KATHLEEN'
"ASSOUAN.

"Oh, what a pleasure have we had to-day! It was early —I had not risen—when I thought I heard English voices singing an English hymn. A pause—it must be a dream! again the voices rose. I sat up—looked around to be sure that I was awake: a child's voice, clear as a bell, I distinguished. This is too much joy!—and there was silence. Could I refrain from weeping? though reasoning how mercifully such dreams are sent to us, reviving, as they do, so vividly past happiness, and with them the hope that brighter days will come again. How often have I been lured into the belief that I saw you all! and though the vision was too soon dispelled, the happy thoughts long remained.

Petherick returned from an early ramble: I told him my fancies; and, observing the tearful eyes, he went on deck to inquire. Soon a bright face peeped in at the doorway, and the cheery voice said, 'You are right: there is a fine *dahabyeh* moored near ours; she carries the American flag, and a fair-haired child runs about her deck.' Thus was our first Sabbath after the perilous journey heralded in.

"We went on board the newly arrived *dahabyeh* and introduced ourselves to Mr. Ewing and his wife; their dear little girl was soon in my arms. Mr. Ewing, an American, is connected with the American Mission-house established at Cairo.

"The Ewings evinced much sympathy towards us; and during our stay of a few days at Assouan I was the recipient of sundry little dainties prepared by Mrs. Ewing: home-made bread, baked in tins such as are used in England, corn-flour, blanc-mange, all so fresh and nutritious that I became strong (having then a great appetite), and was able to get about and hold revels in those grand ruins on the island of Philæ, picturing glorious Cleopatra loitering on its terraces or reposing beneath the palm trees. In this sunny clime imagination runs riot; I gave the reins to mine, and such golden, crimson, and purple-tinted clouds crowned my fancies. One day I picked up a tiny bronze eagle: we thought it might have been the ornamentation on the top of a Roman standard-lance; another day a wonderfully perfect granite head, well chiselled, became a prize.

"On our way down the Nile we visited, for the first time, magnificent Edfoo, now partially cleared of the ponderous encumbrance of sand which for ages had almost concealed it from view. His Highness Said Pasha gave orders for this undertaking to be commenced, and to him all lovers of antiquity must be ever grateful.

"At Luxor we next arrived, bright with reminiscences to us, though darkened for a moment when my poor horse, 'Luxor,' was thought of. At that place, in July, 1861, we had first seen him, curvetting and prancing, during the *fantasie* which Petherick gave to celebrate the anniversary of my birthday, and, because I had admired him, was purchased.

"Once more we were induced to visit grand Karnac, and were accompanied by the Consular Agent, Mustapha Aga, who kindly lent us gaily-caparisoned horses. He pointed out the house built on a ruined temple, at Luxor, usually occupied by Lady Duff Gordon: she was then absent.

"On our return to the 'Kathleen,' wearying for home tidings, I asked Consul Mustapha if he could let me see any newspapers. His son went to their home for a few in his possession. Such a treat it was to see the dear English type again! but almost the first paragraph which attracted my attention was the one relating the awfully sudden death of Captain Speke. For his untimely end sorrow came over me like one tremendous wave, sweeping away the bitterness which had filled my heart against him. Petherick, utterly subdued, spoke tenderly of the man he had once deemed a friend.

"The subsequent morning I was unable to rise; fever held me fast: they say I was delirious, but ever and again I recognized the gentle nursing and tending of a woman's delicate hands, cool lips oft impressed upon my burning forehead, wet clothing deftly removed, to be replaced by fresh garments, and all to the tuneful, cheering babble in our own tongue, such as a nurse utters when soothing an ailing child; a whispered hope of better health, a word or two of prayer, a verse of thanksgiving, and an encouragement to try to rouse myself for the dear husband's sake.

"Who was my ministering angel? you will say. Gratefully I record it is to Mrs. Ewing, the American lady, I owe so much.

"I think we must have remained some time at Luxor, but it was pleasant to feel that once more the 'Kathleen' was on her way. A brother-in-law of Captain Grant's, who is connected with a missionary society, about this time solicited a passage down stream in our *dahabyeh*: he had intended proceeding to the first cataract, but illness attacking him, as it does many in these parts, he was anxious to return to Cairo. Petherick could not accede to his request, in consequence of my illness; and we fear that this refusal will be deemed discourteous and inhospitable."

"THE 'KATHLEEN,'
'OFF THE ISLAND OF RODA, OPPOSITE OLD CAIRO,
"*November 26th*, 1864.

"SISTER DARLING,

"I hardly know how to write to you—I cannot nerve myself to it. We arrived here yesterday afternoon, and in the evening received from the Consulate letters of yours, from February to October: they are not yet all read. I have been very ill, but it is over now."

[*Continued by Petherick.*]

"My dear Kate's excitement after receipt of our voluminous post yesterday at five p.m. (which kept us up until two a.m., and again was recommenced at five a.m. by candlelight) is such that, in her own words, 'I cannot write more: I am too excited; it makes me ill.' So you see, dearest Mona, it is again my agreeable task to be your 'pet' correspondent, only, I believe, now, under the present circumstances, but for a very short time longer, as, thanks to a good, gracious, and bountiful God, poor Kate's health is undergoing a great and decided change for the better. I thank you, dear Mona, from my heart for your precious letters; Kate is indeed the dear, brave, matchless wife you so truly and sisterly describe her.

"The post leaves to-day, and I am anxious to proceed at once to Cairo, to report myself at the Consulate; you must please, therefore, excuse a lengthy reply to your and Peter's welcome letters. Thank him, and beg him to convey heartfelt thanks to my invaluable friends, Mr. Macqueen and Mr. Tinné, for their generous and manifold services, accorded, no doubt, often at serious inconvenience to themselves. It will be an easy but highly cherished task to convince them that I was not unworthy of their support, during absence, in peril, and through evil and false report." Do not expect to see us very soon, as we purpose remaining here some time to recruit."

"THE 'KATHLEEN,'
"AT RODA ISLAND,
"*December 1st.*

"SISTER DEAR,

"I am permitted to write a wee bit daily, so I dare say, ere the post leaves, this will be almost a letter. I send you a leaf of the myrtle and a rose which formed part of a bouquet dear Petherick brought to me. The old familiar perfume was almost a pain: you can understand, dear.

"I am indeed shaken—such a wreck! The last few days of our river journey I remember not; but I know that wherever we stopped kind, generous people gave Petherick many dainties for me. I was then too weak to be able to walk, and was always carried to the deck. All the letters have been read and re-read—some of the papers too. How can I love your darlings well enough? God heard their touching prayers. You cannot yet know that we are in safety here, but I think that you must *feel* it. I want you, dear, to give thanks, with ours, in your church to Him who has brought us so far."

"*December 21st.*

"We have left the 'Kathleen,' and reside now in the house of Hassenein Effendi, and are so much more comfortable. Rapidly I regain strength. Dr. Paterson and Dr. Ogilvie have paid me a friendly visit. It is uncertain when we leave for England. Unpleasant rumours have been circulated against Petherick with respect to the slave trade: the calumny is so utterly absurd that he waits with impatience to be formally accused."

"BOULAC,
"January, 1865.

"SISTER DEAR,

"Still no hope of leaving yet awhile. Peth. very busy with his papers. The servants whom we brought from Khartoum have been systematically robbing us. For some time past we have been missing small sums, and knew not whom to suspect; but the other day, when dining with your kind friends the Mosses, at Shepherd's Hotel, Rechan, our cook, was found coming from one of the apartments; a struggle took place, his scarf or sash became unfolded, and from it fell articles of jewellery, gold coins and dollars; a key also, which was a duplicate of Petherick's secretaire. Rechan was taken to prison, but escaped next day; at least he, it is supposed, bribed the keepers, and so got free. The boy Binc, hearing of the arrest, quickly packed up his things and ran off; the *reis* of the 'Kathleen' did the same: all were in league.

"'The wild donkey had been neglected, his food-money not being so expended, and he died: the groom then joined his fellow-servants. We now have only an old woman of Boulac to wait upon us. Polly parrot, who dislikes strangers, hides herself, and when the poor woman attempts to touch any of our belongings, either to dust or for any purpose, out rushes the parrot from her concealment to bite the servant's feet or to seize her garments, which if she succeeds in doing, Polly is happy, and testifies her delight by laughing loudly, winding up with a prolonged shriek. This bird is a great source of amusement to us: when the cloth is prepared for breakfast or dinner, she calls for her own particular chair to be placed near the table; she then climbs to the top bar, whistles for a plate, and expects to be first served. Sometimes, to teaze her, Peth. assists me, when she, indignant, scolds him. Twice the bird has nearly met with a sad end. When off the Island of Roda, she was perched high on a mast of the 'Kathleen;' Petherick, who was about to proceed to Boulac on his donkey, forgot to give his usual salaam to Polly, she made an attempt to fly at him, but fell heavily into the hold of the boat: for a long time she remained senseless. Again, at this place, she tumbled from the balcony under similar circumstances, as Peth. was riding off to Cairo; the bird was picked up and brought to me. For two hours she was insensible, I grieving all the time, and Petherick, ignorant of the accident, away. Three of the fowls we brought with us from Central Africa have their liberty, and never stray from the yard. One only of the tiny long-tailed doves have we, and it is the last of our fine collection of birds.

"I have been to the palace and gardens of Shoobra with Mrs. Moss, and much enjoyed myself. I now ride and drive without fear—at first I was too timid to do so. Mr. and Mrs. Tinné have been here, and I spent a day with Mrs. Tinné at their hotel. Mrs. Ewing and her little darling I often see. At their house I met the Maharanee, the wife of H.H. Dhuleep Singh. All these little incidents will convince you what progress I have made towards recovery. Miss Tinné lives in a quaint house not far from here, and we see her occasionally.

"I have peeped at Captain Grant's book: it angers me so, he misrepresents facts as far as dear Peth. is concerned; but time will show. No more on this subject at present.

"Herr Binder, who was Austrian Consul at Khartoum, is now at Cairo; he is a visitor—also the Baron Heuglin, and many others—though I dare not yet venture into much society.

"Of all dear Petherick's business affairs he can best communicate them. He has indeed been wronged, and still is so sanguine of redress. I, therefore, will not speak of his hopes."

"BOULAC,
"April.

"We really are to leave for England this month!!! As no charge has been made against Petherick by our own or the Egyptian Government, he feels at liberty to depart. The Ewings have kindly invited us to spend the last few days with them in Cairo. Our desert traps will then be sold: a purchaser was soon found for the 'Kathleen.' Did I tell you that whilst we were in her, at Roda, Lady Duff Gordon came to inspect her? but she was too small for her requirements. Lady Duff Gordon is a remarkably handsome woman: she is charmed with life in the East."

"AMERICAN MISSION-HOUSE,
"CAIRO,
"April.

"We are with our kind friends, the Ewings. Such a happy calm is experienced in this Christian, genial community!

"Polly and the fowls will go with us *home*, but the dove died this morning; driving here, the coachman accidentally whipped out one of the eyes of the little bird: all our care was of no avail; it was, however, a solitary bird since the death of its companion.

"The Consul-General, Consul Reade, and his wife have called to see us, and many more. You remember 'little Dorrit,' as we called her, who was to have accompanied us to Khartoum and the interior, but who fell in love and married here, declaring that the hazardous journey would kill her, and therefore she would not proceed? Alas, Mona! she is dead. At my request her husband called to give me particulars. Cholera carried her off in a few hours: she is interred in the Protestant Cemetery outside Cairo."

"HOTEL ABBÄT,
"ALEXANDRIA,
"*Easter Monday*.

"Yesterday morning we left Cairo, carrying with us the affectionate farewells of the good, kind Ewings; and several friends assembled at the railway station to bid us 'God speed.' Fairly on our way, there rose not in any church Hallelujahs more fervent than those from our hearts and lips; and when, approaching Alexandria, the bright blue sea appeared, which we had thought never to have beheld again, reverently we returned thanks to 'The Almighty,

" 'Who sitteth in the heavens, over all, from the beginning.' "

APPENDICES.

APPENDIX A.

I HAD been fifteen years in Africa prior to my return home in July, 1859. My occupation during these years has been given to the public in my book entitled "Egypt, the Soudan, and the White Nile," published by Messrs. Blackwood and Co. in 1861.

My visit to England was owing to the natural desire I entertained of again seeing my relatives and friends after so long an absence, and also for the purpose of acquiring firearms, principally large-bore rifles for elephant shooting on the White Nile.

One of my earliest calls in London was on Sir R. Murchison, whose acquaintance I had made, many years previously, by rendering him and Professor Sedgwick—then on a geographical tour—some trifling attention, in showing them the neighbourhood of Dillenburg, in the Duchy of Nassau, where I then resided.

Captains Burton and Speke had just discovered the Tanganyka and Nyanza Lakes. Then, as now, African geography was the favourite topic of the Royal Geographical Society, of which Sir Roderick was Vice-President. His reception of me, after my giving a brief account of my wanderings in Africa, was as warm as I could wish, and, without being consulted on the subject, resulted in my being proposed and elected a member of the Royal Geographical

Society. Sir Roderick also introduced me to Captain Speke, who had but recently returned to England from his expedition with Captain Burton.

It was far from my thoughts to court notoriety either as a traveller or as an author, and one of the most urgent of my new acquaintances to induce me to overcome my prejudices with respect to publishing, was Captain Speke.

Although unable to attend the meeting of the British Association about to be held at Aberdeen, I could not resist the pressing request of Sir Roderick Murchison, Captain Speke, and many others, to write a paper for it, which I entrusted to be read by Dr. Norton Shaw, the then Assistant-Secretary of the Royal Geographical Society. I had also acceeded to Captain Speke's desire to give a rough-hand sketch of my travels, which he thus acknowledges:

"EDINBURGH,
"*September* 25*th*, 1859.

"My dear Petherick,

"The map, unfortunately, did not reach Mr. Blackwood in time for insertion in the magazine. I say unfortunately, because I feel that it would have been of material service to the world at large had it appeared there; but, as regards myself, you have satisfied me entirely, and I feel very much obliged to you for it.

* * * * * * *

"My paper on the discovery of the Nyanza followed yours, stating that there was such a close analogy to the habits of all Central Africans, that I was pleased your paper had preceded mine, for by it they would understand what the people were like who occupied the country of which I was about to give a short, dry, geographical description only.

"It has just struck me that you could not do better than

write a short description of your travels in Africa, well loaded with amusing anecdotes and fights with the natives: the thing would tell admirably just at present, and for the future would keep the world looking anxiously for your peregrinations.

"Excuse the hint, and take it only as it is meant. I, for instance, shall be very proud if you will condescend to accept this advice, and wish you as good success in the undertaking as I feel confident you would merit if you only take the trouble."

Captain Speke again writes thus from York, but without a date, simply "Sunday." The letter was received by me at Cardiff, October 12th, 1859:

"MY DEAR PETHERICK,

"Since I dispatched my last to you, I have seen your map, which you so kindly and cleverly drew up for me. It was lying in Mr. Blackwood's office, and is there now; for I told him that I would again write and ask you to publish it in his magazine yourself. You would have my experience to join with your knowledge of Africa, and if you will only trouble yourself to put them together, you would be a world-wide benefactor.

"The interest of the matter must be much more intense than you suppose, or I am sure you would not withhold from the public what they want so much, and which is now kept secret within yourself.

"The Royal Geographical Society have not the means of spreading anything about, whereas Blackwood has a larger circulation than anybody else. Again, the Royal Geographical Society are slothful to the last degree, but Blackwood does not want a week to produce a map, a paper, or anything else."

On the other hand, I acceeded to the desire of several of the leading members of the Royal Geographical Society, that I should write a paper for their next meeting on January 9th, 1860; thus my intended return to Africa in the month of October or November, 1859, became indefinitely postponed. In the meantime Captain Speke and myself corresponded frequently, and from Rheola, in December, 1859, he writes:

"My dear Petherick,

"Were you ever thinking of looking after the Nile's source yourself? I infer by your letter that you may have had it under consideration, and if so, it strikes me that my going up the Nile may possibly be injurious to your prospects. In that case I withhold from interference. But again, should it meet your views that we could manage by combined exertions, either in company or separately, to settle the question of the White River, I would readily work with you. If you think, as I do, the Nyanza is, in all probability, the true source, our object evidently should be to bear at once directly on it from any point on the river which is most convenient for breaking off from. It is obvious to me, from the great altitude of the lake, compared to Gondokoro, that the river must cease to be navigable after a certain distance above that station, and then the mode of proceeding would be to form a strong party, by which we could push through the large tribes that may be to the south of Gondokoro."

The following letter, which I give in full, will speak for itself:

"'JORDANS,'
"*December 22nd*, 1859.

"My dear Petherick,

"I have just received a letter from Sir R. Murchison, and

am delighted to find he has accepted my plan for opening Africa favourably. I proposed to him that I should not go up the Nile, but round by Zanzibar, whilst you, supported by the Foreign Office, should go up the Nile, and meet me at some fixed point which I could determine. What a jolly thing this would be to accomplish! *You could do your own ivory business at the same time that you work out geography.* I shall be in town about the 6th or 7th proximo, and will call on you to make further arrangements. I hope you will yet come down to 'Jordans' some time before you depart again.

"Yours very truly,
"(Signed)   J. H. SPEKE."

Shortly after this I accepted his invitation to go down and spend a day or two at his father's residence in Somersetshire called "Jordans," and Captain Speke informs the Secretary of the Royal Geographical Society thereof thus:

"'JORDANS,'
"*January 2nd*, 1860.

"MY DEAR SHAW,

"Petherick is coming here on Wednesday, when we shall run over his paper on the Nile, and concert measures for meeting in the direction of the Nyanza at some future date."

Referring to his design for following up his discoveries in Central Africa, he stated he felt certain the Government would support him; and, in accordance with his warmly-expressed desire (provided the Government would sanction my absence *and supply me with a grant to cover the bare expenses of the expedition*), I expressed my willingness to meet him at any given point. With this understanding we journeyed to London, and from the discussion which followed the reading of my paper (given in the " Proceedings" of the Society, Vol. IV., No. II., January 9th, 1860), the following extracts will show how eagerly the subject was advocated and distinctly declared to be designed by the Royal Geographical Society:

"The PRESIDENT was sure he should express not only his own feelings, but those of the meeting also, when he said that they were very much indebted to Mr. Consul Petherick for the very interesting paper which he had just read. It was marked by that spirit of commercial enterprise which was peculiarly the characteristic of our country, and from which undoubtedly the Society had upon so many occasions derived the greatest advantage.

"He was happy to announce that Her Majesty's Government had been pleased to grant £2,500 in support of Captain Speke's intended expedition, and he trusted that Mr. Petherick would continue, in an opposite direction, the explorations of which he had just given an account; and he hoped the time might not be far distant when these two distinguished explorers might meet and greet each other, arriving from different directions on the banks of the White Nile.

"SIR RODERICK MURCHISON believed that civilization could only be introduced into Africa by showing to its inhabitants that we were anxious to deal with them fairly and equitably. Dr. Livingstone had often told him that the first step to be taken in civilizing the African was to barter fairly with him, and teach him that he could gain much by attaching himself to an honest Englishman. In conclusion, he heartily hoped that the scheme of developing the true source of the White Nile, which they had in hand, might be so accomplished that we should be the first people who really discovered the sources of the great historical river. Whether the main source was the great Lake Nyanza, or farther west, he was quite sure that by the new co-operating expeditions which were designed by the Geographical Society, and which he hoped the Government would assist, the discovery would greatly redound to the honour of the nation, and would greatly advance geographical knowledge.

"COLONEL SYKES, V.-P.R.G.S., entertained great hopes that when Mr. Petherick and Captain Speke renewed their travels, they would meet and embrace each other on the Equator."

Shortly after this meeting, at the suggestion of some of the officiating members of the Society, I penned the following letter to Sir R. Murchison:

"*January*, 1860."

"SIR,

"The flattering reception of my paper on the White Nile by the members of the Royal Geographical Society, and the comments thereon by the Chairman, the Earl de Grey, yourself, and Colonel Sykes, have induced me to address to you, the Vice-President of the Society, a few brief remarks on the existing state of trade on the White Nile and the Egyptian dependencies of the Soudan in connection with geographical researches.

"It would be superfluous in me to make any general remarks upon the advantages to this great manufacturing country of any extension of its trade with Central Africa by increased facilities for obtaining additional supplies of cotton, gums, ivory, India-rubber, cochineal, oils, and a variety of articles of minor importance; but perhaps you are not to the same extent aware of the benefits that an additional export trade, that I trust at no distant period is likely to present itself to us in the shape of a market for cotton manufactured goods in the same regions.

"Although the negroes of the White Nile accept at present

6—2

only glass beads, cowrie-shells, and copper wire in exchange for the raw produce of the country they inhabit, I have discovered a growing desire for clothing. As to chiefs of tribes and others to whom I have been indebted for some service or assistance rendered, I have invariably presented them with a cotton shirt, of which they are not only proud, but value more than the ordinary glass ornaments; and it is my opinion that as soon as the trade now established shall have glutted their desire for beads, cotton cloths, as in the case at Darfour, will become the principal object of exchange.

"When I first visited the Soudan provinces, the annual export of gum arabic thence to Europe did not exceed eighty tons annually, and the quantity of ivory from Central Africa by the White River was confined to twenty tons. Now one hundred tons of ivory and five hundred tons of gum arabic, of the value of £80,000 per annum, are exported, the greater part of which is returned to the Soudan in the shape of British manufactures.

"In justice to myself, I might also state that during a period of eleven years' residence in these remote points, my own humble efforts and example have in no slight degree contributed to the realization of the above results. The Royal Geographical Society, through its influence with Her Majesty's Government, having obtained a grant to enable Captain Speke to follow up his discoveries northwards, and in consequence of the desire expressed that I should meet Captain Speke on the confines of his lake, and assist him on his way north of the Equator and down the Nile, I am happy to state that from several years' experience of the tribes, and feeling a lively desire for adventure, particularly when connected with the noble pursuit of scientific discovery, I believe myself to be in a position to render that gentleman very material assistance; and, provided it will meet with the approbation of Her Majesty's Government, I shall be happy to devote my time and services to meet and assist Captain Speke as far as I am capable in the discovery of the sources of the Nile."

On the 30th of the same month (January) the Council of the Royal Geographical Society applied to the Foreign Office for a special grant to enable me to afford assistance to Captain Speke in his approaching expedition; this grant, as will be subsequently seen, the Government refused to make. If any further corroboration were needed to show the manner in which I became connected with Captain Speke's expedition, the following extract from Vol. IV., No. III., of the Society's "Proceedings" (March 26th, 1860), would be conclusive.

"CAPTAIN SPEKE said since returning to Europe he had met Mr. Petherick, who, unknown to himself, and while he had been exploring close to the southward of the Equator, was also travelling amongst the tribes to the northward of it, and had brought back names, such as he had heard of and inserted in his map, as Barri and Wangara; the latter, probably, meant for his Wanyaro. These tribes, he was informed by Mr. Petherick—quite in conformity with the Arabs' account of them—were hostile to one another, that they never mixed, and that penetration amongst them would be most difficult. He (Captain Speke) had consequently proposed to Mr. Petherick to make a combined advance simultaneously with him on those tribes which lie in a short compass of two or three degrees immediately to the northward of his lake, and due south of Gondokoro, the German Mission-station on the Nile; Mr. Petherick to come towards Uganda from the north, while he went northwards to the Nile, hugging any river he might find running out of the lake. Now, as Mr. Petherick had readily assented to co-operate with him, and as so much hung upon the security or otherwise of the undertaking, he hoped that that gentleman would receive the same support from the Government which he had done.

"Mr. Consul Petherick said . . . and although he was engaged in trade, and had five or six establishments to look after, yet he would not allow his friend to remain in the lurch while it was in his power to assist him. He was also firmly persuaded that unless Captain Speke were met by himself, or by boats duly armed and provisioned, he would not be able to bring his party down the Nile, owing to the absence of food and conveyance. For only two months in the year did boats remain at Gondokoro, and unless he arrived within these two months, December and January, he would find no boats there to bring him down to Khartoum. He would also find himself among the Barri, a most savage tribe who would not give themselves the trouble to cultivate grain, and for the last five or six years had been so unable to sustain themselves that they had been compelled to barter ivory for grain.

"In assisting Captain Speke, the only thing he required of the Government was that they should allow him sufficient money to enable him to place a couple of well-armed and provisioned boats at the service of Captain Speke, and to retain them at Gondokoro until his arrival."

On or about April 18th, pursuant to invitation, I accompanied Captains Speke and Grant to "Jordans," in order to spend in their company the last few days of their sojourn in England. I cannot refrain here from mentioning the most amicable relations that existed between us; and it was upon this occasion that I personally promised Speke, not only to do my utmost to support him in his arduous undertaking, but, as long as life lasted, never to desert him. They left England on April 27th; and how I kept my promise these pages will show.

APPENDIX A. 87

On May 18th following, I received from Mr. Francis Galton, the Foreign Secretary of the Royal Geographical Society, a letter to this effect:

"MY DEAR SIR,

"Speke has written for 'instructions;' I am drawing them up, and we have an Expedition Committee on Wednesday to finish them off. I want to append to the paper a short letter from you, saying what he ought to do if he arrives at Gondokoro, and giving the times when the wind would be favourable to him for going down the Nile, and any local facts that in the absence of all assistance he might find of use. Would you please word it so that I can have time to read it before the Expedition Committee meets (on Saturday at three p.m.)?

"What about the Consulate?* Supposing you succeed in getting it, what would your White Nile arrangements be, so far as they would affect Speke?

"Very truly yours,

"(Signed) FRANCIS GALTON.

"J. PETHERICK, Esq."

The following is a copy of my reply:

"*May* 18*th*, 1860.

"DEAR SIR,

"In reply to your favour of the 15th inst., which I did not receive until last evening, I beg to state, that, unless arrangements are made with me to provide Captain Speke and his party on their arrival at Gondokoro with provisions and the means of transport, consisting of not less than two boats, he ought to

---

* This was with reference to the Abyssinian Consulate, vacant by the decease of Consul Plowden, and applied for in conjunction with the one I held, the Consulate for the Soudan.

endeavour to arrive at the point above stated in the month of December or January, when he will, in all probability, find the boats of the Arab traders from Khartoum, which will afford him a passage down the Nile to Khartoum.

"On the other hand, if Captain Speke cannot make the Nile at Gondokoro in either of the months stated, his difficulties will be very considerable: the season of the ivory trade will have expired, he will find no more boats there; and in consequence of the invariable great scarcity of grain in that part of Africa, he will have to encounter hunger and the hostility of the tribes, who, finding him unprovided with the means of escape by boats, will doubtless pursue him, and attempt to murder the whole of the party, for the gratification, innate in them, of destroying any stranger intruding on their territory, and to possess themselves of any articles of value wherewith to purchase grain for their half-starving families.

"To advance under these circumstances would be ruinous; and I should then advise Captain Speke to endeavour to retire to more favourable regions, to some agricultural tribe, where, if his means hold, he might support himself and party until the proper season arrives for him to approach the Nile, and when to a certainty he will find the boats of the Khartoum traders.

"I am not yet in possession of any official communication from the Government regarding my application for the vacant Consulate of Abyssinia; but whether I should be honoured by obtaining the appointment or not, I shall under any circumstances be happy to meet the views of the Geographical Society and the Government by placing myself, men, and boats, at their disposal, for the purpose of rendering any assistance to Captain Speke in his perilous undertaking.

"Yours, &c.,
"(Signed)   J. PETHERICK."

APPENDIX A.

At the meeting of the Society held June 11th, 1860, (see Vol. IV. No. 5, page 222), the President, in announcing that Captains Speke and Grant had started on their expedition, added they would be exposed to great dangers. "Consul Petherick, from Khartoum, could meet him with a large force, and escort him through the country. *But Consul Petherick could hardly be expected to do this at his own expense;* and, as the Government declined making any further grant, the Council of the Society had departed from their usual rules, and had headed a subscription with £100 towards defraying those expenses. He only hoped that many gentlemen *would contribute towards so good and just an object.*"

The exact nature and limit of the assistance that I might be able to afford Captain Speke not having been decided on, in compliance with the request of one of the Council, now unfortunately no more, I put forward some proposals which, by reference to the Secretary's "Proceedings," will be found in Vol. IV., No. 5, page 223. The following are extracts therefrom:

"In order to afford the greatest possible assistance to the expedition of Captains Speke and Grant, I consider it necessary to place three well-provisioned boats, under an escort of twenty armed men, at the base of the cataracts beyond Gondokoro, in the month of November, 1861.

"With forty armed men, natives of Khartoum or the adjoining provinces, I would then undertake personally to penetrate into the interior as far as the Lake Nyanza, with a view to effect a meeting with the expedition, and assist it through the hostile tribes between the lake and the Nile, and return thence by the boats to Khartoum.

* * * * * *

"I believe that, with the facilities at my command in the shape of boats and arms, the expense of such an expedition would amount to about £2,000. *In the event of so large a sum not being available, I would then propose to place two well-provisioned boats, under the superintendence of one of my own men, on whose integrity I could confidently depend, to await the arrival of the expedition at the above-named cataracts from November,* 1861, *until June,* 1862. This precaution I consider most important to the success of Captains Speke and Grant, and the expense would be, on a moderate calculation, £1,000."

The Vice-President, Sir R. Murchison, in reference thereto at the meeting held June 25th, 1860 (Vol. IV. No. 5, page 226), said, "they would all participate in the sentiments which Mr. Petherick had so forcibly, succinctly, and ably expressed," adding, that "it was in order to assist Captains Speke and Grant in the most difficult portion of their journey that Mr. Petherick had offered his services." Sir Roderick concluded by saying, "He (Mr. Petherick) was willing to abandon his other occupations, and to give up his time, to meet his fellow-countrymen in this region of the interior. He had only to repeat the expression of his admiration of the proposal—and he did most earnestly hope that British geographers would by their subscriptions support this noble enterprise."

At the meeting of the Royal Geographical Society on November 12th in the same year (see "Proceedings," Vol. V., No. 1, page 20), according to the desire of the President, I again pointed out what the probable difficulties of Captain Speke would be on his way from the Nyanza to Gondokoro, and thence down the Nile; and the President concluded by announcing that subscriptions in aid of my expedition would be received at the Royal Geographical Society's offices. Similar announcements were made at the subsequent meetings of the Society; and in January 1861, £1,000 having been subscribed, an account of my intended expedition, evidently written under some misconception as to its scope, was published in the "Times," and I consequently addressed the following note to the President and Council:

"*February 4th*, 1861.

"GENTLEMEN,

"My instructions not having been read at the last meeting of the Society, and the allusions to the proceedings in the 'Times,' stating my expedition to extend to the discovery of the sources of the Nile, I fear many of the subscribers may be under a false impression respecting the real object thereof, and, at a future time, may express disappointment at my proceeding no farther in the interior than it will be possible for me to accomplish in the time agreed upon—viz., from November, 1861, until July, 1862.

"With the greatest desire to carry out the instructions of the Royal Geographical Society and to satisfy every subscriber, I shall consider it a favour if the Council will publish a brief statement of my approaching expedition; with an explanation that the programme, as put forward in the printed circular, has necessarily been curtailed, owing to the amount therein stated not having been subscribed.

"Wishing to start fair, and on a satisfactory understanding with one and all of my supporters,

"Believe me, &c., &c.,
"(Signed) J. PETHERICK."

An agreement between the Royal Geographical Society and myself then took place, which, with the necessary instructions and subscription list, were published under the date of my letter in the "Proceedings" (Vol. V., No. 1, page 40), and which, for the information of those subscribers who may not have seen the "Proceedings," or who are not members of the Society, I quote in full.

AGREEMENT

Between Consul Petherick and the Royal Geographical Society.

"*February 4th*, 1861.

"I. Consul Petherick undertakes, in consideration of the receipt of £1,000, towards the expedition up the Nile, to place two well-armed boats, during November, 1861, at Gondokoro, with a sufficient stock of grain to ensure to Captain Speke and his party the means of subsistence upon their arrival at that place.

"II. If Captain Speke shall not arrive in November, 1861, that Consul Petherick shall proceed with an armed party southwards towards Lake Nyanza to meet him.

"III. If Captain Speke shall arrive at Gondokoro before June, 1862, Consul Petherick promises to assist Captain Speke to make any explorations which Captain Speke may deem desirable.

"IV. It being further understood that in the event of Captain Speke not having arrived by that time at Gondokoro, Consul Petherick shall not be bound to remain beyond 1862."

INSTRUCTIONS

for Consul Petherick's proposed Expedition up the White Nile in aid of Captains Speke and Grant.

"*February 8th*, 1861.

"The President and Council of the Royal Geographical Society, having ascertained that the amount of subscriptions will not be sufficient to enable you to remain two years to the southward of Gondokoro, and thus to carry out your proposition in full, proceed now to give you instructions whereby the great object of their desire—the rendering assistance to the expedition under Captains Speke and Grant—can be best accomplished with the means at their disposal.

"By leaving England in March, you will be enabled to reach Khartoum in time to equip two boats with a supply of provisions sufficient for your own and Captain Speke's party until July, 1862. With these you will proceed to Gondokoro, where it is very desirable that you should arrive early in the month of October, that is to say, as soon as possible after the cessation of the rains. You will then, in the event of Captain Speke not having arrived, leave a trustworthy person with a sufficient force in charge of the boats—the maintenance of these until June, 1862, at Gondokoro, being of primary importance. The next object the President and Council have in view is, that you should proceed in the direction of Lake Nyanza, with a view of succouring Captain Speke, and bring him and his party in safety to the depôt at Gondokoro.

"The President and Council do not attempt to lay down any limit to this exploration, but, fully trusting in your known zeal and energy, feel assured that you will do all in your power to effect the above-mentioned object without serious risk to the lives of the party under your command. Should the junction with Captain Speke be effected, which there is every reason to believe will be, previous to June, 1862, you will consult with him as to the best means of employing the period which will elapse before the change of the Monsoon will permit you to descend the Nile of extending our knowledge of the adjoining region.

"In entrusting you with the sum which has been subscribed for this purpose, the President and Council, considering themselves accountable to the subscribers for its proper expenditure, will require an account of its disbursement. If circumstances should prevent your meeting with Captain Speke's expedition, they consider that you are entirely relieved from the responsibility of remaining yourself, or detaining the boats, longer than July, 1862, at Gondokoro.

"The President and Council desire to impress upon you the necessity of obtaining, as frequently as possible, astronomical observations for the ascertaining of your geographical position, and that you forward, as often as opportunity offers, copies of your journal to the Secretary of this Society.

"A list of instruments, together with instructions respecting their use, and notices of such phenomena as it it is likely you will have an opportunity of observing, is herewith appended, to which also are added manuals on ethnology, botany, and zoology; to each of which sciences as well as geology, you will have an opportunity of adding much new information. In addition to the 'Hints for Travellers,' published by this Society, particular instructions relative to the peculiar character of the great river you are about to explore have been prepared, and which, it is hoped, will assist you in making observations which will throw much light on the geography of this region.

"The President and Council take this opportunity of expressing their admiration of the spirit of enterprize which has induced you at great personal risk, and, possibly, considerable pecuniary loss, to undertake the charge of this expedition; and they hope, under God's providence, you may not only succeed in affording succour to the Zanzibar Expedition at a period when it will be most in need of it, but that you will succeed in opening a new field to the civilizing influences of commerce."

I may here state, upon one occasion at the "Monday Evenings at Home" of my greatly lamented friend the late Admiral Murray, in the Albany, I first met with Mr. (now Sir Samuel) Baker, and, prior to my departure from England, I received the following communication from him:

"CONSTANTINOPLE,
"*November 20th*, 1860.

" My dear Sir,

"Will you oblige me by giving me as much information as you can upon the route between Cairo and Khartoum?

"I should much like to have had the pleasure of seeing you again before I started, but, being so near to Alexandria, it is too far out of the way to return to England prior to a final start.

"I do not intend to limit myself to time; but I shall (D.V.) pass two or three years in the elephant districts, and try and combine an extensive exploration with my old amusements.

"If Burton could have accompanied me I should have been much better pleased. I have written to him; but, whether or no, I shall start from Alexandria about the first week in March; and if you will kindly address me here as soon as convenient, to care of C. Hanson and Company, Constantinople, they will forward the letter to me in Asia Minor, where I am going for a couple of months' shooting.

"If you could give me a letter to any one in Khartoum who could put me up to the right men and the right plan for a first go at the elephants, I should be exceedingly obliged. What are your movements personally? and when do you expect to return to Khartoum? I shall look forward with much pleasure to meeting you somewhere in those parts, and I think I might manage to help you in your ivory transactions when we meet.

"Very sincerely yours,

"(Signed) SAMUEL W. BAKER."

This was followed by several others, dated at Cairo, expressive of a wish to meet and travel with me. From on board his boat at Boulak on April 14th, 1861, he reports his departure from Cairo as follows:—

"NILE BOAT, BOULAK,
"*April 14th*, 1861.

"DEAR PETHERICK,

"I sail to-day, and five minutes ago your note of March 24th was delivered to me. I need not say how glad I shall be to see you.

"All my guns, &c., &c., are arrived, with 100 lb. of gunpowder; but I expect 150 lb. more of the latter from England. Should this be in Alexandria before you leave for the Upper Country, will you be kind enough to bring it up with you, or to leave instructions, if it be not then arrived, that it be forwarded to you at Khartoum?

"Upon opening a case of nautical instruments, I was terribly disappointed in not finding the expected chronometer. I hope you will make arrangements to secure a right good one somehow or other, and bring up the Greenwich mean time with you. Mr. Thurban can, I think, assist you in this. Do not forget to get a note of the rate of the chronometer and to use the instrument like a young baby, otherwise we shall be bothered for longitude. I think rockets and blue lights would be most useful. If you are not supplied with these, the Peninsular and Oriental Company can supply them from their stores at Suez.

"I have no beads nor anything for exchanging up the White Nile, as I depend upon you for all assistance in these matters. I should have been deceived in both price and quality, having no local experience of the tastes of the ebony ladies of the White Nile. I go to Korosko by boat, then across desert to Abu Hamed, and on to Berber, and then take boat again. I shall be delighted when I have the pleasure of meeting you.

"Very sincerely yours,
"(Signed)   SAMUEL BAKER."

The preliminaries for my departure to aid and assist the Speke Expedition having been completed by the receipt on my part of £1,000, subscribed for this purpose, as before stated, I and my party left Liverpool on April 17th, and arrived at Alexandria on May 2nd, 1861.

Owing to the unaccountable non-arrival of our ammunition, which had left London by sailing vesssel three months prior to our departure, we were detained at Cairo until its arrival on June 30th.

During our stay at Cairo I purchased a quantity of glass beads, and a variety of articles adapted for presents and barter, and superintended the fitting up and rigging of a new boat, the "Kathleen," for the expedition. Another unforseen detention of upwards of a month, from August 1st to September 7th, took place at Korosko, consequent on a deficiency of camels for transport across the desert of Aboo Hamed to Berber. This arose out of the extraordinary demand for cattle by the Egyptian Government to facilitate the transit of troops to the Soudan. From this place, on August 9th, I reported progress to the Royal Geographical Society, and related the circumstance of my having met at Luxor M. de Jean, who was thus far on his return to France from Gondokoro. The means contributed to him by the French Government, he said, were so slender that at the point mentioned he had been obliged to abandon his search for the sources of the Nile. We also met Miani on his return from Khartoum at the Cataracts of Assuan. His expedition, with a similar purpose in view, had, he stated, come to grief at Khartoum by the foundering of his boat and consequent loss of stores.

At this point Dr. Murie joined us in the "Kathleen" from Cairo. He left England to join my expedition in the capacity of photographer and amanuensis, and brought with him an elaborate photographic apparatus. He accompanied us across the desert on the 7th, the boat having been sent forward on September 3rd, to take advantage of the increase of the Nile, in order to surmount the Cataracts of Wadi Halfa, Dongola, and Berber.

On the 29th September, at Berber, I was put in possession of the following letter, dated Cassala, 11th July, 1861, and in consequence I took charge of twenty-eight rather formidable packages, consisting of guns, ammunition, three portmanteaux, seven deal cases of sundries, water-barrels and camel litters, independent of the hippopotami-skins and skulls therein referred to.

"CASSALA,
"11th July, 1861.

"MY DEAR PETHERICK,

"I send you a few lines in the hope of catching you at Berber, on your way to Khartoum. At this time of the year there is no pleasure in travelling through such a continuation of deserts as exist to this spot, and I propose to start on the 13th, and bivouac for a few weeks in a good elephant country of the Atbara, now two days' journey on the road to Katariff, which latter place is on the line to Khartoum. When you are there,

I shall hope to get into communication with you, as I shall send a man there with a letter in about five weeks' time, on the chance of your arrival.

"I sent a soldier to Berber with a couple of hoppopotami-skins and skulls to be added to my baggage, left in charge of Suliman Effendi. Will you kindly let them go on to Khartoum? The teeth I took from the skulls. I have had no sport but antelopes, and the said hippo's, up to this spot; but from all accounts I have now reached a good country. I arrived here on the 8th instant. Pray give my remembrances to Halleem Effendi and Suliman Effendi at Berber, as I received much attention from them.'

"Very sincerely yours,
"(Signed) SAMUEL W. BAKER."

We arrived at Khartoum on the 15th October, prior to the termination of an unusually long rainy season. The south wind was still the prevailing one, and the Nile had never been remembered to have risen so high. Notwithstanding a severe rheumatic attack, I was not long in finding out, and reporting to the proper quarter, the enormous proportions the slave trade on the White Nile had assumed since my departure from the Soudan in the spring of 1859. Although, whilst in England, I had been informed, through Her Majesty's Government, of such a change in connection with the White Nile traffic, I, at the time, believed the statements exaggerated; but now there was no doubt upon the subject. Report stated every ivory trader to be in some way or other connected with this abominable traffic; and, notwithstanding the local government had issued a formal notice prohibiting it, a larger number of men and boats were then employed in the vigorous prosecution of the slave trade on the White Nile than, to my knowledge, had ever heretofore been engaged in any trade on the river.

The affrays that took place between the negro aborigines and the Arabs were described as fearful, and more than one boat's crew of the latter had been assailed and totally destroyed by the exasperated natives. To make matters, if possible, still worse, the ivory traders had resorted to stealing the cattle of the negroes, and turn them to good account. Entire herds were seized by bands of marauding traders, and, taken to adjoining districts, were readily bartered for elephants' tusks, having become infinitely more valuable than the formerly much-coveted glass or copper wares. To the exclusion of everything else, a cow became the sole staple for barter of ivory or food, and was the only medium that could command porters for transport to or from the interior.

To traverse the interior had consequently become considerably more dangerous and difficult, requiring a much larger escort than I had been led to anticipate for the navigation of the Nile, not to mention the additional protection required for travelling inland. In lieu of negro porters, who, according to the new state of things, I was no longer able to remunerate, the obligation of taking with me beasts of burden was of necessity involved, and to prepay, support, and transport additional men and cattle in boats to Gondokoro, and thence into the interior, would evidently entail a much larger and more costly expedition than I had been provided for or had ever anticipated in England.

The difficulties Speke would have to encounter in working his way northwards towards Gondokoro, as soon as he came within the scope of the Khartoum traders' operations, would naturally be proportionate to my own, and I firmly believed that, unless relieved, he would never be able to push his way through such serious and numerous obstacles. I felt that, under the circumstances, I had a *double* duty to perform—to comply with my instructions, and to fulfil my promise made at "Jordans"—to do everything in my power to meet and assist Captain Speke. That Speke also felt he could rely upon me, see his letter inviting me to Uganda, dated Karagwa, March 28th, 1862, and published in "Proceedings," Vol. VII., No. 5, page 235. Speke says: "I will go across the Masai country at once to Zanzibar, but, considering your promise to keep two or three boats two or three years for me, I sacrifice everything to fulfil the engagement."

I was also in receipt of a few lines from Dr. Shaw, the late Secretary of the Royal Geographical Society, dated June 27th, 1861.

"MY DEAR PETHERICK,

"The last news from Speke was to the effect that the party was advancing up the hills into the interior, and hoped to meet you all well at Gondokoro. Go ahead! take observations for our gold medal. With kind regard to Mrs. Petherick,

"Yours, &c., &c.,

"(Signed) NORTON SHAW."

I now dispatched two boats under my agent, Abd il Majid, with instructions, and the following letter, to Captain Speke, dated Khartoum, November 15th, 1861. (See "Proceedings," Vol. VIII., No. 1.

"MY DEAR SPEKE,

"I pray God this may be delivered safely to you, by my agent, Abd il Majid, who, with a strong party, consisting of some seventy men, well armed and equipped, will proceed in search of you the moment he arrives at Gondokoro. We—that is to say, my wife and self, accompanied by a medical man and photographer —after a tedious journey up the Nile, and a vexatious delay of several weeks at Korosko, owing to a deficiency of camels necessary for crossing the desert of Aboo Hamed, arrived here a month ago. Had it not been for a serious illness, from which I am now recovering, we should have left at the same time as Abd il Majid to attempt a meeting. The latter has also been detained by the unheard-of rise of the Nile this season, and the consequent backwardness of the north wind and cool season.

"Abd il Majid's instructions are to proceed to meet you from Gondokoro, *viâ* my establishment at Neambara, on the west bank of the Nile, some four or five days' journey in the interior, where he will reinforce himself with some thirty men, in addition to the forty he proceeds with from here, and unless he meets you in the neighbourhood of Gondokoro, he is to continue due-south in the direction of the Lake Nyanza, which, as he proceeds, he is to inquire for, until my wife and self come up with him. Should Abd il Majid effect a happy meeting with you prior to my arrival, he is to place himself and men at your disposal, return and conduct you to the boats, and make them over to you for your disposal. The bearer has in charge some provisions, quinine, &c., which latter I trust you will not require, and clothing for your immediate requirements; and hoping that all may go well, with my best wishes to Grant and yourself,

"Believe me, &c., &c.,

"(Signed) JOHN PETHERICK."

For reasons that will be easily understood, I did not wish to trouble Speke with the particulars of our difficulties, but merely alluded to my illness to account for our not accompanying Abd il Majid.

At the time, owing to every boat available for the purpose having been engaged by the traders, and the inundation of the arsenal rendering it for a month or two impossible to repair and render ship-shape several disabled boats, I availed myself of a third boat, destined for my trade on the Bahar il Gazal, and ordered the person in charge of it to proceed thither. I instructed him to withdraw from my establishment at the Djour, forty-three men, and to convey them to Gondokoro, to support Abd il Majid and enable him to carry out my instructions with regard to his proceedings in the interior.

Surely this is a sufficient contradiction to the wicked insinuations made against me, when I could not defend myself, that I had made my expedition subservient to my trade. Unfortunately for my interest, the contrary, to a greater extent than I can well describe, was the fact, of which, in its proper place, further information will be given.

The reasons for Abd il Majid seeking for Speke *viâ* my station, are as follows:

(1.) It was agreed between Captain Speke and myself that I should meet him on the west side of the Nile.

(2.) Abd il Majid had not a sufficiently powerful escort to attempt to force a passage through the tribes directly south of Gondokoro; but the same difficulty did not exist, I presumed, south of my station, where he was better known.

(3.) At the same time that he placed well-stored and provisioned boats for the relief of Captain Speke at Gondokoro, he could supply my trading station with every requisite, and I could divide the expenses of his expedition—one-half to the Speke Expedition, and the other half to my trade.

The responsibility of my promise made at "Jordans" to Speke

and his family, to do everything in my power to support him, and not to desert him, weighed heavily upon me; and in duty to myself, and what I considered the spirit rather than the letter of my instructions, I set to work to fit out another expedition of four boats. Although the expense that it would entail would be a serious item, I trusted to trade and the spirit of the Society at home to hold me finally harmless. In order to raise the means to meet this expense, I disposed of ivory and European goods at any price; and in the early part of March, 1862, I succeeded in procuring sufficient for the purpose. How could I have acted otherwise? What would have been thought of me in England, had I, instead of proceeding on my own responsibility, written to ask for more money?

Several letters from Khartoum, addressed to Sir Roderick Murchison and Dr. Shaw, conveyed the purport of the foregoing to the Council of the Society—the last of which, dated, I believe, in March, 1862, contained the following paragraphs:

"MY DEAR SHAW,

"If the spirit of geographers at home is to be measured by my own, you will have a large balance in my favour.

"My expedition now numbers seven boats, and to be independent of the negroes for transport, I take with me thirty donkeys and three horses for own riding. The greatly troubled state of the interior calls for this formerly unanticipated addition to the requirements of the expedition, therefore you will perceive, as far as I am concerned, expense will be no object."

Lest my expedition should be considered unnecessarily large, let us see what is said upon the subject of explorations from Gondokoro southwards in an article entitled the "Sources of the

Nile," in No. 241 of the "Edinburgh Review" (for July, 1863), page 239: "A traveller *could obtain no porters* at that place, (Gondokoro), beasts of burden did not exist; yet a strong party was essential to security and progress. Success was only possible to an able leader, who could command means to take out with him an imposing expedition, so completely organized as to be independent of the natives.

The author of this article being anything but complimentary towards myself in respect of my former travels, or, if I guess aright, disposed to allow me credit for anything I have since done to relieve Captain Speke—the above quotation is an important confirmation of the justice of my views with regard to the requirements of my expedition.

In the midst of my arrangements I received the following letters from Baker:

"SOFI,
"*August* 28*th*, 1861.

"MY DEAR PETHERICK,

"I am located here until the rains are over, having taken Abou Sin's advice to shoot through the country when the fine weather commences. Thus I have planned my shooting trip to Khartoum as follows:

"I cross the river here and work through the country between this and the Settitte river; then across through the Hamran country; then through Nimmur's country and into the Basé country; then on to the rivers Rahad and Dender, to the Blue Nile, and to Khartoum.

"This will occupy some time, and I do not think I can be in Khartoum until December. I am anxious to hear from you and to know your plans for a southern expedition; at present I am not sure of your arrival at Khartoum. Thus I have cut out a good sporting route for myself until I reach Khartoum and begin operations on the White Nile. *The latter route will mainly depend upon your guidance.*

"I am short of a few things, and I shall feel much indebted to you if you will kindly send me per parcel the following list of sundries AT ONCE to Sofi. If you are at Khartoum, all my things that were left at Berber are doubtless there also. These please send of *my things*:

"2 barrels gunpowder.
"1 piece lead (it is about 70 lbs.—the *cut* piece left at Berber and marked with twelve punch-marks at the cut end).
"2 bags of BB shot (this is packed in mat bags with other shot).
"1 black leather or canvas case of guns.
"1 single-barrelled gun } belonging to my servant.
"1 pair pistols }
"1 long narrow deal case of fishing-rods.
"3 lbs. tea (this is packed in a small deal box with about 11 lbs.; you can smell it, and then easily find it).
"2 heads sugar } these are in the same box together, and the soap can be seen through the openings in the wood.
"10 pieces soap }

"SUNDRIES.

"25 lbs. beads, suitable for the Basé country.
"12 steels for striking fire.
"12 blue cotton cloths for the women.
"12 red cotton handkerchiefs.
"If you can spare me the following, I shall be much obliged, as no caps were sent for my large rifle from Holland's in Bond Street:
"1 box 500 *large military* caps.
"1 dozen rockets and blue lights.
"Please let me know the price of all these things.

"If you know any good servant, who can speak either English, French, or German, and, of course, Arabic, I shall be glad to take him on my arrival at Khartoum in December, as I am by no means content with my Cairo plague.

"I am afraid I am giving you a vast amount of trouble; but pray excuse me, as my wants are urgent, and I hope to make a most successful trip through the countries mentioned.

"I met a German named Florian here, who will accompany me through the route to Khartoum. When I receive the things from you I shall have 13 guns and rifles and 5 pistols;
Florian has . .   5 ,,   ,,   4 ,,
                18 ,,   9 ,,

thus there will be nothing to fear in the Basé country from the people. I hear it is a wonderful place for elephants.

"I shall have completed a *pont volant* here in a few days, when I can daily cross the river and get good shooting, as immense herds of giraffes are constantly grazing a couple of miles or so on the other side, and also elephants, while on this side there is literally nothing.

"The post from Katariff to Khartoum is now stopped; thus this letter must go by a circuitous route, unless I can get a man to take it direct, in which case I will send a soldier from a neighbouring village; and please start him off, in company with the camel-load of things, as soon as possible direct to Sofi. If I am not here, the *sheik* will forward the things to me; but I shall be here, backwards and forwards, for the next five weeks, until the rains cease. I have a firman from Said Pasha, and his signature saves me a world of trouble; thus there will be no fear of the things going astray if once safe in these parts. Will you be so kind as to see that they are all so packed as to be waterproof, especially the powder, &c. ?

"I wrote to you from Cassala, but I cannot be sure of my letters reaching you; thus, if I can, I will send this by special messenger, when I shall hope shortly to hear from you.

"Ever very truly yours,
"SAMUEL W. BAKER."

"KATARIFF,
"*November 28th*, 1861.

"MY DEAR PETHERICK,

"I received your letter of the 29th October on the 16th inst., and I regret much to hear that you and Mrs. Petherick are suffering from fever. I trust the cool season will do more than medicine, and restore you thoroughly. I thank you and her most heartily for your welcome, so kindly offered. Thank God, my medicine-chest has been used only for relieving the people of this fever-stricken country, and its contents have been all but untasted by me for many months. The German, Florian, is a great sufferer, and nearly all the natives have enlarged spleens—the effect of repeated fever.

"I am here only for a few days. I shall not hurry on to Khartoum, as I should be sure to miss you, as you leave during next month; but after having gone through the Basé country and visited Nimmur (who sent me a polite invitation a few days ago,) I shall cross the Rahad and Dender far south, and, crossing the Blue Nile, I shall keep a south-west course to reach the White Nile in some distant point, and then wait for the return of the Khartoum boats, when I may have the good luck, D.V., to meet you and give you the hearty shake of the hand that two Englishmen delight in when so far from the old mother.

"Will Mrs. Petherick accompany you up the White Nile?

"If this letter catches you, will you kindly, *if it be possible*, send me on a man who can speak either English, French, or

German, as Arabic interpreter and servant; wages not to exceed fifteen dollars a month, and if less it will be more agreeable. My servant is a useless brute, and I pay him £5 per month: he has been very saucy, having had eight months' advance of wages in Cairo; a good thrashing cured his sauce, but I will not keep him a minute, if you can kindly procure me a substitute on the terms mentioned, and send him to Katariff, from which place he will be directed to me. Will you kindly let him bring the large package of *carpet*, &c., as it will serve as a present to some *sheik*, otherwise the moths will swallow it? I have some very good servants; thus the interpreter will have no actual servant's work to do if he be a superior kind of a fellow, but will merely have to superintend everything.

"Will you kindly forward the enclosed letters to Mr. Colquhoun in Cairo or Alexandria? and he will send them to their destination.

"God grant that we may meet in good health somewhere or other in this wild land, when I shall be truly glad to see you. Has anything been heard of Speke? If so, please let me know, as I am anxious to hear. I made his acquaintance, some years ago, on board the 'Precursor,' on a voyage to England from Ceylon, when we dropped him at Aden.

"Believe me,
"Ever very sincerely yours,
"SAMUEL W. BAKER."

After having supplied him with the required articles, and in reply to his letter of the 28th November, I strongly urged upon him the prudence of giving up his project of travelling south-west from the Blue Nile through the Dinka district to the White Nile, and coming down the latter river to Khartoum. In lieu of such a course, I suggested his coming down the Blue Nile to Khartoum, and, if in time and so disposed, I should be glad if he would join me on my expedition up the White Nile; or in the event of his arrival subsequent to my departure, I begged he would consider my house as his own, and, it being my intention to provide a boat, to furnish me with supplies and any home letters, to follow me at a subsequent date he might take advantage of it to join me.

My reasons for persuading Baker to give up that portion of his project of proceeding through the Dinka district and coming down the White Nile was the smallness of his escort and the hostility of the Dinkas to strangers, of every denomination, traversing their district from the Egyptian territories, in consequence of the great havoc that had been committed upon them by unprincipled ivory traders and professed slave dealers from Khartoum.

Prior to leaving Khartoum, an American, Dr. Brownell, from New York, with a vague idea of crossing the African continent, called upon me and presented a letter of introduction from my friend Hekekian, Bey of Cairo. He wished me to assist him, and, upon inquiry, learning that his means were totally inadequate for the purpose, I took some pains to dissuade him from so rash an attempt. For some time he rather amusingly persisted in the request that I should give him a passage in my boats to Gondokoro, and there drop him, and he would trust to a continuance of his hitherto good fortune to eventually turn up somewhere. On learning that he possessed a good knowledge of botany, with a view to render my expedition as complete as possible, and feeling that I should secure an ardent assistant, I, to our mutual satisfaction, concluded an arrangement with him to accompany us as botanist; he to give me the advantage of his knowledge, and I to bear all expenses.

As a further accessory to our probable requirements in the interior, I took with me some artizans, i.e., a smith, two ship-carpenters, sawyers, caulkers, &c., and every necessary for their work with the exception of timber, which I hoped to find on the spot where we should require to build boats, either to navigate the Nile above the reported cataracts beyond Gondokoro, or any lake we might happen to strike.

Our expedition, the most extensive belonging to a private individual that had ever left Khartoum, having at length surmounted all difficulties, on the 28th March, 1862, started on its mission.

Everything went as well as might have been expected until our arrival at the Sobat, when the premature setting in of the rainy season caused occasional vexatious calms, and, to our dismay, contrary winds, and towing became necessary.

On April 17th we passed the confluence of the Bahar il Gazal; and on the 28th met an Arab trader's boat from Gondokoro, that could give us no tidings of the expected advent of Speke, but informed us that our exploring party under Abd il Majid had penetrated the interior, and were, as far as they knew, all well.

On May 12th, at Aliab, finding a small space of muddy land, the highest point scarcely a foot above the flood, we availed ourselves thereof for discharging our thoroughly saturated stores of every description to repair our damaged spars and rigging, and to refit our leaky craft. We were joined by two parties from Gondokoro with four boats; two of which, with their owners, Hhurshid Aga, an ivory trader and famous for slave kidnapping and cattle lifting, and Amabile Musa de Bono, a Maltese, made fast alongside; the remaining two boats anchoring at a considerable distance down the stream. They were but six days from Gondokoro, where Amabile had been a week, and had left his station at

Faloro ten days previously. He was accompanied by an escort of one hundred and fifty men, and notwithstanding this force he had frequent affrays with the natives, who obstinately contested every day's march. He said that he had penetrated the hilly districts some three or four days' march farther southwards from his station, and had unusually prolonged his stay at Faloro on account of the chance of meeting and assisting Captain Speke and his party. The rainy season had been of the same unexampled violence as experienced by us, and it was his opinion that Speke, if he attempted to reach Gondokoro by the route he had traversed, would find it impossible to cross the Assua river, which had been a source of great risk to themselves. Since their passage, that river would doubtless have swollen so considerably that on that account, and the strength of the current, it would frustrate any attempt that Captain Speke might make to cross it with the necessarily imperfect means at his command. His agent in charge of the station had been, through him, instructed, in case of the possible advent of Captain Speke, to afford him assistance, but under no circumstances to accompany him, or furnish him with any part of their force to assist him through the tribes to Gondokoro. This he was compelled to refuse, he having left no more men at that station than were necessary for its protection; and unless Speke was accompanied by a sufficiently strong force to overcome all obstacles without assistance, he had given positive instructions to his agent to offer to Captain Speke the hospitality of their station until the arrival of reinforcements some six or seven months hence from Khartoum, when there would be no difficulty in assisting Captain Speke to complete his journey. He also prepared me for meeting with Abd il Majid, whom he had left at Gondokoro, but could afford me no particulars of his proceedings in the interior. At the moment of the departure of Amabile and Hhurshid, it was discovered that both of those boats, anchored at some distance from us, one of which belonged to Amabile and the other to Hhurshid, were full of slaves. In consequence of this discovery, and the stringent instructions I had received from the Foreign Office with respect to the slave trade, I considered it my duty to order Amabile's arrest on his arrival at Khartoum, and furtherance to H.M. Consul-General in Egypt on the charge of slave traffic.

Notwithstanding it appeared clear to me from the statements of Amabile, that Speke could by no possibility reach Gondokoro by Faloro and the Eastern Nile-bank, I was most anxious to effect a meeting with Abd il Majid, as I wished to learn from him the results of his investigations directed from our station. It appeared to me now beyond a doubt, that Speke, not having been heard of as far as about 3° north of the Equator on the eastern side of the Nile, would inevitably have stuck to his original plan agreed upon between him and me before our parting at " Jordans," that he would traverse the country on the *western* shores of his lake, and continue his journey on the west side of the Nile to Gondokoro. My search for him, therefore, by Abd il Majid, appeared to me more forcibly than ever to have been directed in the right direction. As a further proof I may here perhaps cite, in corroboration of this arrangement, that Speke evidently intended I should traverse the western side of the Nile, his statement at Faloro to Kidgwiga the guide, furnished him by Kamrasi (see his work, " Journal of the Discovery of the Source of the Nile," page 585). He states: " I would send another white man to him (Kamrasi), not by the way I had come through Kidi, but by the left bank of the Nile."

I was not long in suspense, for on May 16th—that is, four days after my interview with Amabile—we met Abd il Majid and his three boats on his return to Khartoum. In defence of his disobeying my instructions and returning before he was overtaken by me, he repeated the same reasons for leaving Gondokoro as assigned by Amabile.

The history of his movements had been as follows:

In the absence of any intelligence of Captain Speke or his expedition, on his arrival at Gondokoro about the end of December, 1861, Abd il Majid proceeded to my station at Wayo (formerly misnamed Neambara), and after supplying them with their requirements, was attacked by illness, which incapacitated him from any exertion. He therefore deputed in his stead Mussaad, the agent of the station, to proceed southwards in the direction indicated, with as many men as could possibly be spared from the station, in search of Captain Speke and his party. Mussaad, who accompanied Abd il Majid down the Nile, informed me that this search was prosecuted during seventeen marches (a direct distance of about eighty-five miles), through Jawila, Baga, Fegalo, into Rakoa. The districts of Fegalo and Rakoa were found in an exceedingly disturbed state, owing to the incursions of the Neam Neam: whole populations had fled from their settlements, agriculture had been neglected, and a state of destitution and famine hitherto unwitnessed prevailed; to that extent, that after four consecutive days' subsistence on bulbs, roots, and the wild fruits of the forest, the escort, hearing no tidings of better prospects in advance, expressed themselves determined to give up the search. Mussaad, having learned the existence of a large expanse of water but four days' journey distant, and in his direct line of march to the southwards, expressed a hope that it might be the Victoria Nyanza, and was most anxious to push for it. This lake, formerly reported by me to the Royal Geographical

Society (see "Proceedings," Vol. VIII., No. IV., page 150), has been subsequently named by Sir Samuel Baker the "Albert Nyanza."

The same state of desolation having been reported to exist on the line of route to the margin of the lake, his half-famished men rebelled against further advance, and the party consequently retraced the route they had pursued, and returned to our station at Wayo.

The statement of Amabile, in the first instance, and now corroborated by Abd il Majid and Mussaad, proved to me that the time appointed by the Royal Geographical Society for the arrival of Captain Speke (June, 1862), could not be kept. It therefore appeared to me that my engagement with the Royal Geographical Society was virtually fulfilled, as stated in Paragraph 4 of my instructions ("Proceedings," Vol. V., No. 1). "It being further understood that in the event of Captain Speke not having arrived by that time at Gondokoro, Consul Petherick shall not be bound to remain beyond June, 1862."

Although at this stage I believed myself perfectly justified, as far as my connection with the Royal Geographical Society was concerned, to have given up any further proceedings and returned to Khartoum, yet, in consideration of the ties of friendship connecting me with Captain Speke, the promise I had made to him during his last days in England, "that I would under no circumstances as long as I had life desert him in the interior, and that I would keep stores and boats for him at Gondokoro for an indefinite period," I felt it my duty under any circumstances, however adverse, to proceed to his relief.

That Speke evidently was under the impression that I would continue my search until I met him, even if that took two or three years to achieve, and that he could thoroughly depend upon me, see his letter, addressed to me from Karagwé, March 28th, 1862, in "Proceedings," Vol. VII., No. 5, as follows:

"My dear Petherick,

"I wrote a letter from Karagwé to send it by my Balyüz Baraka, through Unyoro, to ask you how you were. Now I am a great deal nearer you, and send another Balyüz Mabruk, together with some men from M'tessa. This is to invite you up to Uganda, for the King is very anxious to see you. I dare say this may somewhat interfere with your trade, and so create some pecuniary loss; but depend upon it, whatever that loss may amount to, I will ask the Government to defray it, for it is of the utmost importance that the country should open to trade, &c., and no opportunity could be better than the present. You will have to drop your dignity for the present, and to look upon me as your superior officer; for on asking M'tessa what presents I should write for, he said, 'Don't say anything about it, lest he should think that I, M'tessa, coveted his property more than himself.' So to quiet him, I said he did not understand the matter—that I ordered you to come up the Nile to look for me and bring me away, and that three vessels were mine as well as their contents, and you could not disobey my orders. I do not know what things you have; but bring a lot of pretty things, such as cheap jewellery, toys, pretty cloths, glass and china ware; one or two dogs of any sort, for the King's emblem is a dog; and any quantity of powder and lead, for he shoots cows every day. Mabruk can best select these things. Don't bring uniform, for I have none, but bring a lot of common red cloth and fez caps for my men to wear as a guard of honour. I have lots of muskets, and have given several guns and rifles to M'tessa; so bring no spare guns here, though your men may be armed up to the teeth. I have lots of beads for the way back to the boats.

Grant is at Karagwé with a game leg, and I am sending boats for him. His last letter to me is enclosed, also a map of the country, which you had better send to England, together with this, by the first opportunity. I would go across the Massai country at once to Zanzibar; but considering your promise to keep two or three boats two or three years for me, I sacrifice everything to fulfil the engagement. A photographic machine would be very useful here, for the Court is very splendid. You need not trouble yourself with a sextant, for I have three, but compass your route carefully. If Baraka reaches you, bring him up this way; we will then all go in boats to Rumanika's, King of Karagwé. Mind Rumaniki and Kamrasi, King of Unyoro, are brothers-in-law, but M'tessa is Kamrasi's enemy. However, I am trying to patch up their war by telling M'tessa he is the King of the Luta Nzigi, and Uganda is his grazing-grounds; that he should send a present to Kamarasi and become friends with him. You may tell Kamarasi this; and say I am a very great man, anxious to see him, if he will let you come here and fetch me away. I am very hard up for tobacco, and have neither brandy nor tea. All the things I have asked for are for myself, nobody else need give a present. I cannot write any more letters, for I have a whole year's collection. Unyanyembe waiting for an opportunity to reach Zanzibar.

"J. H. SPEKE."

The effect of this, the most fearful rainy season any one attached to our expedition now collected at this point—two hundred and twenty men—had ever experienced, was to produce climatic fever and sickness of various descriptions. To this the first to succumb was our botanist, poor Brownell, who died on the 20th May, and whom we buried in about the 8° North latitude, at a bend in the river, in an ant-hill, the only piece of ground above the water that the eye could compass in every direction as far as the horizon. A few days afterwards another invaluable man, one of the artizans accorded to us by the Viceroy of Egypt, followed in his wake. To describe the melancholy prospect around us beggars description. Baker, in alluding to it (see "Proceedings," Vol. X., No. 1, page 7), says, "Far as the eye can reach, in that land of misery and malaria, all is wretchedness. . . . . One dry spot I saw slightly raised above the boundless marsh: there some white man was buried."

A second most unpleasant circumstance in connection with the slave trade now occurred by the detection of Abd il Majid in complicity therewith, and his connection during his stay at Gondokoro with the notorious Hhurshid Aga and the young Maltese. He was forthwith handcuffed and sent under arrest, with the particulars of the circumstances, to Khartoum, to be judged by the Egyptian Government, of which he was a subject.

After thirty-eight days' monotonous towing, with occasional rough sailing before tempestuous winds occasioned by thunderstorms astern, our men, worn out with fatigue and ill health, reached Lohnun, or the "Abu Kuka" of the Arabs, in the Kytch territory (July 2nd), in latitude 6° 54' 35" N., and E. longitude 32° 28' 42". To convey to the reader the best idea in my power of the toilsome progress under circumstances so adverse as those we necessarily experienced by the unforeseen early setting in of this exceptionally rainy season, by reference to the map he will find that we only made good, in a direct line during the thirty-eight days quoted, little more than seventy miles, or less than two miles per day. Under ordinary circumstances, with a fair wind, we might easily have reached Gondokoro from this point in six days; but now, with my men so thoroughly worn out from the exertion of towing, sleepless nights, and the depressing effects of malaria and its consequent fevers, in addition to the most serious obstacle of all, the utter worthlessness of our entire stock of cordage for the purpose of towing, further progress by water became utterly impossible.

With a determination to vanquish every obstacle, and keep my appointment with Speke at whatever hazard, I decided to abandon my boats and proceed to Gondokoro by land. In order to carry out this determination, it was a primary object to place stores at Gondokoro, in anticipation of the requirements of Speke or myself. With this view I re-shipped a cargo, consisting of a variety of necessaries, into the least damaged of the boats, and stripped the three others of their standing rigging to serve as towing-lines, to enable the former to proceed to the Shyr, where I knew a capital material for rope-making was available from the leaf of the delaeb trees, that abound in the vicinity.

On the 25th July this boat, assisted by a spurt of wind occasioned by a thunder-storm, set sail; and the *reis* was ordered to proceed to Gondokoro, and remain there until the arrival of myself or Captain Speke. In the event of their meeting, the *reis* and storekeeper were particularly instructed not only to supply my countrymen with everything available that might be required, but the *reis* was to place himself, crew, and boat, at the absolute disposal of Speke. The three other boats, being perfectly useless, were, after being temporarily caulked and refitted, to return to Khartoum. In the meantime, by instalments in proportion as negro porters presented themselves, our stores were forwarded along the route we intended to take.

In order to reconnoitre the route leading to the interior, I had several times proceeded on horseback, many miles distant, up to my middle in water. I was always accompanied by a few men of my escort; and, although occasionally much inconvenienced by the depth of water we encountered, the practicability of proceeding, although at a terrible discomfort, was agreed to; the more so as, having an India-rubber punt requiring but one man to carry it, I could, if necessary, ford the party and our stores over any deep water that might intervene in our route. The task was, however, by no means an easy one, as we could not see the termination to this fatiguing journey; nor could the natives give us any definite idea of the extent of the inundation, it being far beyond their territory. In the first instance, a march up to the middle, with an occasional swim across some ravine, to a trading station of the Poncet Brothers, called Adôr, some miles due-west of us, was a certainty; but how far the flood extended beyond that point we had no means of ascertaining.

Notwithstanding these difficulties, I was nobly supported by my wife in the determination to proceed, and the men, although sullen, coincided with my views. Everything being prepared, and the necessary instructions written for the securing of a fresh supply of boats and provisions, to return from Khartoum with the following season commencing in October, and to proceed to Gondokoro, we mounted our horses. At this juncture the men forming our escort, as I had been privately informed, made up their minds not to proceed with us, but to seize the boats and either insist upon our returning with them to Khartoum or to return thither without us. After so many years residence among them, and naturally possessing a knowledge of the Arab character, I well knew how keenly susceptible they were to praise or reproach from a woman, and that there was nothing they would shrink from if taunted by the example of a being whom, by their creed, they were taught not only to consider inferior to themselves in intellect, but immeasurably beneath them in point of courage and endurance. My wife was equal to the emergency, and on the roll being called I instantly assisted her into the saddle, and forthwith, with an encouraging cheer and a wave of the hand, she pushed her horse into the swamp and incited them to follow. The example, instantly followed by myself, communicated itself, as if by electricity, to our men, and, as they afterwards good-humouredly explained to us, they were irresistibly forced to abandon all thought of their preconcerted revolt, and for very shame, against their dearest wishes, at least follow where a woman led. Had the attempt been made without the assistance and presence of mind of my wife, it would certainly have resulted in signal failure, and perhaps have cost me my life; as it was, we were all on the best of terms.

The boats had started very shortly afterwards for Khartoum, and at our next bivouac the men, relieved of the presence of the sick thus sent home, feeling it now more than ever their interest to stick to me, cheerfully promised to encounter every difficulty that might present itself on our new mode of progress.

After six weeks' disastrous toil through marsh, mud, and water, encounters with the natives, entailing loss of life and much valuable property, including photographic apparatus and a host of necessaries, we succeeded in reaching Adael in the Rhol, the extreme point to which the inundation had reached at right angles from the Nile, in latitude North 6° 35′ 53″ and longitude East 30° 8′ 4″; in other words, 170 miles of tortuous travel from Lolnun or Aboo Kuka, and within about three miles of the river Nam. Our inability to obtain porters so soon as we expected, and serious illnesses, entailed a sad delay, and on the 13th November our departure took place, now in a southerly direction, and about parallel with the Nile, through the

Djour and Moro districts to the Neangara, in the Morokodo, in latitude North 5° 22′ 41″ and East longitude 30° 6′ 26″, where we arrived on the 30th of the same month.

At this portion of our journey, at about thirty-five miles south of Adael, at a village called Jirri, at another point twenty-seven miles farther south at Dagwara, we came in contact with the Nam, a large and important tributary to the White Nile, rising, I was informed, in the hilly Neam Neam district, in about 3° North latitude, and proceeding nearly due-north, adds its waters to the Nile in the district of the Aliab, in about 8° 27′ North latitude, where previously, in a morass of reeds, I had observed its outlet.

For our hospitable reception at Neangara and the means of further progress we were indebted to my ten-days'-distant trading station, called Wayo. Had we not had this source wherefrom to supply our wants, I know not what would have been our fate. A great number of our men—no novices to the hardships of travel—must have succumbed to ill health and fatigue had it not been for a small number of our animals that still retained sufficient strength to carry them occasionally. The best men amongst them, with but an apology for clothing, without a change of any kind, and under the influence of the worst of climates, had become desponding and weary. Our means, too, had dwindled to an alarmingly small compass; and it was only the keen appreciation of the utter helplessness to which my wife, self, and party had become reduced, that occasioned the ablest of my men to cordially hail my proposal to tarry with the invalids at this place, whilst they went forward to seek the trading station (misnamed Neambara, but properly Wayo) which I have been so erroneously and unjustly accused of visiting for the purposes of my private trade (see Captain Speke in his "Journal of the Discovery of the Source of the Nile," page 603):

"But what had become of Petherick? He was actually trading at Neambara, seventy miles due-west of this, though he had, since I left him in England, raised a subscription of £1,000 from those of my friends to whom this journal is most respectfully dedicated." Thus, though not actually avowed, it is, I fear, implied, that my trade was benefited at the expense of the Speke Expedition, to support which, with a singleness of purpose and an utter disregard of consequences, I was devoting my utmost energy and the entire means at my disposal.

On December 15th, in lieu of the wearied men who had proceeded thither, a powerful escort, with porters from Wayo, by forced marches had hastened and arrived to our relief. They found me in a sad plight: the rest had acted beneficially on most of the sick, but I had become a helpless invalid from gastric fever. Had it not been for the medical skill and great attention of Dr. Murie, and the careful nursing of my wife, I must have succumbed. It was not until a month afterwards that I was enabled to leave the Neaugara.

Our welcome station Wayo, in latitude 40° 46′ North, and East longitude 36° 20′, at the junction of the rivers Bibio and Ayi, in the Moro territory, was reached January 25th, 1863.

Now that I have arrived with my narrative into the heart of the Moro district, it may not be inopportune to notice what during my absence had taken place at the meeting of the Royal Geographical Society on May 26th, 1862.

My deceased friend Dr. Peney, in 1861, had been in this district, and in his report thereon, addressed to Monsieur Jomard, and published in the "Nouvelles Annales des Voyages," and referred to at the above meeting, quoted several names of places, such as Mundo, Moro, and Neam Neam, which coinciding, so far as the names were concerned, with other places laid down by me much farther south and west in my previous journey directed from the Bahar il Gazal to the Equatorial district in 1858, led the President of the Society into the error that the district in which I now found myself, and reported on by Dr. Peney, were identical with my farthest point in 1858. With reference thereto, the President in his address at the anniversary meeting, May 26th, 1862 (page 177), was induced to state "the penultimate stage of Petherick's route undertaken from the Bahar il Gazal, from the year 1853 to 1859, was sixty miles westward from Gondokoro, and if that be the case, an enormous rectification became necessary in the estimated extent and direction of his itinerary." If the reader, however, will refer to the Society's Journal for 1865, he will find the most ample confirmation of the accuracy of my first itinerary, as in the map of "The Nile and its Western Affluence," founded on my astronomical observations, and constructed by Mr. Arrowsmith, the error of identity in the places visited by Dr. Peney in 1861, and myself in 1858, is self-evident; the Mundo, alluded to by me in 1858, being therein acknowledged to be in 3° 40' North latitude, and 28° 50' East longitude; therefore, in lieu of being sixty miles, as stated by the President, from Gondokoro, it has been recognized, as the crow flies, at two hundred miles from that spot.

To return to my narrative. Our sojourn at this point was limited to the shortest possible time for obtaining a sufficiency of porters for our personal requirements, and the carriage of the stock of elephants' tusks, that, in conformity with the routine of my business, had been collected at this station during the preceding trading campaign. A fortnight sufficed to complete that arrangement, and on February 12th we were on the desired road to Gondokoro.

APPENDIX A.

In proceeding to Gondokoro, where Speke, had he arrived, would have found every requisite in my boat sent on from Aboo Kuka in July last, my object was in any case to replenish myself with stores and provisions, of which I was now destitute, and in the event of his non-arrival to proceed thence southwards in search of him. So far from having abandoned the interests of the Speke Expedition, I now—as previously, when I withdrew a portion of my men from my trading station, the Bahar il Gazal, for the support of Abd il Majid—again prejudiced my commercial interests by ordering the whole of the disposable men, short of an entire abandonment of the station, to accompany me in my search for Speke. The necessity for thus collecting so strong a force was necessitated by the more than usually turbulent state of the tribes, consequent on the raids made on them for cattle and slaves by the traders that infested the locality to be traversed.

In the territory of the Neambara, when about half-way on our journey, we rejoiced in meeting about sixty of our men. The men in question, in conformity with my orders from Aboo Kuka, were reinforcements from Khartoum, and, with three boats for the Speke Expedition, and one for the requirements of my trading station, had arrived at Gondokoro on January 20th. In reporting the arrival at that place of Mr. (now Sir Samuel) Baker, on the 2nd of the following month, they handed me a letter from him dated February 9th, in which, after thanking me for the hospitality of my roof during six months' stay at Khartoum, and reverting to the irritation caused at the place by my arrest of Amabile Moussa, the Maltese, and of my own man Abd il Majid, on a charge of slave trading, he says, "an accusation was sent to the Consul-General against you, signed by nearly all the Europeans at Khartoum, including the official declarations of the two Consulates, charging you with some former participation in slavery. Of course the seals of numerous natives ornamented the document."

With reference to this subject, the men reported that the arrests above alluded to, and my reports to the local Government charging every native trader that I had met with participation in that traffic, had created great excitement and indignation at Khartoum, and that they had heard it currently stated that, in revenge, some paper charging me with a similar offence at some former period had been put into circulation for signature amongst the traders. They further informed me of the circulation of the report of my death and party, and that they had set out from Gondokoro to ascertain the truth of that statement, and expressed the greatest joy in meeting me. They now returned with me to Gondokoro, where we arrived on February 20th, 1863.

When within sight of this long-desired haven, I cannot express the gratification and intense relief we experienced at thus having at last realized our object. It had seemed to us something like a phantom: the more we advanced and toiled, the farther it appeared to recede. When leaving our boats at Aboo Kuka, we had buoyed ourselves up with the hope of reaching this place in the course of a month, or six weeks at the outside. Alas! how vain were our hopes! In lieu of travelling some one hundred and fifty miles, we had, owing to ignorance of the extent of lowland flooded by this untoward and unexampled inundation, traversed four hundred miles; thus this journey, instead of six weeks, took us seven months' arduous exertion to accomplish, and, attended as it was with loss of life to some of our followers, and with more sickness, privation, pain, and misery to all concerned than it ever has been my ill fortune to have experienced, it proved an undertaking of greater difficulty to accomplish than it is in my power to explain.

My readers will recollect that at the outset of this journey I was deeply indebted to the presence of mind and courage of my wife at this critical juncture; and, indeed, but for her intrepidity it could never have been undertaken. Ignored as all our efforts have been by the parties most interested, and for whose sole advantage all this toil was endured and persisted in; and also that at a subsequent period, on our return to England, all recognition thereof was entirely refused by the President and Council of the Royal Geographical Society, I cannot refrain, at this stage, from paying a passing tribute to one whose untiring energy, courage, and devotion most materially assisted me in vanquishing all impediments and carrying the object I had in view to a successful termination.

Before stepping on shore at Gondokoro, we found not only Baker, according to our expectation, but, to our most agreeable surprise, also Captains Speke and Grant, who had arrived five days previously, and the former was in possession of our *dahabyeh*, the "Kathleen." There also was the boat sent on by us in July from Aboo Kuka, and awaiting up to this date the advent of Speke or myself. Instead, however, of the cordial meeting I had anticipated from the ardently sought-for, and now successful, travellers, we were met with coolness and a positive refusal to partake of more of our stores or assistance than would satisfy their most urgent requirements, and that elsewhere could not be obtained.

Without any intimation of his reasons for so doing, Speke immediately removed his effects from the "Kathleen," and, in reply to my urgent solicitations that he should retain possession of her and accept of as many of the other boats as he wished, to proceed on his voyage down the Nile, he coolly replied, "I do not wish to recognize the succour dodge, and friend Baker has offered me his boats." At a subsequent meeting he, with a view to ignore his connection therewith and his letters to me from "Jordans" (see page 80), with great effrontery, asked me who it was that had prompted the "succour dodge"!

With reference to the subject of our meeting, as quoted in his work (page 603), of which no mention was made at the time, he accuses me of trading at the Neambara; but for a refutation of this most extraordinary statement I must merely beg to refer the reader to the body of this work, and without further comments upon the memory of one now no more, request the public to draw their own inferences with regard to the truth of this statement, and leave to their consideration the merits or demerits of his conduct. But were it true that I had been trading, was it not in connection therewith that I first became known to the Royal Geographical Society? and was it not in accordance therewith that this very expedition was planned? and had Captain Speke forgotten his letter to me from "Jordans," dated December 22nd, 1859, wherein he suggested that geography and trade might be combined? and referred to page 80, Vol. II.

With reference to Captain Grant, who, on the contrary, was most friendly at Gondokoro, a change in his sympathies had evidently taken place since his return to England, and I was not a little surprised to find the following passage relative to our meeting at Gondokoro in his book, "A Walk across Africa," page 366. He says:

"But where was Petherick? Had he made no preparations for us? or, finding we were not able to keep time, had he despaired and given up the search? A handsome *diabeah* and luggage-boat of his were here, but there were neither letters nor instructions for us. He himself was not at Gondokoro, and had never been there.

APPENDIX A.

Instead of co-operating with our expedition, he had gone to his own ivory depôt in the west, and only arrived at Gondokoro four days after ourselves. We learned from Baker that kind friends in England had placed £1,000 in the hands of Mr. Petherick for our succour, and were doubly surprised he had made no effort to meet us. It was to M. de Bono's men, and not Mr. Petherick's, that we were indebted for our escort. I feel it due to the memory of my companion to state these facts, and to say that I had the same feeling of disappointment he had, and that our meeting with Mr. Petherick was by no means the cordial one we anticipated. Having been previously supplied with all necessaries and three return boats by Baker, for conveying us to Khartoum, we required nothing, save a few yards of calico, to replace the bark-cloth of our twenty Seedees, and this we obtained from the stores of Mr. Petherick."

Now, I cannot but think that the impression conveyed to the public must be that I not only neglected my duty to the Speke Expedition, in pursuit of my own interests, but that, with respect to the £1,000 contributed, I made no use of it for that purpose, rendered no services, nor made any return whatever for it. Any casual reader, after perusal of the above passages, would, it strikes me, lay down the book with that impression upon his mind.

Before dismissing with an emphatic denial the truth of Captain Grant's statements, I may remark that in accordance with my letter, appended as it was to the instructions of the Royal Geographical Society, and forwarded for Captain Speke by the Colonial Office, June 11th, 1860, to the Cape in the Governor's bag—the Speke Expedition had no right to expect more than two boats and men to await them with supplies at Gondokoro. Instead of two, they found four boats awaiting them, one of which had been there for that purpose upwards of four months previous to their advent to that place, and the four were there eight months beyond the term June, 1862, after which (see "Proceedings," Vol. V., No. 1) I was no longer bound to provide for them. To give the reader an idea of the manner in which I had provided for the travellers, I venture to quote from a pamphlet, by John A. Tinné, Esq., May 12th, 1864, and entitled, "Geographical Notes of Expeditions in Central Africa by Three Dutch Ladies." The ladies say "they never saw a more disappointed man than Mr. Petherick. He and his wife have had dreadful ill luck. He had made the best arrangements to meet Captain Speke, and his boats were loaded and dispatched with all sorts of good things for his use. They set off too late from Khartoum, in March, 1862, and the winds being then adverse, caused much delay and damage to their boats, and they were consequently obliged to abandon them and proceed by land from Aboo Kuka. This was the end of August,* 1862; and it being then the rainy season, that place proved impracticable. They were delayed from August to February by rain, by deep morasses, by affrays with inhospitable natives, and by illness; and only arrived at Gondokoro in February, 1863, five days after Captain Speke, who had previously accepted Mr. Baker's provisions and boat, and refused further aid from Mr. Petherick, so that he had to retain all he had sent forward for Captain Speke's requirements, which was fortunate for us, for we were thus provided with wine, pale ale, tea, soap, pearl barley, Lemanns' biscuits, an India-rubber boat—nay, we cannot say what. It is strange to find these luxuries here, and we enjoy them greatly."

That the boats were there Captain Grant himself partially admits, by acknowledging "a few yards of calico" from my stores; and

---

* Should be August 1st.

that they were not made use of for the downward voyage to Khartoum—nor but a trifling quantity of stores accepted—was surely no fault of mine.

Captain Grant says that he had learned from Baker that "kind friends in England had placed £1,000 in the hands of Mr. Petherick for our succour, and were doubly surprised that he made no effort to meet us." Captain Grant might have added that I placed in his own hands the prospectus of the Royal Geographical Society concerning the subscription fund of the so-called "succour dodge." Moreover, prior to the date of the publication of his work, the Royal Geographical Society were in possession of the accounts of my expedition, by which Captain Grant might have seen that, in lieu of the £1,000 referred to, the sum total of the expenditure I had incurred in my efforts to assist him had amounted to upwards of five times that sum.

The excess of £4,600 and upwards, over and above the sum subscribed, was with no slight effort and sacrifice obtained entirely from my own resources; and I venture to hope, that if Captain Grant is at a loss to appreciate the efforts I had made, and the preparations at Gondokoro for the arrival of Captain Speke and himself, the subscribers to my fund and a just public will view the subject in a different light. They may regret, with myself, that I was not on the scene five days earlier in person; but they must, I think, admit the injustice of Captain (now Colonel) Grant's assertion that I had made no effort to meet him.

But when it is considered that the advent of the Speke Overland Expedition from Zanzibar was sixteen months behind its appointed time at Gondokoro, considering also the unprecedented rainy season which commenced two months earlier than usual, with its accompanying southerly and contrary winds, inundating thousands of square miles, and that my means of meeting him were confined chiefly to sailing boats up the Nile, I think I have a fair claim to the consideration of the Royal Geographical Society for having kept my appointment within half that loss of time, viz., seven months, after the estimated period of my arrival.

With reference to Speke's acceptance of supplies and boats from Mr. Baker, however praiseworthy in the first instance the motive may have been, upon the rumour of my death at Khartoum, for Mr. Baker to get up an expedition to replace my loss to the Speke Expedition, I feel that with his knowledge that my boats, with every requisite, had, prior to him, left Khartoum for Gondokoro to support the Zanzibar Expedition and our own, and my personal subsequent advent at that place in sufficient time for every practical purpose, when I imparted to him the great efforts I had made to keep my appointment, he should have felt in duty bound to give way, and permit me to complete the programme I had undertaken.

There is no doubt in my mind that it was the report of my death that induced Mr. Baker to undertake this expedition; and that, although not admitted at the time, he was also encouraged so to do by the Royal Geographical Society, I think the following letter, received by me at a subsequent date from Captain Speke, will prove:

"KHARTOUM,
"BRITISH CONSULATE,
"*April 15th*, 1863.

"MY DEAR PETHERICK,

"We came down the Nile all right, the last *nugger* arriving on the fortieth day, and have lived ever since very comfortably under the tender care of your fair Fatma.* To-morrow we hope to be well away in the early morning, consigning your small packages to their destination in as good order as you gave them to us. The spades you were good enough to give me, I have made over to Fatty, as our *reis* bought sheep on the way with dollars. I was sorry to find, on arrival here, that the townspeople had reported you dead, and in consequence of it the Royal Geographical Society had determined on sending the second thousand pounds to Baker, with a view to assist him in looking after us.

"This now was too bad, for Hhalil † never gave the slightest credence to the report brought down by the merchants, and said so in answer to his brother's inquiries concerning it at Cairo.

"To make the best of the matter, and to do justice to all, I wrote home a full explanation of our conversation at home before we left England, and the position in which we met at Gondokoro.

"Should you feel inclined to write a full statement of the difficulties you had to contend with in going up the White Nile, it would be a great relief to the mind of every person connected with the succouring funds, and also to myself, as the peoples' tongues are always busy in this meddling world.

"With Grant's best wishes, conjointly with my own, to Mrs. Petherick and yourself, for your health and safety in the far interior,

"Believe me,
"Yours truly,
"J. H. SPEKE."

The unpleasantness with Speke was but a preliminary to my ill fortune at Gondokoro. Hhurshid and Agâd's men, a few days in

---

* My housekeeper. † Hhalil, my Arab agent at Khartoum.

advance of us, from their station adjoining my own at Wayo, had committed abominable outrages on the negroes during their march. At their urgent request to protect them, I brought with me to Gondokoro some Barri men, in order to reclaim for them some girls that these Arabs had captured. This circumstance, in addition to the previous steps I had taken to arrest this abominable and, to legitimate trade, most ruinous traffic, like the application of a match to a powder-magazine, produced a most bitter explosion against me on the part of Arab traders, their representatives, and several hundred of their interested servitors. This excitement is alluded to in Dr. Murie's letter, quoted in the body of the work, page 314, Vol. I.; but any description of mine can give only a faint idea of its intensity.

My own men, some two hundred and fifty in number, either blood relations or otherwise closely allied to the traders, although on entering my service they had bound themselves to keep aloof from slave traffic, joined in the commotion, and the upshot was the breaking open of my stores, an indulgence in *araki*, spirits of wine, &c., and the stealing of ammunition. To such an extent were their reckless fusillades carried that a boy on board the "Kathleen" was shot, and, but for their arrant cowardice, they would have deliberately accorded to me the same fate.

Furnished as I was with the most elaborate materials for exploration ever collected at this spot, owing to my exercise of the duties of British Consul in the prevention of the slave traffic, I now had the mortification to see them crumble away. Some hundred of the men, regardless of my orders to the contrary, decided to return forthwith to my trading station at Wayo; others, principally hunters, would do nothing but proceed down the Nile, nominally to shoot elephants, but in reality to deprive me of their services and do just as they pleased; a third party, more straightforward than the rest, seized a boat, and, protesting in strong language that they would serve no man unless permitted to capture slaves, they forthwith let go from the shore and proceeded direct to Khartoum.

Bad as they were, I must give a few of them the credit they deserve of showing good feeling. Seeing that they were abandoning us in very ill health, with two boats and but five men to guard them, eleven of the deserters stepped out, and generously declared "for the sake of 'bread and salt,' go where I would, my fate should be theirs."

Baker, known as my countryman, was supposed to be as antagonistic to the slave trade as myself, and experienced, in conseuqence, a similar inconvenience. He had brought an escort of forty-six men, far too small for anything in the shape of independent exploration; but of those only sixteen remained faithful to him, Soon after this event I received the following communications from him:

"GONDOKORO,
"*21st March*, 1863.

"SIR,

"This morning my escort openly mutinied, refusing to proceed upon the journey, and threatening to shoot the *vakeel* and desert me if I insisted upon their accompanying me. I am thus stopped in my intended exploration after a large outlay, and having no authority over my men, who are Egyptian subjects, I apply to you as Consul for the necessary assistance under the circumstances.

"(Signed) SAMUEL BAKER."

"GONDOKORO,
"*March 25th*, 1863.

"J. PETHERICK, Esq.,
"*H.B.M. Consul, Soudan.*
"SIR,

"The mutiny of the men specially engaged by me in Khartoum as escort for my expedition to the sources of the Nile has prevented me from attempting a forward movement from Gondokoro.

"The expedition fitted out for the object above mentioned is therefore, frustrated at its very commencement by the mutinous refusal of the men to proceed.

"These men are, therefore, individually and collectively responsible for the outlay of the expedition, which has failed through their mutiny.

"I, therefore, request you to make known my claim to the Egyptian authorities against the men composing my escort, they being Egyptian subjects, for whom the Government is responsible.

"The amount of this claim is, for the present moment, £700 sterling; from Khartoum to Gondokoro.

"In addition to this, I claim for all expenses I have incurred from Constantinople to Khartoum, and for those that I shall incur from Gondokoro to Alexandria.

"I am,
"Truly yours,
"SAMUEL W BAKER."

From being in precisely the same fix with my own more numerous escort, I was not only powerless at the time to afford the slightest assistance, but had I made the attempt the probability is it would have proved disastrous to us both.

Baker, anxious to do something, had been incited by Speke to explore the Little Luta Nzigi; and from the fact of my having reported a nameless sheet of water, described as a "deep and wide river," west of the locality, flowing west, during my travels from the Bahar il Gazal in 1858 (see "Proceedings of the Royal Geographical Society," Vol. V., No. 1, page 39), and Mussaad, in his search for Speke from my station at Wayo, having also heard of the Luta Nzigi, I was naturally anxious to see and explore the waters myself. But for the mutiny of my men, it would have been an easy task to accomplish. Now, however, reduced to equal forces, and to make the best of them, my proposal to Baker to combine and push for the latter was no sooner made than accepted. He, however, literally calculated without his hosts; for no sooner were his men informed of the project than the rascals protested that they would not move an inch in my company, and in the hour of its birth the infant project expired.

My last hope for further exploration had received its death-blow; and Baker, who had been previously sorely disappointed by De Bono's agent disgracefully leaving him in the lurch after having promised him safe convoy with his powerful band to Faloro, was at his wits' end. There remained no choice but to attach himself to a large body of Hhurshid's men, about to proceed to their station, some five days' journey to the eastward of Gondokoro. His ambition pointed south; but, like myself from Aboo Kuka to Gondokoro, he could do nothing but submit to the inconvenience of an immense *détour*, with the hope of eventually alluring the traders to extend their operations towards the field of his ultimate hard-earned and well-merited success.

In order to insure his expeditious return to Khartoum, on the 13th of March, 1863, for the consideration of 6,240 Egyptian piastres, equal to £64, I engaged to supply him with a large *dahabyeh* and twenty *ardebs* (about twenty imperial quarters) of dourra at Gondokoro, not later than the 1st of June, 1864. The last communication, on the eve of his departure, is as follows:

"GONDOKORO,
"March 25th, 1863.

"MY DEAR PETHERICK,

"Will you be good enough to send me a line, receipted, for the amount I am indebted to you for the fat? and I also add a dollar for the auger, if you will include that in the note.

"(Signed)   S. W. BAKER."

Speke and Grant had previously left in Baker's boats for Khartoum. The former, although consigned by me to Grant, had taken charge of from five hundred to six hundred plants, which he promised in my name, and under similar conditions to the collection made by Grant, to present to Kew Gardens "in as good order as you gave them to us," as he remarks in a letter already quoted.

I may here state that upon a recent application to the proper quarter for the nomenclature of my plants, with a view to append it to this work, to my dismay I was informed that my plants had been passed into the herbarium with my name attached, but no list of them had been made out, and that it was not possible to accede to my request. During a further correspondence, in which I expressed my disappointment, considering the expense I had incurred by the employment of two professional gentlemen, Drs. Murie and Brownell, for the collection of plants, I drew a comparison between this treatment and that received at the hands of the authorities at the British Museum, to whose kindness I owe Appendices B and C of this work.

Unlike Speke, I could procure no particulars of my plants; and it is the more vexatious inasmuch as I believe my party to be the only one that ever culled and preserved the desert Flora of Aboo Hamad. The district on the confines of the tropics is so seldom favoured with rain that it is perhaps the most scorched and barren desert it has ever been my fate to traverse. On the eve of our crossing the desert from Korosko, in August, 1861, it had not been moistened by rain for nine years, when two days' heavy thunder-storms thoroughly drenched it, and not only cooled the almost intolerable heat, but produced a delightful vegetation, covering the immense plains with a refreshing tint, and giving all a pleasant occupation in gathering and preserving the newly grown flowers. These, instead of being enumerated in the present work, it appears to me, adorned another's collection.

After a succession of fevers and a variety of illnesses that fastened upon my wife and myself during our return voyage and residence at Khartoum, as a substitute for the excitement of travel, I was laid up with a series of guinea-worms revelling in the fleshy part of my right leg and foot. Whilst in this state, a paragraph from the "Overland Mail" was placed in my hands, descriptive of a banquet in honour of Captain Speke on his return to Taunton. In that portion of his address touching upon the slave trade, he (as it was broadly stated in another paper) obviously referred to me when saying, "men with authority emanating from our Government, who are engaged with the native kings in the diabolical slave trade." My experience of Speke at Gondokoro, and also the tone of his last letter, written under my roof at Khartoum, and quoted a few pages back, ill prepared me for so wilful an effusion of slander and calumny. The blow was as hard as I could well bear; therefore, in accordance with the advice of friends at home, and considering the distance I was from the scene of action to answer through the press, I decided, in lieu thereof, at a future date to enter proceedings against Captain Speke. His subsequent deplorable death, while on my way home, unfortunately deprived me of this satisfaction.

With a view to embrace the whole of these unwarrantable aspersions, I must again refer to Mr. Baker's letter of 2nd February, 1863, wherein he states: "An accusation was sent to the Consul-General against you, signed by nearly all the Europeans at Khartoum, including the official declarations of two Consulates, charging you with some former participation in slavery. Of course the seals of numerous natives ornamented the document."

Without further comment upon the absurdity of my prosecuting others in the event of my ever having exposed myself to a similar charge, I will simply lay before an impartial public a few of the most important documents I thought, under the circumstances, it would be to my interest to acquire.

To understand the first two documents, it will be necessary for me to carry the reader back to the year 1859, when, for the first time, I left Khartoum for England. Twelve months afterwards, the Austrian Consular Agent, Dr. Natterer, now deceased, reported at length, in German, to his Consul-General at Alexandria upon the horrors of the recently established slave trade on the White Nile. Translated into French by Her Majesty's Agent, his report reached me through the Foreign Office in December, 1860. In it the following passage occurs:

"Hereusement qu'aucun Autrichien et soit dit a l'honneur de

APPENDIX A. 141

l'Allemagne, jamais un Allemand ne se rend vers le Nil Blanc; ils sont tous établis ici; de toute le colonie de Khartoum il n'y a que les Français, et de plus un Anglais, et un Maltais, qui trafiquent d'esclaves, et se rendent coupables des actions honteuses dont je viens de parler."

Now, as I was the only Englishman that traded on the White Nile, there could be no doubt that the slave accusation partially referred to myself. Therefore, upon my first meeting with Dr. Natterer at Khartoum, on my return in 1861, I sought an explanation of the offensive paragraph in question, with this result:

"KHARTOUM,
"*March* 14*th*, 1862.

"With respect to my report of the 5th April, 1860, No. 76, to the I.R. Austrian Consulate-General, I beg to inform you that in the translation of that report into French an unpleasant error has crept in. After I had described the bartering trade with the negro populations as having suffered in consequence of the slave trade, I said that the Germans were settled here in Khartoum, and that Frenchmen, Italians, one Englishman, and one Maltese carried on *trade* upon the White River. The translator has erroneously taken this to mean *slave trade*. At that time I did not at all know who was carrying on the slave trade on the White River, and therefore not the slightest imputation was intended to be cast upon you, which fact I hereby acknowledge.

"(Signed) Dr. JOSEPH NATTERER,
"*Administrator of the Imperial Royal Austrian Consulate.*

"JOHN PETHERICK, Esq."

"KHARTOUM,
"*May* 19*th*, 1864.

"SIR,

"In compliance with the request addressed to me that I should afford you an explanation respecting a denunciation to the effect that you at one time were engaged in the slave trade in the Soudan, I have the honour of declaring most conscientiously:

"That no accusation to that effect against your respected person has ever at any time come to my knowledge, nor have I ever heard anything to this effect during the period when I acted as Austrian Vice-Consul here, from 1852 to 1858, or since that time during our many years' acquaintance in Khartoum and Kordofan.

"I have already expressed myself two years ago to the same effect, respecting a similar unworthy insinuation in reports which had been published in the 'Geographical Journal' of A. Petermann.

"As I hear, the deceased Imperial Royal Austrian Consulate Administrator, Joseph Natterer, has preferred an indirect complaint against you on this subject to his Consul-Generalate in Egypt, concerning which you have had to render explanations to your Government.

"I take the liberty also of declaring further that the preferrer of the said complaint was designated by his chief, the Imperial Royal Austrian Consul-General, Von Schreimer, in presence of myself and the Imperial Royal Austrian Ministerial Councillor, Von Auber, as, a person upon whom no reliance could be placed, and consequently the accusation alluded to can possess neither legal value nor influence.

"I am quite ready, in case of need, to confirm the above statements by oath.

"(Signed)   THEODORE VON HEUGLIN,
"*The Royal Wartemberg Court Councillor.*"

APPENDIX A.

"KHARTOUM,
"February 24th, 1864.

"SIR,

"I am astonished to learn that you have been accused of having carried on an illicit trade at Kordofan and on the White River. I can positively state that, having been for many years your neighbour in Kordofan, I have seen nothing in your conduct that would warrant such a defamation of character. Like an honest man you engaged in the regular trade of the produce of the country, such as gum and ivory.

"I never went to the White Nile while you were there. I know that you had several establishments which furnished quantities of ivory; and I never heard it reported that you were carrying on a trade forbidden by law.

"I do not doubt but that you will be able to confound the false reports which may have been circulated against you.

"(Signed) G. THIBAUT,
"*Administrator of the Imperial Vice-Consulate of France.*

"JOHN PETHERICK, Esq."

"KHARTOUM,
"January 28th, 1864.

"SIR,

"I have the honour to declare that during the last ten years, my having been at Khartoum, and spent an entire year at Gondokoro, where you had an establishment, I have never heard of your being engaged in slave traffic, or of your agents engaging in such trade on your account.

"(Signed) M. L. HANSAL,
"*Pro Manager of the I.R. Consulate of Austria for Central Africa.*

"JOHN PETHERICK, Esq."

It will be seen, with reference to dates, that I have followed up this subject irrespective of their order of succession, and to dispose of it I must beg to continue in the same manner as far as other subjects are concerned, and now retrace my steps to 1863.

The "hue and cry" that had been raised against me vanished on my return to Khartoum, and I had no difficulty in procuring men for the equipment of the "Kathleen" for Baker, and two other boats for the requirements of my trade. When all preparations had been organized and the men prepaid, some new regulation on the part of the Egyptian Government for the future conduct of the White Nile trade were unexpectedly issued. They were designed, it was stated, "for the better suppression of the slave trade;" but, in reality, as it was evident to every one conversant with the subject and the ways and means of the Egyptian Government, the design was to monopolize the ivory and "ebony" trade, and by the exclusion of private traders from the locality, to secure for the Egyptian Government total exemption from the occasionally troublesome supervision of what were termed "meddling Europeans."

These measures, under the name of *Werko* (poll tax), were so directly opposed to the stipulations of the International Commercial Treaty, that in conformity with my instructions as British Consul, and my interest as a trader, I could not assent, but to the utmost of my power opposed them. It was in vain that, in order to make matters smooth, I offered, under protest, to comply with the arbitrary demands of the Egyptian Government, and to remit the subject for the consideration and decision of a superior authority. Nothing would do but my immediate personal obligation for the amount due in taxes on my men, a written statement that the amount was paid of my own free will, and that I acknowledged the justice of the measure!

This was too much! and withholding my assent, I was officially informed that "I might do what I liked with my boats, but that not a man in my employ should leave Khartoum." In order to keep my arrangements with Baker, I conformed without further demur, and paid the tax; but, with regard to my trade, it was thus summarily stopped. I, however, resolved that as soon as my wife's and my own health would permit, to proceed to seek that redress from Her Majesty's Government to which, as a British subject, I felt myself entitled.

Moosa Pasha, the then Governor-General of the Soudan, a thorough tyrant and great tactician, knowing that I had hitherto met with no support whatever from my Government, either with respect to commercial questions or the steps I had taken in prosecuting persons engaged in the slave trade, had presumed upon the probability of their continued inaction, and had allowed matters to take their course as described. But so soon as it was known to him that Earl Russell had abolished my Consulate, then there were no bounds to his unmitigated rage for my ruin. After our departure from Khartoum he issued instructions to his sub-governors to prevent our obtaining the necessary number of camels wherewith to cross the desert of Aboo Hamad.

Two months were frittered away in fruitless endeavours to obtain twenty-five camels by promises of unheard-of high rates of pay. As a last resource, intimidation prevailed upon a local despot to send us eight camels. Thus, in addition to our own two dromedaries, and by the abandonment of every dispensable article of luggage it was thought we might, with safety to our lives, succeed in crossing the most sterile and forbidding of deserts. We *did* cross it; but our sufferings from the excessive heat, diminished rations of water, and the fatigue induced by eighteen hours a day in the saddle, it is out of my power to describe.

Knowing that my Government held slavery in the greatest abhorrence, this Pasha judged that if he could commit me of it, both my ruin and his revenge for my opposition to the *Werko* tax would be accomplished. How he set about it the following translations of French documents will show:

<p style="text-align:center">"BERBER,
"<i>August 9th</i>, 1864.</p>

"Sir,

"We have received the letter you wrote on August 6th, to-day, and by which you inform us that during your forced sojourn here (at Berber) for want of camels, one of your elephant hunters, named Gandil Nast, has arrived here, and has been presented to you, and has given you a verbal report of the events which have taken place at Khartoum after your departure from that city, and you add that as these events appear to be of a very grave character when taken in connection with the infamous accusations brought against you by His Excellency the Governor-General, Moosa Pasha, you request us to have the said servant called for the purpose of cross-examining him, and reporting to you the result of our interrogation, so that in case of need you might, at any future time, be able to enlighten your Consul as to the means the Governor-General has resorted to for the purpose of obtaining false evidence detrimental to your honour from your servants.

"In conformity with your wish, we have had before us Gandil Nast, the person in question, and the following, Sir, is a faithful report of the details he has given us, relative to the events that have taken place at Khartoum during your absence.

"1st. During the return to Khartoum of your servants, who were upon the White River (in June, 1864) the boat that conveyed them stopped at different military posts established on the White River for the purpose of preventing the slave trade, and supported by the Egyptian Government; the boat was minutely inspected, and the servants were questioned several times, and at length, finding nothing illegal, the officers commanding these different posts gave the boatmen a passport, by which means they were enabled to reach Khartoum.

"2nd. The same servant states that on arriving at Khartoum, the local Governor demanded from your servants the immediate payment of the personal tax or duty called ' *Werko*.' This payment having been made, the Governor-General ordered that this said servant, as well as your special agent Abdel Rahman, should be thrown into prison and separated one from another.

"After five days' detention, this hunter was examined by Moosa Pasha, who asked him if he had not taken any slaves, and if you had not expressly ordered him to carry on the trade. The hunter replied that he had never seen slaves either bought or sold, and that, on the contrary, you had always energetically forbidden him to carry on this dreadful trade.

"This reply made the Governor-General order five hundred blows of the ' *courbatch* '—(a whip of hippopotamus-hide)—to be given to the servant; and we have ourselves learned that the above-mentioned hunter or servant still bears upon his head, back, and shoulders, the marks, more or less deep and still unhealed, of the blows of the ' *courbatch*.' After this, the same Governor-General ordered baked bricks to be placed on the inside of his elbow-joints, the bricks being retained in that position by lashing the wrist to the arm below the shoulder, and he then exposed him for six hours to a burning sun, forbidding any person to give him water to drink; and finally, this same servant adds that for five consecutive days the same questions were again and again put to him, and they being followed by the same reply, he was again submitted to the same torture.

"3rd. On the sixth day, the said Governor-General had the said servant brought before him, and informed him that if he did not declare in writing that you had ordered him to carry on the slave trade, he would place with him in his prison five Albanian soldiers, and subject him to treatment unfit for publication; to which your servant replied that he would prefer to be placed at the mouth of a loaded cannon and die rather than submit to it. The Pasha then despairing of obtaining from him the avowals he desired, again gave him a new application of the 'courbatch,' and spitting in his face, had him thrown out of his divan, and he thus obtained his liberty.

"4th. The same servant declares that the so-called Faki Mahommed, your Arab secretary, was carried away from his house at Halfaya by five soldiers, with a pronged fork round his neck, and dragged to the feet of the Pasha, by whom he was examined, and was then put in prison.

"Such, Sir, are the explanations furnished by your native hunter as to the events which have passed at Khartoun after your departure, and we trust that they may help to enlighten the persons called on to judge the grave case between you and His Excellency the Governor-General of Soudan.

"We have the honour to be, Sir,
"Yours truly,
"FERD LAFARGUE,
"Mr. THEODORE DE HEUGLIN,
"*Aulic Counsellor of His Majesty the King of Wurtemberg.*

"To Mr. JOHN PETHERICK,
"&c., &c., &c."

"BERBER,
"*August 9th*, 1864.

"We, Consul of Prussia at Cairo, certify that the signature of Mr. Theodore de Heuglin written above is that of his own hand, in testimony of which we have signed these presents, and have fixed the seal of the Consulate thereto.

"The Consul of Prussia,
"BRUGSCH.

"Cairo, January 24th, 1865."

On November 25th we moored our boat alongside the island of Roda, opposite to Old Cairo; and on the other side of the island—within a few hundred yards—lay Moosa Pasha's steamboat. Strange to say, at an early hour on the following morning the Pasha left for the Soudan; and so unexpected and hurried were his movements, that some of his attendants were left behind.

That he had done his worst was soon made apparent by Mr. Reade, our acting Consul-General, on my reporting myself, informing me that His Highness the Viceroy had verbally accused me of slave trading. On this, Mr. Reade invited His Highness to make a formal charge, so that he might act accordingly. In compliance with Mr. Reade's suggestion, I waited the return from England of Mr. (now Sir Robert) Colquhoun, and then officially urged the advancement of the charge.

Two or three communications (during as many months) having met with no response from the Egyptian Government, Sir Robert advised my proceeding to England for the purpose of pressing my claim for compensation from the Viceroy, for the loss of my trade, which he himself could not entertain. As I had given ample opportunity to the Egyptian Government for the advancement of any charge against me, he considered me exonerated; and that if, even at any future time, proceedings should be instigated, he could no longer take notice of them.

To conclude this subject. In reply to my earnest request that Her Majesty's Government " would grant me the closest investigation, in order to afford me an opportunity to refute any charges or misstatements that may have been made with reference to any connection on my part with the slave trade, or derogatory to my honour," I hope I may be pardoned for quoting the following letter:

" FOREIGN OFFICE,
" *June* 21*st*, 1865.

" SIR,

" I am directed by Earl Russell to acknowledge the receipt of your letter of the 1st instant, stating that you have reason to believe that reports have been made against your character in connection with the slave trade, during the time you were employed as Her Majesty's Consul for the Soudan, and requesting that an inquiry may be instituted, in order to enable you to refute any charges or misstatements that may have been made derogatory to your honour.

" In reply, I am to state that Her Majesty's Government have been informed that no trade has hitherto been carried on by native and European traders on the White Nile, and in the Soudan, without an indirect, if not a direct, encouragement being given to the slave trade; and that this traffic in slaves is incidental to, and arises out of, the ivory trade along that river.

" A proof of this is furnished by the fact of slaves having been conveyed in your own boats; although—as you stated at the time, and as Her Majesty's Government are willing to believe —without your knowledge or sanction.

"I am to add that there is no evidence before Her Majesty's Government that you had any direct participation in this traffic; and Her Majesty's Government acquit you of any such participation.

"(Signed)   A. H. LAYARD.

"JOHN PETHERICK, Esq.,
&c., &c."

The above document will, I think, be more to the purpose than anything I could say, and therefore I dispense with further comment, and allow the reader to form his own judgment of the value of the charges which directly or indirectly have been launched against me.

I must now beg to retrace my steps to Khartoum.

On the 31st December, 1863, I received the first intelligence of Consul Cameron's imprisonment by Theodore, and I at once communicated it under flying seal through Her Majesty's Agent to the Secretary of State for Foreign Affairs. In concluding my letter, I say:

"If Her Majesty's Government believes me competent, I place myself at its disposal for the execution of any mission to the Court of Abyssinia."

From the circumstance of some slight attention that I had been enabled to show the Emperor, through the medium of the visits of occasional Abyssinians of rank to Khartoum, and his knowledge of the steps I had officially taken, in 1856, to endeavour to induce the Egyptian Government to restore a number of captured individuals and cattle that had been seized by Egyptian troops on a *razzia* in the free territory of Bogos, the position I held in the Soudan was well known to him; and from my knowledge of the habits of semi-barbarous chieftains and African despots, I flattered myself that the mission of my wife and self, both personally acquainted with Cameron, would prove successful.

Not doubting that my proffer of services would be accepted, I selected as presents a variety of English firearms, including elephant rifles and ammunition, a couple of watches, amber mouth-pieces, a variety of Bohemian glass, and a shirt of mail.

The treacherous behaviour of a *friend*, whose subsequent untimely end no one can have greater cause to regret than myself, had, however, in the meantime unsuspectedly, and without the slightest provocation or foundation, so thoroughly poisoned the minds of authorities at home against me, that to my utter surprise, instead of any recognition of my offer to free Cameron, I received the following terse communication:

"FOREIGN OFFICE,
"*October* 31*st*, 1863.

"Sir,

"As the public interests no longer require the retention of a British Consul at Khartoum, Her Majesty's Government are of opinion that the time has arrived to abolish the post.

"I have accordingly to state to you that on and after the 1st of February next, your functions as Her Majesty's Consul for the Soudan will be at an end.

"You will, on the termination of your services under this Department, seal up and deliver to Her Majesty's Agent and Consul-General at Alexandria the whole of your official archives.

"I am, &c.,

"(Signed) RUSSELL."

My last effort for the relief of Consul Cameron, at the time *when the Abyssinian war was in contemplation*, was thus:

"THE TOOKUL, HENLEY-ON-THAMES,
"*July* 7, 1867.

"My Lord,

"In conformity with the wishes of your Lordship, expressed to me by letter on the 5th instant, that it would be more convenient if I would put my suggestions with respect to the relief of the captives in Abyssinia in writing, I beg to submit the following brief statement of the most inexpensive, and to my mind, according to the present position of our relations with Theodore, the safest means to coerce him to release the prisoners in his possession.

"Your Lordship is aware of the absence of salt in Abyssinia, and that it has to be imported from the coast. Of the importance of salt as an article of consumption I need not dwell; but perhaps it may not be so well known that in Abyssinia proper, and many of its dependencies and neighbouring territories, it is so valuable as to form an universal object for barter, and is equivalent in value to coin.

"The plan that I have the honour to suggest for the consideration of your Lordship is, that Her Majesty's Government, in concord with his Highness the Viceroy of Egypt, should establish and entertain a small but efficient naval and military force at Massowah, so disposable as to establish a blockade for the prevention of all communication between Abyssinia and the coast on the one hand, and with the Egyptian dependencies of the Soudan on the other.

"It would be a matter for consideration whether the blockade should be so stringent as to annul all possible intercourse between the above-named points, and comprise the seizure of merchandise and individuals as counter-hostages to guarantee the safety of the prisoners, or whether it should be confined to prevent the transit of salt into Abyssinia.

"It seems to be beyond a doubt that Theodore of late has met with many reverses, and it is to be concluded, in proportion that he is losing power, the several native chieftains must acquire it.

"Therefore, as soon as the avowed object of the blockade shall have become apparent, and that it will last until the conditions thereof shall have been complied with, in my humble opinion the effect will be that not only the energy of the chieftains, but that of entire populations, will be directed to consummate the safety and release of the captives.

"The limits of a letter necessarily restrict me to brevity, and it was with a view to a more elaborate communication of my ideas that I ventured to solicit an interview with your Lordship.

"I can only add that in the event of the foregoing being deemed worthy of your Lordship's consideration, I shall be happy to contribute any further information in my power in connection with the subject.   "I have, &c.,

"(Signed)   JOHN PETHERICK.

"The Right Hon. Lord Stanley, M.P.,
"*Secretary of State for Foreign Affairs.*"

In reply I was honoured thus:

"FOREIGN OFFICE,
"*July* 11*th*, 1867.

"Sir,

"I am directed by Lord Stanley to acknowledge the receipt of your letter of the 7th instant relative to the best means of procuring the release of the British captives in Abyssinia, and I am to thank you for the suggestions made by you, which shall be duly considered.   "I am, &c.,

"(Signed)   JAMES MURRAY."

To the majority of the traders, European and native, at Khartoum, the tidings of my consulate being abolished were a source of great satisfaction, but to none so much as the principal officers of the Egyptian Government—who, enraged with my official proceedings generally, regarded the bulky despatches that passed through their hands, addressed to Her Majesty's Consul-General at Alexandria, with mistrust and hatred.

Some far-seeing Mussulmans there were, however, who acknowledged unhesitatingly — notwithstanding their differing with my opposition to the slave trade—their participation in many benefits conferred upon them by my not unfrequent successful opposition to oppressive inroads that, during my official residence in the Soudan, since 1849, had more or less been directed by every succeeding Governor against one branch or other of the commerce and produce of the country.

Neither did all the Europeans express the satisfaction that may be imagined; and, as a parting tribute to one now no more, who held very contrary views from those first quoted, I give the following communication that appeared in the "Athenæum" of April 9th, 1864, headed

"OFFICIAL ENGLAND ON THE WHITE NILE.

"KHARTOUM,
"*January* 21*st*, 1864.

"A few days ago, we received intelligence that the English Government had resolved to abolish the Consulate which it established in the Soudan in 1849. This decision has troubled the sound portion of our colony; because, under the painful circumstances in which it is placed, it found in the experience and character of the British Consul a favourite rallying-point.

"To the slave dealers and men of their class—to whom the presence of a British Consul was a restraint—it is of course a triumph. It appears to me that, if in 1849 the British Government had sufficient motives for establishing a Consulate in the Soudan, there exist, at the present time, much more powerful reasons for maintaining it. The recent discoveries of Captains Grant and Speke must result in the organization of other scientific expeditions, of which Khartoum will form either the point of departure or that of arrival. England, which may lay claim, and with justice, to the honour of nearly all new discoveries in Africa, will certainly take the lead in these expeditions; and I cannot conceive it possible that she will willingly deprive them of the protection of a British Consul at Khartoum. This protection will become especially indispensable to those expeditions which require Khartoum, or some other place in the Soudan, as the point of departure; for in the absence of Consular intervention with the local authorities, or the mediation of a man of local experience—who, from his position, is under obligations to render service—I am of opinion that it will be impossible to organize any expedition there. They will be scandalously fleeced, or leave badly provided, and so will fail. It would not be difficult to cite instances in support of what I advance.

"A higher motive renders it desirable to maintain at Khartoum a British Consulate. The slave traffic in the While Nile country (for a long time held in restraint sufficiently feeble) has had for years—thanks to the encouragement of certain high functionaries who find their profit in it—an extension truly frightful; and it is exercised with such horrors, that I hesitate to describe them.

"Every year more than one hundred vessels leave Khartoum for the purpose of hunting down the negroes; and slaves, who formerly were brought in by stealth, are now dragged publicly along the highways of the country, and even through the streets of Khartoum, with the yoke upon their necks.

"The British Consul, Mr. J. Petherick, initiated measures

which would have soon placed a limit to this traffic; unfortunately, owing to the aversion of four-fifths of the Khartoumers, who live by it, he saw his reputation tarnished by false accusations, his fellow-citizens, and friends misled on his account—he found no sufficient support, even before his superiors, who were doubtless prejudiced against him.

"The non-success of Mr. Petherick in his proceedings against certain persons accused of this traffic has given license to these slave dealers. Assured, henceforth, of impunity, and of the inefficiency of the law, they have thrown off the mask.

"It is an everlasting scandal to civilized Europe thus to authorize, by her silence, the infamous piracy which has stained the White Nile with blood; and for anti-slavery England, who, instead of declaring herself impotent by abolishing her Consulate at Khartoum, should have surrounded it with all the prestige possible, authorized severe measures, and extended a hand to enforce their execution.

"From a review of the interests involved in the question, it may still be said there was a time when neither the number of British subjects established in the Soudan, nor the importance of English commerce in these countries, required that England should maintain a Consul at Khartoum. But now financial societies are being formed for the exploration of the Soudan, which, in a triple point of view—agricultural, industrial, and commercial—already attract the attention of Europe.

"New routes of communication by land and, perhaps, by sea, will soon be opened. In this movement, ought not the commerce of England to have a large interest, and will she be able to dispense with a Consulate in a country much more in its infancy as relates to the law and its administration, than to its industry and commerce? Although personal considerations may be for us of secondary importance—and we are not the defenders of

Mr. Petherick—we ought to add, that this Consul (a man of intelligence, possessing a knowledge of the Soudan from a long experience) has performed the duties of his office with an integrity and firmness that may well serve as an example to his colleagues. In the blow which has deprived Mr. Petherick of office, that which is the most distressing is the fact that his deposition followed quickly upon energetic measures taken by him against this traffic, and against that oppression which the local authorities endeavoured to bring to bear upon Europeans. I repeat, this deposition of Mr. Petherick passes current through the country as a disavowal of these measures, and is regarded as a censure publicly inflicted upon Mr. Petherick by his superiors in consequence of the attitude he assumed.

"I am ignorant whether the British Government can now reconsider the decision it has taken; but I do know that the re-establishment of a British Consulate at Khartoum would be a measure which all those who have at heart the triumph of the principles of civilization in this barbarous country would receive with joy.

"(Signed)   Dr PRUYSSENAERE,
"*Belgian Resident at Khartoum.*"

The recent disclosures by Consul Reade of Cairo, that will be fresh in the memory of every one, of the extent to which the slave trade is carried on in the heart of Egypt, must surely satisfy the public of the desirability of the establishment of a British Consulate at Khartoum—the hotbed of the Egyptian slave trade—if not for the entire suppression of the trade, at least for its contraction within less shocking limits. Its entire abolition, I believe every-one with a knowledge of the domestic habits of Mussulmans will agree with me is next to an impossibility. Nothing less than the subversion of their religion, for the suppression of polygamy and its consequent usages, will conduce to the complete prevention of that slavery which, to every Mahommedan, is a domestic necessity. If the French and English Governments were to combine, and put the screw on the Egyptian Government, there is nothing to prevent the imposition of such burdens upon the trade as speedily to confine it within limits; and by gradually curtailing these limits, slaves will become too great a luxury for any but the wealthy to indulge in. Thus, by introducing the thin end of the wedge, a change of domestic habits may, in course of time, be realized.

Upon our return to England, to my very great surprise, I found, from a circular of the Royal Geographical Society, dated May 3rd, 1865, that Baker, by exceeding his instructions and arrogating to himself, as far as was in his power, the supplying of boats and necessaries at Gondokoro, not only met with the approval of the Council, but was to be rewarded by the Society's gold medal for supplanting me in the services wherewith I, the Society's envoy, was specially charged, and which, to all intents and purposes, I succeeded in carrying out after unprecedented reverses.

The following is a quotation from the circular; and of one clause, in italics, I complain in particular:

"The Patron's medal will be awarded to Mr. Samuel Baker for his vigorous explorations, entirely at his own cost, in the interior of Africa, whereby he first determined the course and position of the Atbara, a great eastern tributary of the Nile; *next, for having fitted out at Khartoum an expedition by which he relieved Speke and Grant;* and thirdly, for the further explorations of Equatorial Africa in which he is now engaged."

That I have just cause of complaint against both Sir Samuel Baker and the Council of the Royal Geographical Society I think an extract from a letter addressed to the "Times," January 29th, 1863, by the President, will certify. For Baker, in lieu of supporting me, and in opposition to his instructions and my wishes, when he had ocular proof at Gondokoro of the untruth of my reported death, and of the preparations I had made for the succour of Speke and Grant, still persisted in the continuation of those duties which had been assigned to me, and which he was in the event of my death only authorized to perform. That the Council of the Royal Geographical Society, after they had by my report been placed in full possession of the circumstances of my successful efforts to place the boats, grain, &c., agreed upon at the disposal of Speke and Grant at Gondokoro, should continue to support Baker in this act of usurpation, and even to reward him for superseding their own representative, is a step which every impartial person must condemn. The President says:

> "It may surprise many persons that these ladies, who have thus penetrated by the White Nile into Central Africa beyond Gondokoro, and about one thousand miles by water beyond Khartoum to nearly 4° North of the Equator, should have made no mention of Mr. Petherick, who had preceded them in his voyage to Gondokoro. This seems to be explained by the fact, announced by Mr. S. W. Baker in a letter from Khartoum, that Mr. Petherick having met with disaster on the river, through a continuous south wind and incessant rain, had sent all his boats back to Khartoum, save one, and was proceeding by land to Gondokoro.

> "It is therefore probable that the telegram announcing the death of this bold traveller and his spirited wife by drowning is inaccurate.

> "The next post will probably solve this painful mystery; but

if it should unhappily prove true that the adventurous Petherick has lost his life, the Council of the Royal Geographical Society has in that case assigned to Mr. Baker all the charge which they had confided to Mr. Petherick.

"Having fitted out an expedition at his own cost, Mr. Baker was about to proceed, by the last accounts from Khartoum, to Gondokoro, there, as he thought, to meet and support Petherick, whose replenished boats and stores he had taken charge of.

* * * * * * *

"For the successful accomplishment of this task in exploring a large unknown region in Central Africa, Mr. Baker has the hearty good wishes of all geographers, including

"Your obedient servant,
"(Signed)   RODERICK I. MURCHISON."

No allusion whatever having been made at the meeting of the Society with respect to the efforts I had made for the relief of Speke and Grant, I considered it incumbent upon me, prior to the award of the medal, to read and place upon the table the following protest :

"THE PRESIDENT AND COUNCIL OF THE ROYAL GEOGRAPHICAL SOCIETY.

"GENTLEMEN,

"Without any desire to interfere with the distribution of the Patron's medal, I consider it necessary in the present instance, in vindication of my own character, to state that the reasons given for the award of it to Mr. Baker are incorrect, inasmuch as, in compliance with the orders of the Royal Geographical Society, the relief of Speke and Grant was virtually accomplished by myself, and in a manner far exceeding the instructions I had received, and before the arrival of Mr. Baker or his expedition at Gondokoro.

"These facts are stated in my report of January, 1864, communicated to the Council, and I respectfully request that this my protest against the reasons assigned may be recorded in the minutes of this meeting, and subsequently published in the 'Proceedings' of the Society.

"(Signed) JOHN PETHERICK.

"LONDON, 22nd May, 1865."

Two days after the first meeting of the Society I had attended since my return from an eventful and disastrous journey, and no recognition in any way having been bestowed upon me, I addressed a note to the President to this effect:

"*May* 24*th*, 1865.

"DEAR SIR,

"Will you kindly permit me an interview, at your own convenience, in order that I may justify myself in your estimation and good opinion?

"That I shall obtain justice at your hands I am convinced, and I feel certain that knowingly you would never wrong any man, much less one who has exerted himself to the utmost of his power to carry out your own desires. All I ask is fair play and to be allowed an opportunity to defend myself. I have returned to England for the purpose of regaining my good name, which during my absence, as you are aware, has greatly suffered from gross misrepresentations.

"I regret not having had an opportunity of seeing you when

APPENDIX A.

I called, and to express that I entertain no bad feeling towards yourself; but I felt it my duty to protest against a printed statement so prejudicial to my honour and interests.

"(Signed)   JOHN PETHERICK.

"SIR RODERICK IMPEY MURCHISON.
   "&c., &c., &c."

On the same day I received the following reply:

"*May 24th*, 1865.

"MY DEAR SIR,

"In reply to your letter of this day, I hasten to say that I shall be happy to see you to-morrow, Thursday, at the Museum in Jermyn Street, at three p.m.

"I am of course desirous to see fair play and complete justice done to you; but you must give me leave to observe, if you think the words used by the Council in awarding a medal to Mr. Baker reflected in any way discredit to yourself, you are clearly under a misapprehension of our meaning and wishes.

"Recollect what I said at the meeting. From what Baker stated from Khartoum, we were under the impression either that you had lost your life, or that your expedition had met with such disasters as would prevent your succouring Speke and Grant. Hence the *motive* of Mr. Baker appeared to me to be truly noble. It would be very painful for me to have to act as umpire between Captains Speke and Grant on the one hand, and yourself on the other. But few distant expeditions are conducted without some disagreements among the parties; and I cannot see that in anything which the Royal Geographical Society has done you have cause for complaint.

"The imputation to which I presume you allude, came from

and *through other channels*, and are wholly irrespective of your labours as an envoy on a special service.

"(Signed)   RODERICK IMPEY MURCHISON.

"J. PETHERICK, Esq."

Notwithstanding the verbally repeated assurance of the President that he was anxious to see fair play and justice done to me, another meeting of the Society was held without the slightest notice being taken of the return of my brave wife and self from our perilous expedition. Considering the allusion made to her previously to our departure at the meeting of February 25th, 1861 (see Vol. V., No. 3., p. 107) : "And as Mrs. Petherick is to accompany him, he (the President) felt confident that, with the usual spirit of geographical research which animates the ladies who have honoured us with their presence, she would warmly second and support the resolve of her daring and distinguished husband," I could not help feeling that much discourtesy and great injustice had been committed towards one who, whatever had been my shortcomings, should have been considered deserving of some recognition. I, therefore, as envoy of the Society, made this last appeal :

"TO THE COUNCIL OF THE ROYAL GEOGRAPHICAL SOCIETY.

"*June* 12*th*, 1865.

"GENTLEMEN,

"I anticipate that at the last meeting of the season, some recognition of my services with regard to the expedition to aid and succour the late Captain Speke and his party, may be made.

"I failed not in what I undertook: stores, boats, and every-

APPENDIX A. 165

thing requisite were placed at the disposal of the travellers, Speke and Grant; thus faithfully fulfilling to the utmost my compact with yourselves.

" (Signed) JOHN PETHERICK."

Shortly after, I received the following reply:

" 15 WHITEHALL PLACE,
" *June* 17*th*, 1865.

" SIR,

" I am desired by the Committee appointed in consequence of your letter to report to the Council whether any recognition is due to your services, to submit the following Memorandum to you, preparatory to their coming to a decision on the subject.

" An early reply from you is solicited.

" (Signed) H. W. BATES,
" *Assistant Secretary to the Royal Geographical Society*."

"The Committee understand from the documents in their possession, that the following short statement gives a just account of Mr. Petherick's establishment at Gondokoro, between the months of November, 1861, and June, 1862. Before proceeding further, they desire to submit it to Mr. Petherick's perusal, in order that he may have an opportunity of pointing out any misapprehension into which they may have fallen. They request an answer as soon as possible, and, at the latest, within a week.

" (Signed) H. W. BATES,
" *Assistant Secretary to the Royal Geographical Society*."

"MEMORANDUM.

"It appears that the first boats dispatched by Mr. Petherick to Gondokoro after his return to Africa, were two in number. They were sent to Khartoum in November, 1861, immediately after his arrival at that place, and they reached Gondokoro in January, 1862.

"The Egyptian who had charge of these boats proceeded westwards, to a trading station belonging to Mr. Petherick, whence he (the Egyptian) dispatched a trading expedition southwards. On its return, the whole party went back to Gondokoro, taking with them some slaves which the Egyptian had been buying on his own account. They quitted Gondokoro early in May, and sailed back towards Khartoum.

"On the way, they met Mr. Petherick, who discovering the slaves, put the Egyptian in irons, and sent him in one of the boats to Khartoum. He ordered the other boat back to Gondokoro, where it arrived after June, 1862.

"It would appear, therefore, that Mr. Petherick had boats at Gondokoro during the four and a half months of January, February, March, April, and part of May, but at no other period during the time of his agreement with the Royal Geographical Society, from November, 1861, to June, 1862."

"To H. W. BATES, Esq.,
"*Assistant Secretary to the Royal Geographical Society.*

"*June* 23rd, 1863.

"SIR,

"With reference to the Memorandum communicated to me on the 17th instant, permit me to express great surprise at the very limited view the Committee has therein taken of the extent of my exertions to relieve the Speke Expedition. By reference to the documents alluded to, it will appear that for reasons therein assigned, in order to hope for a successful result, an expedition on a much larger scale than the one agreed to had become indispensable; therefore, during the greater part of the time originally contemplated for its duration, instead of two, I had *seven* boats employed for the relief of Captain Speke and his party.

"One of these boats, laden with stores of various descriptions, reached Gondokoro against unprecedented difficulties in October, 1862, and, according to instructions, it remained there until the arrival of Captains Speke and Grant, from which they drew a certain amount of stores and grain, which Mr. Baker had it not in his power to supply.

"Another expedition of three boats left Khartoum in December, 1862, and arrived at Gondokoro in January, 1863, prior to Mr. Baker. One of these (the 'Kathleen') had been taken possession of by Captain Speke, a portion of whose effects were on board on my arrival at Gondokoro.

"The expedition from my trading station southwards, I beg to say, was an *exploring* and *not* a *trading* one; and notwithstanding the return of two boats under the charge of Abd il Majid, in disobedience to my orders, on the 10th May, 1862, from Gondokoro, and seven weeks prior to the date fixed for the termination of my agreement, it took place consequent on the certain information conveyed to him by the person in charge of De Bono's station, of the impossibility of Captain Speke reaching Gondokoro before the following season.

"Again permit me to state, the slaves discovered by me in the possession of Abd il Majid, were not brought by him from my station, but were, in conjunction with other traders, carried off from the vicinity of Gondokoro.

"Upon a reconsideration of the question, I feel the Committee will give me credit for continuing my exertions beyond the allotted time as expressed in the agreement, but in full accordance with the interpretation of the real views of the Council of the Royal Geographical Society, as conveyed to me in their instructions for my guidance.* Captain Speke not having been able to keep time,† and the object in view being his relief, the continuation of my efforts to attain that end must at the time have met with the approval of the Society, inasmuch as, on the report of my death, its wishes are distinctly recorded by a Minute of the Council, dated January 26th, 1863,‡ and to which, for a just appreciation of my efforts, permit me respectfully to refer the Committee.

"(Signed) JOHN PETHERICK."

On the following day I received a communication to this effect:

"15 WHITEHALL PLACE,
"*June* 24*th*, 1865.

"Sir,

"The Council of the Royal Geographical Society having yesterday taken the subject of your letter, dated June 12th, into

---

* In the instructions occurs this paragraph: "The President and Council do not attempt to lay down any limit to this exploration, but, fully trusting to your known zeal and energy, feel assured that you will do all in your power to effect the above-mentioned object without serious risk to the lives of the party under your command."

† He was sixteen months behind the time appointed for his arrival at Gondokoro.

‡ This occurred nearly seven months after the date fixed for the termination of my contract with the Society. The Minute in January 26th, 1863: "When on the subject of the reported death of Consul Petherick and wife, the President was requested to communicate with Mr. Baker at Khartoum, requesting him to act for the Society, should the report of Consul Petherick's death be confirmed."

their full consideration, have instructed me to transmit to you the following statement as their reply to the said letter.

"(Signed) H. W. BATES,
"*Assistant Secretary to the Royal Geographical Society.*

"J. PETHERICK, Esq."

"MINUTE OF COUNCIL.

"In June, 1860, Mr. Consul Petherick, then about to revisit the White Nile for the purpose of trade, suggested that his expedition might render important service to Captains Speke and Grant, if the Royal Geographical Society were pleased to avail themselves of the opportunity. He represented that Gondokoro was deserted by traders, and even by natives, for part of the time between November and June, and that Captain Speke's party would risk starvation if they arrived during that interval. After that, the only practicable route to Khartoum lay by river, and the boats were not to be procured at Gondokoro except by a chance from the ivory traders. Lastly, that Captains Speke and Grant would find themselves in serious difficulties if unsupported by persons who were familiar with the language and customs of the northern tribes. The good-will of many Fellows of the Society, as evinced by voluntary subscriptions, to which the Council contributed £100 on the part of the Society, finally took the shape of an agreement (see Appendix) between the Royal Geographical Society and Mr. Petherick. A sum of £1,000 was placed in his hands, and he engaged, on his part, to station as a depôt two well armed, provisioned boats at Gondokoro, in November, 1861, with a supply of provisions sufficient for his own and Captain Speke's party until July, 1862, 'the maintenance of these until June, 1862, at Gondokoro, being of primary importance.' (Instructions, 'Proceedings,' Vol. XL.) Also Mr. Petherick undertook, in the event of the non-arrival of Captain Speke, to go southwards as far as he could, to endeavour to meet and succour him.

"Lastly, Mr. Petherick was entirely relieved from the responsibility of remaining himself or detaining the boats longer than the end of June, 1862.

"In considering how far Mr. Consul Petherick has fulfilled his engagement to the Society, it is proper to make allowance for the disasters which befell him when engaged in his own trading pursuits, and rendered him incapable of reaching Gondokoro till many months after the latest of the above dates. Difficulties of transport in Egypt, partly due to the absence of camels at Korosko, delayed Mr. Petherick's arrival at Khartoum till November, 1861, at which date he had undertaken that the boats should have been stationed at Gondokoro. However, immediately on his arrival at Khartoum, he dispatched two boats, which reached Gondokoro in January, 1862.

"A misconception now appears to have arisen on the part of the Egyptian under whose charge they were. Instead of maintaining the two boats till the end of June, 1862, with stores to await Captain Speke's arrival, the Egyptian proceeded westward, six or eight days' journey from the White Nile, to a trading station belonging to Mr. Petherick. Thence he dispatched an agent southwards, in order, Mr. Petherick states, to search for Captain Speke's party, and carrying letters for them; but, as they did not follow the course of the river, they were not travelling in the direction from which that expedition might have been expected to arrive.

"Stores were bartered on Mr. Petherick's account, and the Egyptian captured slaves on his own. He then sailed back from Gondokoro towards Khartoum early in May, and met Mr.

Petherick, who, discovering the slaves, sent the Egyptian in irons to Khartoum. Mr. Petherick ordered back one of the boats to Gondokoro: he himself, travelling overland, did not reach that place till February, 1863, four days after Captain Speke's arrival, and seven months after the termination of the agreement with the Royal Geographical Society.

"The boat Mr. Petherick had ordered back to Gondokoro was stationed there when Captains Speke and Grant arrived; but, according to the statement of Captain Grant, the agent in charge of her made no offer whatever to assist them gratuitously with provisions. They bought certain articles as any other customers might have done, at the store belonging to Mr. Petherick, which was established like that of other traders at Gondokoro; but nothing whatever was offered by Mr. Petherick's men, who seemed entirely occupied on their master's business. They were wholly silent as to any orders having been given by Mr. Petherick to afford succour to the travellers; and they gave no letters, nor did they bring any other communication to them.

"It was through Mr. Baker that Captains Speke and Grant became aware that a subscription of £1,000 had been raised in England at Mr. Petherick's solicitation, and placed in his own hands for the purpose of establishing a depôt to relieve them on their arrival at Gondokoro.

"The Council are of opinion, from these facts, that Mr. Petherick complied with his agreement with the Society, to keep boats at Gondokoro between November, 1861, and July, 1862, to the extent only of having provisioned boats at that place, with communications for the travellers between the months of January and May, 1862.

"The Council are satisfied that he used considerable exertion in endeavouring to recover the time he had unhappily lost between Alexandria and Khartoum. They are also aware that his efforts were the more praiseworthy on account of the difficulties due to an exceptionally early change of the monsoon, and to unusual floods on the river, and also on account of the existing disturbances among the populations of the White Nile.

" Mr. Petherick's proposal to search in his own person for the travellers had no result, owing to the above-mentioned causes of delay on his journey. The expedition under the charge of his agent seems to have been little more than a private trading journey, and that in a direction in which the travellers were not likely to be found.

" With regard to Mr. Petherick's enterprises after June, 1862, the date at which his agreement with the Society had come to an end, the Council do not consider that any special recognition is due from the Society to Mr. Petherick. They are unable to satisfy themselves that Mr. Petherick's proceedings after that date were seriously modified by any other motives than his own private speculations in trade."

" APPENDIX.

"AGREEMENT BETWEEN CONSUL PETHERICK AND THE ROYAL GEOGRAPHICAL SOCIETY, February 4th, 1861.

" 1. Consul Petherick undertakes—in consideration of the receipt of £1,000 towards the expedition up the Nile—to place two well-armed boats, during November, 1861, at Gondokoro, with a sufficient stock of grain to ensure to Captain Speke and his party the means of subsistence upon their arrival at that place.

" 2. If Captain Speke shall not arrive in November, 1861, that Consul Petherick shall proceed with an armed force southwards towards Lake Nyanza to meet him.

"3. If Captain Speke shall arrive at Gondokoro before June, 1862, Consul Petherick promises to assist Captain Speke in making any explorations which Captain Speke may deem desirable.

"4. It being further understood that in the event of Captain Speke not having arrived by that time at Gondokoro, Consul Petherick shall not be bound to remain beyond June, 1862."

By the above verdict of the Expedition Committee, opposed as it was to common justice, impartiality, and the "fair play" that the President of the Society had encouraged me to anticipate in his letter of the 24th May, I felt myself temporarily constrained to abide.

That the tribunal by which I was judged was not fairly constituted, nor one, as emanating from the Royal Geographical Society, I had every right to expect, the public will admit when I state that my only living accuser, Captain Grant, was allowed to be present during my trial, whilst I was not accorded a similar privilege.

I had been attacked by unfounded statements and worse insinuations when too far away to defend myself; and now prejudice and preconceived opinions had so far prevailed as to induce a committee of gentlemen to deal me this unfair and overpowering blow at a time when, if permitted, I was fully capable of defending myself.

I protest against this verdict, and although the odds of the prestige and power of a Committee of a highly popular, and one of the leading societies in the world are opposed to me, there is still a higher power—that of public opinion—to which, in the fullest confidence of its impartiality and justice, I unhesitatingly venture to appeal. I feel that an apology is due to my friends and the public at large for the lapse of time which has taken place between the date of the ultimatum of the Expedition Committee and the publication of this statement. The reason has simply been that the inroads made on my health by climatic influences and the severe shock I received from the reverses I have experienced have incapacitated me from persevering in a work that proved too harassing to be dealt with but at intervals. In order to assist my friends and the public in arriving at a just decision in this matter, I beg to recall to their memory the following facts:

The Committee commence with the quotation of a Minute of Council stating that it was at my suggestion the Royal Geographical Society were pleased to avail themselves of my offer to render important services to Captains Speke and Grant. From this it might be inferred that I was a suppliant for employment on this expedition; but the Committee do not state at whose instigation this suggestion was formally made. But to place things as they occurred: in December, 1859, I received a letter from Captain Speke, in which he says:

"Were you ever thinking of going up the Nile yourself? if so, it strikes me that my going up the Nile may possibly be injurious to your prospects. But should it meet your views that we could manage by combined exertions, either in company or separately, to settle the question of the White River, I would readily work with you."

Shortly after, on the 22nd December, 1859, I received another letter from him, in which he tells me:

"I have just received a letter from Sir Roderick Murchison, and am delighted to find that he has accepted my plan for opening Africa favourably. I proposed to him that I should not go up the Nile, but round by Zanzibar; whilst you, supported by the Foreign Office, should go up the Nile and meet me at some fixed point which I could determine. I shall be in town about the 6th or 7th proximo, and will call upon you to make further arrangements."

Subsequently, at a meeting of the Royal Geographical Society (see "Proceedings," Vol. IV., No. 2, page 42), Sir Roderick Murchison remarked that he "was quite sure that the new co-operating expeditions, *which were designed by the Royal Geographical Society*, and which he hoped the Government would assist," &c., &c.

Again, at the meeting of March 26th, 1860, Captain Speke, after narrating how he met me, says, "he (Speke) had consequently *proposed to Mr. Petherick* to make a combined advance, simultaneously with him, in those tribes which lie in a short compass of two or three degrees immediately to the northward of his lake, and the southward of Gondokoro."

The President said, "it was exceedingly desirable that Government should grant that additional power to Mr. Petherick, which would enable him to lend real assistance to Captain Speke at the time of need," &c.

It was then, consequently, at the request of the Secretary of the Society that, in June, 1860, in conformity with the proposals of Captain Speke and backed by the wishes of the President and other leading members of the Council, I made a formal statement of how I thought I could be of service to Captain Speke.

At the meeting of the 11th June, 1860 (see "Proceedings," Vol. V., page 222) the President, in announcing that Speke and Grant had started on their expedition, added, "Consul Petherick from Khartoum could meet them with a large force and conduct them through the country; but Consul Petherick could scarcely be expected to do this at his own cost, and, as the Government declined making any further grant, the Council of the Society had departed from their usual rules, and had headed a subscription with £100 towards defraying expenses." He then urged "*the Fellows of the Society to subscribe liberally for the same purpose.*"

How, then, can the Committee say that it was at my suggestion that the Society availed themselves of my services, when, from the evidence of the "Proceedings," quoted above, it is plain that the idea originated with Captain Speke and the Council, who, unsolicited, sought my aid?

At this stage I offered, in case the sum of £2,900 was raised, to go as far south as the point of the termination of Speke's first expedition.

On the 25th February, 1861 (see "Proceedings," Vol. V., No. 3, page 107) the President announced the subscriptions to exceed £1,000, and said, "Consul Petherick is about to proceed to Khartoum," &c. I then distinctly stated that the sum subscribed was only one-half what would be required for the whole object, and consequently, that found would only suffice for carrying out the first part of the project of the Society, viz., *that of meeting Captain Speke and supplying him with grain and other necessaries at Gondokoro.*

That I did succeed in doing this is beyond dispute—and Speke not availing himself thereof is no fault of mine. The two boats under Abd il Majid arrived at Gondokoro in December, 1861, and not in January, 1862. A third boat, laden with grain and having a crew of forty-three men, arrived at the date stated by the Committee, for the support of Abd il Majid in his search for Speke overland, as advised in my letter to Speke, dated Khartoum,

November 15th, 1861, a copy of which I forwarded to the Society on November 25th.

In a previous letter to Sir Roderick I informed him that it was owing to the powerful opposition Abd il Majid would be likely to meet with by proceeding direct south from Gondokoro that dictated the route *viâ* my station on the west side of the Nile, and that the direction in which they travelled was not, as the Committee affirms, a wrong one. I need only state that upon the occasion of Captain Speke taking leave of his guide, Kidgwiga, at De Bono's station (see page 585 of his work), he describes it as the best route to adopt from Gondokoro.

That there could have been no misconception on the part of my servant I think is evident. On the contrary, during the overland journey he followed his instructions to the full extent of his power; and, considering that the Society had been fully advised of the step, had they disapproved of it, why not at the time have communicated with me? But neither the Society nor Speke, at the time of my entering on this enterprise, really expected more of me than that I should meet and succour the Zanzibar Expedition at Gondokoro.

The following extract from a letter addressed to me by Dr. Shaw, one of the officials of the Society, proves this. He writes:

"*June* 27*th*, 1861.

"MY DEAR PETHERICK,

The last news from Speke were to the effect that the party was advancing up the hills into the interior, and hoped to meet you all well at Gondokoro. Go ahead! Take observations for our gold medal.

"(Signed)   NORTON SHAW."

Why the Committee insist upon calling this a private trading journey I am the more at a loss to understand, as I had previously stated to them its objects; and with reference to the account of expenditure furnished to the Society, I debit myself with one-half of the expenses of this expedition, on account of any trade that might arise out of the search for Speke. I maintain that Mussaad's journey was not undertaken with a view to trade; but if, in carrying out his instructions and without prejudice thereto, he traded when an opportunity occurred (and I should have blamed him if he had not done so), I cannot see why the Committee endeavour to disown its real object and throw discredit on the expedition by calling it a trading journey.

Do not the whole proceedings of the Royal Geographical Society convey to the world that the main object of every journey or voyage of discovery, which they countenance in Africa and elsewhere, is the extension of British commerce? That it was known and expected I should trade, the following quotation from the "Proceedings," (Vol. VIII., No. 4, page 124), amply testifies:

"The President and Council in expressing a hope that you may not only succeed in affording succour to the Zanzibar Expedition, but that you may also succeed in opening a new field to the civilizing influence of commerce."

Again, Speke in his letter to me, dated December 22nd, 1859, said, "What a jolly good thing it would be to accomplish! You could do your ivory business at the same time that you work out geography!!"

With reference to the statement of Captain (now Colonel) Grant to the Committee that my agent in charge of the boat and stores at Gondokoro made no offer whatever to assist them gratuitously with provisions, an extract from Captain Speke's work—which I shall presently quote—will be sufficient to contradict this assertion. He also goes on to say, "they bought certain articles as any other customers might have done." Had Captain Grant been aware of, or recollected, Captain Speke's letter to me, he would have hesitated before making so unfounded an assertion.

In the letter referred to, dated Gondokoro, February 24th, 1863, after asking to be supplied with three pieces of American sheeting and a few other necessaries, Speke says:

"I have already taken from your stores, on account, 96 yards of American sheeting, which, together with the above, I could either repay you at Khartoum, Cairo, or London—just as you please."

Captain Grant also forgot that Speke and himself, when at Gondokoro, were destitute, and naturally unable to pay for anything they might desire to purchase. Speke further says in his work (page 606):

"My men begged for some clothes, as Petherick, they said, had a store for me under the charge of his *vakil*. The storekeeper was then called, confirming the story of my men: I begged of him *to give me what was my own*. It turned out it was all Petherick's, *but he had orders to give me on account anything I wanted*. This being settled, I took 95 yards of the commonest stuff as a makeshift for mosquito curtains for my men, besides four sailors' shirts for my head men."

On the following page he goes on to say:

"At his (Petherick's) urgent request, I took a few yards of cloth for my own men and some cooking fat; and though I offered to pay for it, he declined to accept any return at my hands."

Neither Speke nor Grant have in any form acknowledged that during their sojourn at Gondokoro my stores supplied their men with daily rations of grain; but this is of little importance.

It is, I think, needless to say more upon this subject; but, for the information of my readers, I beg to state that my store at Gondokoro, in this instance, was strictly a depôt for the benefit of the Speke Expedition ; and that the store annually established was not for the sale of articles of any kind, but simply for the accommodation of my trading stations in the interior.

Captain Grant's statement that the agent in charge of the boat at Gondokoro gave them no letters is quite correct. In the belief that I should arrive before the boat at Gondokoro, I took care of the letters for Speke and Grant, and, on meeting the travellers, delivered them personally.

Baker had arrived at Gondokoro before Speke or myself, and it was but natural that Grant should first of all hear through him of the subscription of £1,000; but Captain Grant might have added that on my arrival I placed the Society's "Proceedings," containing a full account of everything relating thereto, in his hands.

With reference to the date fixed by the Committee for the termination of my agreement to keep boats at Gondokoro to relieve the Nile Expedition—that Speke did not expect me to withdraw my assistance in July, 1862, is evident. In his letter to me from Karagwé, March 28th, 1862, and published in the "Proceedings" of the Society (Vol. VIII., No. 4, page 235), he says :

"I would go across the Masai country at once to Zanzibar ; but considering your promise to keep two or three boats two or three years for me, I sacrifice everything to fulfil the engagement."

I likewise "sacrificed everything" to keep *my* engagement; but when Baker appeared upon the scene at Gondokoro, Speke entirely ignored *his* engagement.

The Committee, also, in lieu of giving me a fair trial, preferred to abide by the prejudices they had conceived, and to follow the example of Speke and Baker by not only ignoring the stipulations of the agreement, but by setting aside the acts of their own Council.

Thus, upon the report of my death, the Council of the Society—six months after what the Committee please to call the termination of my agreement—authorized Baker, in the event of my death, to continue the duties that had been assigned to me!

That the Council acknowledged my services beyond the date fixed by the Committee is proved by their acceptance of my accounts of expenditure, which have not only been passed by the Finance Committee for the entire term of the expedition, but have been published in the Society's "Proceedings."

In the accounts submitted to the Society, every item was particularized; but the following curtailed version will, I think, convey a more correct idea of the cost of my expedition than that published in the "Proceedings."

(See balance-sheet, pp. 182, 183.)

My having duly advised the Society, from Khartoum, that additional expenditure would be required to equip a much larger expedition than I had anticipated, and at no time receiving any notice of disapproval thereof—my willingness to advance the requisite funds in the belief that the Society would hold me harmless, as no limit was placed on my efforts to meet Speke—all combine to make me consider the Society virtually and morally my debtor to the amount of £4,172 4s. 6d., the excess of expenditure over receipts, as annexed in the account on the next pages.

Had I met with a fair trial, I make no doubt of the result, and feel sure the President would have considered himself justified in again appealing to the Fellows to charge themselves with voluntary proportions of that balance, the whole weight of which I have been left alone to bear.

EXTRACT OF ACCOUNT RENDERED TO

OF
Expedition to succour

DISBURSEMENTS.
EXPEDITION UNDER ABD IL MAJID.

		£ s. d.	£ s. d.
1861. Nov. 15.	To five months' advance of wages to twenty men, crews of two boats	45 0 0	
	Ditto to Abd il Majid and Escort of forty men	86 8 4	
	Firearms, Ammunition, &c.	259 6 11	
	Glass Beads and objects for barter	319 5 10	
	Grain, Provisions, Stores, &c., &c.	174 13 4½	
	Ditto exclusively for Captains Speke and Grant	49 0 10½	
			933 15 4

EXPEDITION UNDERTAKEN BY MY WIFE AND SELF, ACCOMPANIED BY DRS. MURIE AND BROWNELL AND HENRY FOXCROFT.

1862. Mar. 20.	To five months' advance to fifty-six men, the crews of four boats	127 11 7	
	Ditto to Hunters and Escort, fifty-three men	309 19 10	
	Beads and objects for barter	1572 3 1	
	Firearms, Ammunition, &c.	1969 5 4	
	Provisions, Horses, Donkeys, and sundry Stores	1300 2 0	
June & Sept.	Balance of pay and boat-hire on return of boats to Khartoum, per my Agent, M. Lulf Allah	323 1 2	
			5602 3 0

EXPEDITION DISPATCHED BY MY AGENT FROM KHARTOUM TO REINFORCE THE FOREGOING.

1863. June.	To advance to an Escort of fifty-six men and crews of five boats	363 8 1	
	Grain, Provisions, Stores, &c.	903 16 1	
	Balance of pay and boat-hire on return	582 3 10	
			1849 8 0
	TOTAL DISBURSEMENTS		£8385 6 4

THE ROYAL GEOGRAPHICAL SOCIETY
BY
Captains Speke and Grant.

	RECEIPTS.	£	s.	d.	£	s.	d.
1861.							
Nov. 15.	By subscriptions from the Royal Geographical Society and the public...	1000	0	0			
	One-half the expenses of Expedition under Abd il Majid, on account of my trade	466	17	8			
1863.							
Mar. 20 to April 18.	Sundry Goods to my Establishment on termination of Expedition	1227	1	4			
	Amount realized by the sale of sundry Firearms and Stores	567	3	2			
	Ditto returned to my stores at Khartoum	614	0	2			
	Hire of one boat for the requirements of my trade	63	6	8			
	Amount realized by barter of Tusks with Goods charged to Expedition, 10 crs. of 100 lbs. each, @ £16	160	0	0			
1865.							
Nov.	Balance of Subscription Fund	114	12	10			
	TOTAL RECEIPTS				£4213	1	10
	EXCESS OF DISBURSEMENTS OVER RECEIPTS				£4172	4	6
					£8385	6	4

In answer to the last paragraph of the Committee's statement, if they had referred to my report to the Society they might easily have satisfied themselves that, after June, 1862, I did not possess the means wherewith to trade; and by a reference to my account of expenses they would also have seen that I had given credit for transactions in trade, during the entire course of my journey, to the amount the ivory obtained at Khartoum, viz., £160.

That, at a subsequent date, the Council of the Society entertained a different view of my proceedings after June, 1862, is proved by the insertion in the Journal for 1865 of a short abstract of my "Land Journey Westward of the White Nile." It contains what no other traveller has furnished, for, besides astronomical data, it contains the measurements of the White Nile, and its western tributaries from the Sobât southwards, up to 4° 46′ N. latitude. And although the Expedition Committee could give me credit for no other than personal motives for this journey, the Geographical Society of Gotha thought differently, and Dr. Petermann, in the "*Mittheilungen*," declares that "we must acknowledge it to be the most important journey of all hitherto accomplished in the territory between the Upper White Nile and the Djour;" and in another place he adds, "One also plainly sees that upon this map special importance was laid, and, indeed, it appears to us to be the most important thing in the new volume of the Journal."

In finally submitting myself to the judgment of the subscribers to my fund as to whether I performed, so far as it was in my power, what I had undertaken, I beg to again bring before their notice my last communication addressed to the President and Council of the Royal Geographical Society previous to starting on my expedition.

"*February 4th*, 1861.

"Gentlemen,

"My instructions not having been read at the last meeting of the Society, and the allusion to the proceedings in the 'Times,' stating my expedition to extend to the discovery of the source of the Nile, I fear many of the subscribers may be under a false impression respecting the real object thereof, and, at a future time, may express disappointment at my proceeding no farther in the interior than it will be possible for me to accomplish in the time agreed upon, viz., November, 1861, to July, 1862.

"With the greatest desire to carry out the instructions of the Royal Geographical Society and to satisfy every subscriber, I shall consider it a favour if the Council will publish a brief statement of my approaching expedition, with an explanation that the programme, as put forward in the printed circular, has necessarily been curtailed owing to the amount therein stated not having been subscribed. Wishing to start fair, and on a satisfactory understanding with one and all of my supporters,

"(Signed)   JOHN PETHERICK."

That I went as far as I possibly could, and, notwithstanding unforeseen difficulties, such as the unprecedented overflow of the Nile, *did* eventually carry out to the letter my engagement with Speke and the Royal Geographical Society, I venture to presume will be admitted.

While the Society, in its "Proceedings," admit that from heavy rains and flooded rivers Speke might be unable to get forward, no allowance is made for me, who had not only an unprecedented early monsoon, with its contrary winds, &c., to surmount, but vast floods to overcome—which he had not.

It is also stated that I was detained for want of camels at Korosko, and was too late in the season in leaving Khartoum; but Speke was a great deal later in leaving Zanzibar. I am blamed for being at Gondokoro seven months beyond the time so unjustly quoted by the Committee as the limit to which my attempt to succour Speke was confined, while he was sixteen months after the period appointed for his reaching that place.

Does not this show the folly of any man, or body of men, sitting down in London and fixing the time for the meeting of two expeditions—the one starting from Egypt and the other from Zanzibar, both to meet at Gondokoro at a given period—the latter having one thousand five hundred geographical miles and the former two thousand miles to travel?

And now with thanks to those readers who may have patiently followed me through so much dry and, perhaps, uninteresting matter, I submit to their consideration the justice of the Council of the Royal Geographical Society, who accorded unlimited praise to the one who had the shortest distance to perform, and was the longest about it, while they would neither recognize the efforts of the other to keep his appointment, nor welcome him home!

APPENDIX B.

APPENDIX B.

DESCRIPTIONS OF A NEW SPECIES
OF
FRESH-WATER TURTLE AND CHAMÆLEON.

By Dr. J. E. GRAY, F.R.S.

"BRITISH MUSEUM,
"*July 3rd*, 1869.

"MY DEAR SIR,

"I am very glad to hear that you are about to publish the result of your travels in the Upper Nile basin.

"Among the very interesting specimens which you sent to the British Museum are two very large full-grown, soft-back fresh-water or mud tortoises, which you obtained from Khartoum. When I first received them, I believed that they were identical with the soft-back fresh-water or mud tortoise of the Lower Nile, which is now called *Tyrsa Nilotica*, and gave an account of them in my description of that animal, published in the "Proceedings of the Zoological Society" for 1864.

"The *Trionichidæ*, or mud, or soft-backed tortoises are very unlike the other fresh-water tortoises, the back being covered with a soft skin, that is expanded out on the side, so as to form a short edged cartilaginous flexible shield. They have only three claws on each foot, and the head is covered with a thick soft skin, like the body. They are furnished with fleshy lips, which hide the horny beak that covers the jaws; the lower lip is bent downwards, and the upper ones are dependent over and cover the lower one.

"But I have lately discovered that specimens of the *Trionichidæ* —that are very like externally, especially in the dry and more or less distorted state in which we have them in museums—are in fact distinct species, which are easily distinguished by the examination of the bones of the head, and especially the form of the chewing surface of the jaws. I was induced to soak the head and open the jaws of the specimen which I received from you, and those which we had from Mr. Burton from the Lower Nile, and also the specimens which we purchased of M. Du Chaillu from the Gaboon, under the name of *Aspidonectes Aspilus* (Cope), and I was much pleased to observe that the specimens from the Upper Nile or Khartoum, differing entirely in the form of the masticating surface of the jaws from both the specimens of the Lower Nile and the Gaboon: the skull and masticating surfaces of the two latter were exactly alike, and are the well-known *Tyrsa Nilotica*, while the animals which you sent from Khartoum were so different that I have considered them as the types of a new species, forming a distinct genus in the family, which I have named *Fordia Africana*, after Mr. Ford, so well known for his beautiful lithographic figures of reptiles, fishes, corals, and other animals.

"When the differences in the form of the masticating surface of the jaws were observed, and the attention was called to the difference that existed between the two mud tortoises, it was easily seen that even the stuffed specimens from Khartoum had a shorter and more rounded face than the stuffed specimens of the Nilotic *Trionyx*, though it had previously been overlooked. The alveolar or chewing surfaces of the upper and hinder jaws are very wide and nearly flat, while the same parts of the jaws of the Nilotic *Trionyx* or *Tyrse Nilotica* are attenuated, concave, and sharp edged in front, and only broad and flattened on the sides. The Khartoum mud tortoise may be then described :

" *Fordia*.—Head short, broad; face short; forehead convex, with a narrow linear deep anterior palatine grove in the skull, rather shallow. Alveolar surface of the beak of the upper jaw very wide; the beak of the lower jaw very broad, as wide in front as on the side, quite flat; granular, with a very indistinct indication of a longitudinal central ridge in front.

" The hinder pair of costæ about half as broad as the pair of costæ before it.

Africa. The genus is known from *trionyx* by the flatness and width of the alveolar surface of the beak.

" *Fordia africana*. — The head and neck (and most likely the other parts of the body, limbs, and dorsal shield) olive, minutely and regularly speckled with small regular white spots.

" The hinder sternal callosities triangular, rather longer than wide, straight in front and the inner side very acute behind.— *Fordia africana*, GRAY, P.Z.S., 1869.

" Hab., Upper Nile, Khartoum. Adult male and female in the British Museum.

" The head and neck of these large specimens, when the skin was wet, showed that it is speckled with white, like the true Nilotic mud tortoise, *Tyrse Nilotica*. The sternal callosities differ rather in form from those of *Tyrse Nilotica*; the hinder ones are larger and more acute behind. The last costæ of the ribs are all wider, compared with the others, than in that animal.

"A young specimen in spirit, from the Upper Nile, obtained from Mr. Petherick, probably belongs to this species.

"The head, neck, feet, and dorsal disk covered with close, small, dark-edged circular white spots, those on the side of the head, and especially on the chin and throat, being rather the largest.

"With kind regards, believe me
"Yours faithfully,
"JOHN EDW. GRAY.

"J. PETHERICK, Esq.,
  "&c. &c., &c."

Dr. GRAY has also given the following description of a new species of chamæleon, discovered by Mr. Petherick, in the "Proceedings of the Zoological Society," 1863, p. 94:

"This species is very like *Chamaeleo Senegalensis;* but the scales on the ridges of the back are of the same size as those of neighbouring parts, and therefore do not form any appreciable crest. The occiput is rather differently shaped, the hinder central keel being a little more prominent. The scales of the head, body, limbs, and tail are smaller and less raised. The limbs are longer and more slender.

"This species is very different from the *Chamaeleo affinis* of Rüppell (which is the *C. Abyssinicus* of the Berlin Museum), from Abyssinia, which differs from both *C. senegalensis* and *C. laevigatus* in the scales being much larger and more convex, and in the scales of the ridges of the head and back being larger than those on the neighbouring parts, so as to form distinct crests; and in *C. affinis* the body is grey or blackish, with two or three broad, irregular-shaped, opaque white spots, forming an interrupted streak on each side of the back of the animal.

This species may be thus described:

"*Chamaeleo laevigatus.*—Grey or bluish in spirits. Scales small, flat, subequal, uniform; dorsal line nearly smooth, scarcely crested. Belly with a crest of larger acute white scales. Occiput slightly raised in the centre by a slight keel; the superciliary ridges and the central keel scarcely dentated. The legs elongated, very slender."

" Hab., Khartoum.

APPENDIX C.

THE
FISHES OF THE NILE.
BY
Dr. ALBERT GÜNTHER, F.R.S., F.Z.S., &c.

APPENDIX C.

THE FISHES OF THE NILE.

By Dr. ALBERT GÜNTHER, F.R.S., F.Z.S., &c.

THE extensive collections of fishes made by Mr. Petherick on the Lower and Upper Nile, and deposited in the British Museum, have induced me to comply with his request to give an account of them. Indeed, by so doing I merely fulfil a promise made to him several years ago, when, on his return to Egypt, I directed his attention to this part of the Fauna. It will be seen from the following remarks how much our knowledge of the zoology of the Nile has been advanced by his efforts; and the British Museum may now claim to possess the most complete series of the fishes of the Nile.

But, however gratifying an account of the success of these collections would have been to those immediately concerned in them, I thought it more useful to travellers to the Nile, and to zoologists, to take this opportunity of compiling short descriptions* of *all the*

---

* Most of these descriptions are taken from my general work on Fishes, "Catalogue of the Fishes of the British Museum," Vols. I.—VIII., published by the Trustees, 1859-69. Several of the woodcuts are inserted here from the same work, with the kind permission of the Trustees.

species known from this river, so that the collector may recognize them on the spot, and select those examples which, at present, are most valuable for European collections, or may be unknown to science. In order to facilitate the determination of the species by men not acquainted with ichthyological terms, I have added the Arabic names from reliable sources and Mr. Petherick's lists. However, it must be remarked that most of the species appear to have different names on the lower and upper parts of the river, and I have not always been able to find out whether the name is used at Cairo, or Khartoum, or in some other district. I thought myself entitled to give such a general account, as the species which I do not know from autopsy are but few in number.

The first[*] account of Fishes of the Nile has been given by a Swede, Dr. Friedrich Hasselquist, a disciple of Linnæus, who visited Egypt in the year 1750, and gave excellent descriptions of thirteen species observed by him at Cairo ("Reise nach Palæstina." Rostock, 1762. 8vo.) About twenty years after, Egypt was visited by a Danish naturalist, Peter Forskål, who, like Hasselquist, died before his discoveries were published under the title "Descriptiones Animalium," &c. (Havn., 1775. 4to.) He added nine species to those previously known.

Sonnini, a French officer, who visited Egypt towards the end of last century, has the merit of having first published illustrations of the most common Nile fish, eleven in number. They are perfectly recognizable, and the author has added the vernacular names. ("Voyage dans la Haute et Basse Egypt." Paris. 8vo.)

---

[*] We cannot enter here into the fragmentary notices of ancient and medieval authors.

At the beginning of the present century (1809) the grand work containing the discoveries and observations of the naturalists accompanying the French expedition to Egypt was published. ("Description de l'Egypt." Paris. Folio.) The ichthyological portion was worked out by Geoffroy St. Hilaire (father and son). It contains the descriptions and figures of twenty-seven species, all from the lower parts of the Nile. The figures are productions of great artistic value, though frequently inaccurate in points of detail.

Not less important than the discoveries of the French naturalists were those made by Dr. Eduard Rüppell, who collected in Egypt, on the Red Sea, and in Abyssinia, in the years 1829 to 1835. He treats of the fishes of the Nile in three papers, published in Frankfort-on-the-Maine, and gives a list of forty-five species, thirteen of which were discovered by himself. Like his predecessors, he collected chiefly on the Lower Nile; but he added also six species from Lake Zana, which we shall mention hereafter. Singularly enough, these latter fishes have never been found in the Nile proper,* therefore I need not add here their descriptions.

Two French travellers paid some attention to these fishes almost at the same time as Rüppell. The first, De Joannis, appears to have collected chiefly small fishes, which, unfortunately, are too much neglected by collectors, who depend on the native fishermen, and consequently obtain only the larger and eatable kinds. He describes six species which have not been rediscovered, and are but indifferently described and figured in "Guérin's Magazin de

---

* Lake Zana is 5,800 feet above the level of the sea, and the temperature of its water in March was 16° R. (Rüppell.)

Zoologie." (1835.) The other author, J. J. Rifaud, has figured about twenty fishes in a very coarse manner, in his great work, "Voyage en Egypte depuis 1805, jusqu' en 1827." (Paris. Folio.) Beside a figure, which appears to have been taken from the broad-nosed eel, there is no novelty among them.

The materials which existed in the European collections at the time when Cuvier and Valenciennes's general work on fishes was published, had been so well worked out, that they were not enabled to add much to our knowledge of this Fauna. Also Dr. Heckel, who examined the ichthyological collections made by Russegger during his travels in Egypt and Nubia, and published a most useful historical synopsis of the fishes of the Nile (Russegger's "Reisen." Stuttg., 1847. 8vo. Vol. II.), was not more successful, three of the four species named by him as new having been previously described. In this list sixty-seven species are enumerated (the Lake Zana species, and Cyprinodonts which are not found in the Nile, not included); but nine of them have since been proved to be merely synonyms, so that at Heckel's time not quite sixty species were known to inhabit this great river.

Finally, I have to mention that Sir Samuel Baker has given us the first glimpse of the Fish-Fauna of the great Central African lakes to which the course of the river has been traced. He figures in "The Albert Nyanza," Vol. II., p. 131, two fishes which are evidently *Lates niloticus* and *Lepidosiren*.

How much our knowledge of this Fauna has been advanced by Mr. Petherick's collections is evident from the following list, which contains eighty-one species, of which eleven only were not found by him, or are not known to me from autopsy. On the other hand, eighteen were new additions; and the discovery of genera like *Ctenopoma, Haplochilus, Rhinoglanis*, and the Indian *Ophiocephalus* in the upper parts of the Nile are points of the greatest interest. The British Museum has lately received numerous collections from West Africa; and a comparison of those fishes showed that a most intimate connection exists between these distant Faunas. This analogy has been noticed as early as the year 1834, by Mr. Bennett, one of the Secretaries of the Zoological Society, whose premature death was so great a loss to ichthyology. ("Proc. Zool. Soc.," 1834, p. 45.) I have thought it useful to indicate, in the list, whether the several species belong more properly to the Fauna of the Lower or Upper Nile, the first and sixth cataracts being made the boundaries of the two courses. Mr. Petherick has collected at Cairo, Khartoum, Gondokoro, and on an affluent of the White Nile (B. il Gazal and Djoor) south of Gondokoro. His predecessors have collected chiefly on the lower parts of the river.

LIST OF THE FISHES OF THE NILE.*

	Lower Nile.	Upper Nile.	West Africa.
Lates niloticus	×	×	×
Ctenopoma petherici	o	×	×
Mugil cephalus	×	o	×
Mugil capito	×	o	o

* The mark o signifies that the species has not yet been found in a particular region.

	Lower Nile.	Upper Nile.	West Africa.
Mugil petherici	×	o	o
Mugil saliens	×	o	o
Mugil cryptochilus	×	o	o
Ophiocephalus obscurus	o	×	o
Chromis niloticus	×	×	o
Clarias anguillaris	×	×	×
Clarias parvimanus	×	o	o
Clarias lazera	×	×	o
Clarias macracanthus	×	×	o
Heterobranchus bidorsalis	×	o	o
Heterobranchus intermedius	o	×	o
Heterobranchus longifilis	×	×	o
Schilbe uranoscopus	×	×	o
Schilbe mystus	×	×	o
Schilbe dispila	o	×	×
Schilbe hasselquistii	×	o	o
Eutropius niloticus	×	×	o
Siluranodon auritus	×	o	o
Bagrus bayad	×	×	×
Bagrus docmac	×	×	o
Chrysichthys auratus	×	o	o
Chrysichthys macrops	o	×	×
Clarotes laticeps	o	×	×
Auchenaspis biscutatus	×	×	×
Synodontis sorex	o	×	o
Synodontis macrodon	×	o	o
Synodontis serratus	o	×	o
Synodontis schal.	×	×	×
Synodontis humeratus			
Synodontis membranaceus	o	×	o
Rhinoglanis typus	o	×	o

	Lower Nile.	Upper Nile.	West Africa.
Mochocus niloticus	×	o	o
Malapterurus electricus	×	×	×
Citharinus geoffroyi	×	×	×
Citharinus latus	×	×	×
Alestes dentex	×	×	o
Alestes kotschyi	×	×	o
Alestes macrolepidotus	×	×	×
Alestes nurse	×	×	o
Alestes rüppellii	o	×	o
Hydrocyon forskalii	×	×	×
Hydrocyon brevis	o	×	×
Distichodus niloticus	×	×	o
Distichodus rostratus	×	o	o
Distichodus engycephalus	o	×	o
Distichodus brevipinnis	o	×	o
Ichthyborus microlepis	o	×	o
Ichthyborus bessé	×	o	o
(Coregonus) niloticus	×	o	o
Mormyrus caschive	×	×	o
Mormyrus oxyrhynchus	×	×	o
Mormyrus geoffroyi	×	o	o
Moymyrus hasselquistii	×	×	×
Mormyrus cyprinoides	×	×	×
Mormyrus bane	×	×	o
Mormyrus discorhynchus	o	×	o
Mormyrus bovei	×	o	o
Mormyrus isidori	×	o	o
Mormyrus dorsalis	×	×	o
Mormyrus petersii	o	×	×
Mormurus anguilloides	×	o	o
Gymnarchus niloticus	×	×	×

	Lower Nile.	Upper Nile.	West Africa.
Haplochilus fasciolatus	o	×	×
Labeo niloticus	×	×	o
Labeo coubie	×	×	o
Labeo forskalii	×	×	o
Barbus bynni	×	×	o
Barbus perince	×	o	o
Barilius niloticus	×	o	o
Barilius thebensis	×	o	o
Barilius bibie	×	o	o
Clupna fieta	×	o	o
Heterotis niloticus	×	×	×
Anguilla vulgaris	×	o	o
Anguilla latirostris	×	o	o
Tetrodon fahaka	×	×	×
Polypterus bichir	×	×	×
Polypterus senegalensis	×	×	×
Lepidosiren annectens	o	×	×

All the species, described by Rüppell, from Lake Zana, are Barbels,* viz.,

Barbus surkis.　　　　*Barbus gorguari.*
Barbus intermedius.　　*Barbus elongatus.*
Barbus affinis.　　　　*Barbus nedgia.*

It is evident from the peculiarly simple course of the Nile and the absence of tributaries in its lower portion, which would connect it with systems of other rivers, that the Fauna of this part is

---

* The fish described by Rüppell as *Chondrostoma dembensis* cannot be admitted into the system; Rüppell himself omits it in a later list. It appears to have been some young fish.

merely the offspring of that of the Upper Nile, and therefore the propriety of making a distinction between them may be questioned. When we examine more closely the lower Fauna, we find that it consists

1. Of several species of Grey Mullets *(Mugil)*, one Shad *(Alosa)*, and two species of Eel *(Anguilla)*, which are simply immigrants, or periodical visitors from the Mediterranean, and never ascend beyond the cataracts.

2. Of about thirty-seven species, which are also found in the Upper Nile, some of them at least are evidently carried down by the annual floods, and do not propagate their species in more northern latitudes; but our information on this point is at present extremely meagre.

3. About seventeen species of Siluroids, Cyprinoids, and Characinoids, have been hitherto found below the cataracts only; but whether any of them are peculiar to the Lower Nile is a question which cannot be decided at present.

The Fauna of the Upper Nile is at once distinguished by the absence of the Mediterranean forms mentioned above, and by the presence of fishes typical of tropical Africa, which never, or but very rarely, lose themselves into the lower part, and certainly do not propagate there. Such are *Ctenopoma, Ophiocephalus, Clarotes, Rhinoglanis, Haplochilus, Lepidosiren*, and others. The number of species amounts to fifty-six, and of these not less than twenty-five are absolutely identical with West African species; so that the affinity between the West African rivers and the Upper Nile is not much less than that between the Upper and Lower, the latter having thirty-six species out of fifty-three in common with the

Upper. Further, when we consider that our knowledge of West African fishes is very far from being complete, and that every fresh collection contains some other fish previously known from the Nile, we may venture to state that the Faunæ of the Nile and the West African rivers belong to the same zoological district; that there is an uninterrupted continuity of the Fish-Fauna from west to east; and that the species known to be common to both extremities inhabit also the great reservoirs of water in the centre of the African continent.

On the other hand, there are few fishes known at present which the Nile has in common with East Africa; with the exception of *Chromis niloticus, Malapterurus electricus*, one species of *Mormyrus*, two of *Labeo* and *Lepidosiren*: the affinity is merely generic, there being nineteen genera out of thirty-five in common. The locality nearest to the system of the Nile whence fishes have been obtained is Lake Nyassa, and all the fishes collected there by Dr. Kirk proved to be distinct from those of the Nile, and even from those of the other parts of the system of the Zambezi.

PERCIDÆ. (PERCHES.)

LATES.

Jaws, vomer and palatine bones, with bands of very small villiform teeth; no canine teeth. Two distinct dorsal fins, the first with seven or eight spines; anal fin with three spines. Gill-covers armed with spines; præorbital bone strongly serrated. Scales rather small, with rough borders. Lateral line continuous from the head to the tail.

Lates niloticus, Gmel. (The Perch of the Nile.—*Keschr Homar*, when young).

D. 7 or 8 | $\frac{1}{17}$. A. $\frac{3}{8-9}$. L. lat. 60.

Very similar in appearance to the Bass; it is said to attain to a weight of more than one hundred pounds, and a length of four to five feet, and its flesh to be excellent food. It extends to the West African rivers, and it is evidently this fish which is figured by Sir Samuel Baker in his "Albert Nyanza," Vol. II., p. 131.

LABYRINTHICI.

CTENOPOMA.

Body compressed, oblong, covered with rough scales of moderate size. Lateral line interrupted. Gill-covers serrated; mouth of moderate width; small teeth in the jaws, on the vomer and palatine bones. One continuous dorsal fin, with numerous (15—18) spines; anal fin with about eight or ten spines.

The fishes of this genus are very similar, and closely allied to the Climbing Perch of the East Indies (*Anabas*). The habits are very probably similar, although nothing positive is known regarding them. According to more recent observations the fishes provided with a labyrinth-form appendage in the gill-cavity, appear to be as much dependent on air for breathing as on water. They are of small size, attaining to a length of about six or seven inches. Mr. Petherick has discovered a new species in the Upper Nile.

Ctenopoma petherici, Gthr. (Plate I., Fig. A.)

D. $\frac{18-15}{10-9}$. A. $\frac{10}{0-11}$. L. lat. 29. L. transv. 3/9.

The height of the body is one-third, or a little more than one-third, of the total length (without caudal); the maxillary extends to below, or but slightly beyond, the anterior margin of the eye. Teeth in the jaws and on the palate in narrow bands. The diameter of the eye equals the extent of the snout. Five series of scales between the orbit and the angle of the præoperculum, the outer series covering the præopercular margin. Operculum, inter- and suboperculum strongly serrated. The soft rays of the vertical fins covered with small scales. Brownish olive; many scales with a brown central spot, these spots being less distinct in old specimens than in young ones; a round black spot, sometimes edged with whitish, on the root of the tail.

The largest specimen is six and a half inches long. Collected at Gondokoro.

MUGILIDÆ.

MUGIL. (Grey Mullets. *Bouri, Dabahra.*)

Body oblong and slightly compressed, covered with smooth scales of moderate size; lateral line not marked. Mouth transverse, narrow, without real teeth; lower jaw with a sharp margin. Two short dorsal fins, the anterior with four stiff spines; anal fin a little longer than the second dorsal. Ventral fins with one spine and five rays, inserted behind the pectoral fins.

The grey mullets are inhabitants of the sea, but enter freely fresh waters. None of them are found above the cataracts.

Mugil cephalus, Cuv.

D. 4 | $\frac{1}{8}$. A. $\frac{3}{8}$. L. lat. 42. L. transv. 14—15.

The height of the body is contained five times in the total length, the length of the head four times and a half. The head is very slightly convex superiorly, and the width of the interorbital space is contained twice and one-third in the length of the head. The upper lip is not thick. The angle made by the two mandibulary bones is an obtuse one. The cleft of the mouth is not quite half as deep as broad (between the angles of the mouth). The maxillary is entirely covered by the præorbital. Eyes hidden behind a broad adipose membrane; nostrils rather distant from each other, the posterior being in the middle between the anterior and the orbit. The space at the chin between the mandibles is broadly lanceolate. The vertical fins are not scaly; the first two dorsal spines are half as long as the head; the pectoral extends to about the eighth scale of the lateral line: its base is above the middle of the body; the ventral is inserted midway between the pectoral and spinous dorsal. Dark shining stripes along the series of scales.

I have not seen specimens of this species from the Nile; and it is admitted here on the authority of Cuvier and Valenciennes.

Mugil capito, Cuv.

D. 4 | $\frac{1}{8}$. A. $\frac{3}{9}$. L. lat. 45. L. transv. 14.

The height of the body is contained five times or five times and one-third in the total length, the length of the head four times and a half. The snout is broad and depressed; the interorbital space slightly convex, its width being contained twice and a half or twice and two-thirds in the length of the head. The angle made by the

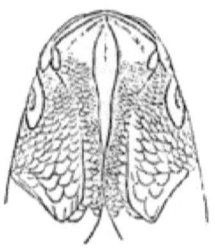

two mandibulary bones is rather obtuse; the præorbital has an obtuse longitudinal ridge, and does not entirely cover the maxillary bone. Eyes without adipose membrane; nostrils close together: they are less distant from each other than the posterior is from the eye. The lips are not covered by the nasal bones. The space at the chin, between the mandibularies and the interopercula, is rather broad, elongate, cuneiform. There are twenty-eight or thirty scales between the snout and the spinous dorsal. The two anterior dorsal spines are nearly half as long as the head. The eighth or ninth, the twelfth or thirteenth, the twenty-fourth or twenty-fifth scales of the lateral line correspond to the extremity of the pectoral and to the origin of the two dorsal fins. The root of the pectoral is above the middle of the body; the ventral is inserted midway between the pectoral and spinous dorsal. Dark stripes along the series of scales; generally a blackish spot superiorly at the base of the pectoral.

Valenciennes, relying upon the authority of Ehrenberg and upon the specimens collected by him, states that, besides the true *M. capito*, another species is found in the Nile closely resembling it, but distinguished by the position of the dorsal fins. "The distance between the commencement of the first dorsal and that of the second is less than in the other species [of Europe], for in the latter it is equal to the distance between the commencement of the second dorsal and that of the caudal, whilst in the *dubahra* it is one-fourth less. Otherwise the species agree with *M. capito*." He calls this species *M. dubahra* (Cuv. & Val., Vol. XI., p. 69). Having examined our European and African specimens of *M. capito* with regard to the position of their dorsal fins, I found that they are intermediate between *M. capito* and *M. dubahra*. The future must show whether the *dubahra* has other characters by which it may be distinguished from *M. capito*.

Mugil petherici, Gthr.

D. 4 | $\frac{1}{9}$.   A. $\frac{3}{10}$.   L. lat. 45.   L. transv. 11.

This species is similar to *M. capito* or *M. dubahra*, C., V., from which, however, it may be readily distinguished by the number of the fin-rays, and by several other minor characters. The height of the body is contained five times and a third in the total length, the length of the head five times. The snout is broad and depressed, much longer than the eye; the interorbital space slightly convex, its width being two-fifths of the length of the head. The upper lip has a series of minute ciliæ. The angle at the symphysis of the mandibles is obtuse, and the cleft of the mouth is twice and a half as broad as it is deep. The præorbital has no longitudinal ridge, a shallow anterior notch, the extremity rounded and the margins serrated. Eyes with the adipose membrane rudimentary, just touching the iris. Nostrils close together: they are less distant from each other than the posterior is from the eye. The space at the chin, between the mandibles and the interopercula, is rather broad, elongate, cuneiform. There are thirty scales between the snout and the spinous dorsal. The length of the anterior dorsal spine is somewhat more than one-half of the length of the head. The origin of the spinous dorsal is half-way between the snout and the root of the caudal. The twelfth, the fifteenth, and the twenty-seventh scales of the lateral line correspond to the extremity of the pectoral and to the origins of the two dorsal fins. The soft dorsal and anal are scaly at the base, and the former commences in the vertical from the fourth soft ray of the anal fin. The caudal fin is deeply forked, the length of one of its lobes being somewhat less than one-fifth of the total. The root of the pectoral is on the middle of the depth of the body; its length equals the distance of its base from the eye; it has a pointed scale in its axil, but it is not very long. The least depth of the tail is less than one-half the length of the head.

Silvery, shining golden, with darker stripes along the series of scales; a blackish spot superiorly at the base of the pectoral.

A single specimen, ten and a half inches long, was obtained by Mr. Petherick at Cairo.

Mugil saliens, Risso.

D. 4 | $\frac{1}{8}$. A. $\frac{3}{9}$. L. lat. 45. L. transv. 15.

The height of the body equals the length of the head, and is contained five times and a half in the total. The snout is moderately broad, somewhat tapering anteriorly; the width of the interorbital space is one-third of the length of the head. The angle made by the two mandibulary bones is a right one; the præorbital does not entirely cover the maxillary. Eyes without adipose membrane; nostrils close together, the posterior being in the middle between the anterior and the orbit. Lips not very thick, not covered by the nasal bones. The space at the chin, between the mandibularies and the interopercula, is elongate, tapering anteriorly. The two anterior dorsal spines are half as long as the head; the pectoral terminates at some distance from the vertical from the origin of the dorsal, and its root is somewhat above the middle of the body. Dark shining streaks along the series of scales.

Mugil cryptochilus, Valenc.

D. 4 | $\frac{1}{8}$. A. $\frac{3}{9}$. L. lat. 45.

The nasal bones are advanced, so as to cover the upper lip when the mouth is closed. The præorbital does not entirely cover the maxillary. The length of the head is one-fifth of the total or thrice the diameter of the eye. Eye without adipose membrane. Pectoral long, falciform, with the lanceolate scale in the axil short; scale at the base of the spinous dorsal long, extending beyond the posterior spine. Caudal deeply forked, with the upper lobe longest.

The single specimen observed is eight inches long.

This is one of the few species which I do not know from autopsy; the description is taken from Cuv. and Val., Vol. XI., p. 61.

OPHIOCEPHALIDÆ.

OPHIOCEPHALUS.

Body elongate, anteriorly subcylindrical, covered with smooth scales of moderate size; head depressed, covered with shield-like scales superiorly; lateral line well marked. Teeth in the jaws, on the vomer and palatine bones. One long dorsal and anal fin, without spines. Ventral fins six-rayed, inserted below the pectoral fins. A cavity accessory to the gill-cavity.

All the fishes of this family are fresh-water fishes from the East Indies, with the exception of one discovered by Mr. Petherick in the Upper Nile. It appears from recent observations that the amount of air which is in solution in the water is not sufficient for the respiration of these fishes, so that they are obliged to come to the surface at certain intervals, to receive an additional quantity of atmospheric air.

Ophiocephalus obscurus, Gthr. (Plate II., Fig. B.)

D. 42. A. 26—29. L. lat. 70. L. transv. 7/14.

The height of the body is nearly one-eighth of the total length, the length of the head nearly one-fourth; the width of the interorbital space is more than the extent of the snout, and one-fourth of the length of the head. The cleft of the mouth is wide, the maxillary extending behind the orbit. The scales on the upper surface of the head are of moderate size, those on the neck small; there are thirteen series of scales between the orbit and the angle of the præoperculum. The pectoral does not extend on to the origin of the anal, and its length is one-half of that of the head; the length of the ventral is three-quarters of that of the pectoral. Caudal rounded, its length being six times and one-third in the total. Blackish, lighter below, with dark streaks along the series of scales; a series of black blotches along the side; head with two indistinct oblique black spots along its base. Pectoral and ventral variegated with blackish. Chin black, with white spots.

Length seventy-seven lines. Collected at Gondokoro.

CHROMIDES.

Chromis.

Body compressed, carp-like, covered with smooth, rather large scales; gill-covers scaly. One long dorsal fin, the anterior portion of which is formed by numerous spines; anal fin with three spines. Lateral line interrupted. Teeth compressed, generally lobate; the anterior teeth form a continuous series, closely set.

Chromis niloticus, Hasselq. (*Bolti.*)

D. $\frac{15-17}{12-14}$. A. $\frac{3}{9-11}$. L. lat. 33. L. transv. $\frac{5}{13}$.

Teeth very small, in several series; scales below the eye in two series; sometimes a rudimentary third series below the præorbital; snout obtusely conical, with the upper profile oblique; caudal subtruncated; the soft dorsal extends to, or nearly to, the middle of the caudal, if laid backwards. The height of the body is contained twice and one-third in the total length (without caudal).

The *Bolti* is one of the most common and best eating fishes of the Nile; it is herbivorous, and attains to a length of twenty-four inches and more.

SILURIDÆ.

CLARIAS. (*Karmouth, Coor.*)

Body eel-shaped, naked. One long dorsal fin, without spines, extending from the neck to the caudal; anal long. Jaws with a band of villiform teeth; a band of villiform or granular teeth across the vomer; cleft of the mouth transverse, anterior, of moderate width; barbels eight; one pair of nasal, one of maxillary, and two pairs of mandibulary barbels. Eyes small. The upper and lateral parts of the head are osseous, or covered only with a very thin skin. A dendritic accessory branchial organ is attached to the convex side of the second and fourth branchial arches, and received in a cavity behind the gill-cavity proper. Ventrals six-rayed, behind the pectoral fins; only the pectoral has a pungent spine.

The African species of this genus attain to a great size, specimens being found of four and five feet in length.

Clarias anguillaris, L.

D. 69—73. A. 53—55. P. 1/9.

Vomerine teeth villiform, forming a band, which in its middle is narrower than that of the intermaxillaries; it has not a process behind in the middle of its concavity. Head densely granulated above, its length being one-fourth, or rather more than one-fourth, of the total. Barbels slender: those of the nostril two-fifths or one-third as long as, and those of the maxillaries rather shorter than, the head. The pectoral fin extends to, or nearly to, the vertical from the origin of the dorsal; its spine is short, two-thirds as long as the fin.

Clarias parvimanus, Gthr.

D. 76. A. 57. P. 1/8.

Vomerine teeth villiform, those in the middle of the band conical. The band of vomerine teeth is in its middle rather broader than that of the intermaxillaries; it has a very short process in the middle of its concavity. Head rather finely granulated above, its length being one-fourth of the total. Barbels slender, those of the nostril one-third as long as the head, those of the maxillary shorter than the head. The pectoral fin does not extend to the vertical from the origin of the dorsal; its spine is short, not quite two-thirds as long as the fin. The dorsal does not extend on to the root of the caudal.

Clarias lazera, C. & V.

D. 77. A. 58. P. 1/10.

Vomerine teeth granular, forming a band, which in its middle is broader than that of the intermaxillaries; it has not a process behind in the middle of its concavity. Head coarsely granulated above, its length being one-fourth of the total. Barbels long: those of the nostril extend nearly to the root of the pectoral, those of the maxillary beyond the origin of the dorsal. The pectoral fin extends to, or somewhat beyond, the vertical from the origin of the dorsal; its spine is short, not quite two-thirds as long as the fin. The dorsal extends to the root of the caudal.

Clarias macracanthus, Gthr.

D. 70—75. A. 54—55. P. 1/9.

Vomerine teeth granular, forming a band, which in its middle is twice as broad as that of the intermaxillaries, and which in the middle of its posterior margin has a very short inconspicuous process. Head coarsely granulated above, its length being a little more than one-fourth of the total. Barbels of moderate length, those of the nostril being two-fifths as long as, and those of the maxillary extending to the end of, the head. The pectoral fin reaches to the vertical from the origin of the dorsal; the length of its spine is three-quarters, or rather more than two-thirds, of that of the fin.

Valenciennes has described a species under the name of *Clarias hasselquistii* (Cuv. & Val., Vol. XV., p. 362., pl. 416.) Among the numerous examples from the Nile which I have examined, I have not met with one which would agree with Valenciennes's description of his *Cl. hasselquistii*: it is said to have very short barbels, the nasal being only one-fourth, and those of the maxillary one-half, of the head. The vomerine teeth are described as villiform, forming a band "*étroite, assez large et rétrécie dans le milieu.*" The figure represents this band with a very prominent median posterior process.

HETEROBRANCHUS. (*Karmouth*).

Very similar to *Clarias*, but the back is occupied by a long dorsal fin divided into two portions, an anterior which is rayed, and a posterior which is adipose; anal long. A band of villiform teeth across the vomer; cleft of the mouth, the eight barbels, the armature of the head, the gill-apparatus with the accessory organs, the ventral and pectoral fins, as in *Clarias*.

These fishes are extremely similar to *Clarias*, and attain to the same large size.

Heterobranchus bidorsalis, Geoffr.

B. 12—13. D. 44. A. 52. P. 1/10.

The length of the adipose fin is rather less than two-thirds of the rayed dorsal; pectoral spine slightly serrated. The nasal barbels are half as long as those of the maxillary, which reach only to the gill-opening. Vomerine teeth villiform, forming a crescentic band.

Heterobranchus intermedius, Gthr.

B. 9. D. 39—41. A. 49—50. P. 1/10.

The length of the adipose fin is rather less than two-thirds of that of the rayed dorsal; pectoral spine scarcely serrated. The nasal barbels extend to, or beyond, the end of the occipital process, those of the maxillaries beyond the root of the ventral fin. Vomerine teeth villiform, forming a crescent-shaped band, which, in its middle, is much broader than that of the intermaxillaries, and which has a short median posterior process. Blackish above, whitish below. Otherwise very similar to the preceding species.

Heterobranchus longifilis, C. & V.

B. 9—10. D. 29—31. A. 44—46. P. 1/10.

The adipose fin commences immediately behind the dorsal and terminates at the root of the caudal; its length is equal to, or not much less than, that of the rayed dorsal; pectoral spine distinctly serrated. The length of the anal fin is nearly one-third of the total (without caudal). The nasal barbels extend to the base of the occipital process, those of the maxillaries to the root of the ventral fin; but they appear to be rather shorter in large specimens. Vomerine teeth villiform, forming an arched band which is as broad as that of the intermaxillaries. Blackish above, whitish below.

Schilbe. (*Schilbe.*)

Body scaleless, elongate. One short dorsal fin with a pungent spine; no adipose fin; the anal terminates close by the caudal, which is forked. Barbels eight: one to each maxillary, one to each posterior nostril, and two to each mandible, the latter being placed one behind the other. The palatine teeth are present, and form, together with those of the vomer, a horseshoe-like band. Nostrils remote from each other, the posterior wider than the anterior. Head covered with skin. Neck elevated, the upper profile of the head being concave; eye behind and partly below the cleft of the mouth. Ventral composed of six or seven rays, behind the pectorals.

The species do not appear to attain to a large size, the largest examples brought to Europe being about eighteen inches long. Like all the Siluroids of the Nile, they are carnivorous, and very voracious: an individual of seven inches had swallowed another fish five inches long. Eaten by the natives, but of a watery taste.

Schilbe uranoscopus, Rüpp.

D. 1/6.   A. 67—71.   P. 1/11.   V. 6.

The height of the body is two-ninths of the total length (without caudal), the length of the head one-fifth; the greatest width of the head is three-fifths of its length. The lower jaw is the longer; the depth of the cleft of the mouth is one-half of its width. Nasal and maxillary barbels of nearly equal length, shorter than the posterior of the lower jaw, which are about one-third as long as the head. The diameter of the eye is one-fifth or one-sixth of the length of the head. The end of the dorsal fin is situated vertically above the root of the ventral, and the width of its base equals that of the latter; its height is less than the length of the head, the length of its spine being two-thirds of the latter; spine finely serrated posteriorly. The anal fin terminates at a short distance from the caudal, which is deeply forked, with pointed lobes. The pectoral spine is stronger than that of the dorsal fin, and terminates at, or close by, the root of the ventral; it is finely serrated along its inner edge. A blackish spot on the origin of the lateral line.

Schilbe mystus, L.

D. 1/6.   A. 55—64.   P. 1/11.   V. 6.

The height of the body is one-fourth of the total length (without caudal), the length of the head one-fifth; the greatest width of the head equals its length without snout. The lower jaw is the longer. the depth of the cleft of the mouth is two-fifths of its width. Nasal barbels shorter than those of the maxillaries, which are half as long as the head; the posterior mandibulary barbels are three times or four times as long as the anterior, and somewhat longer than those of the maxillaries. The diameter of the eye is one-sixth of the length of the head. The dorsal fin is situated entirely before the ventral, and the width of its base equals that of the latter; its height is less than the length of the head, the length of its spine being three-quarters of the latter; spine finely serrated posteriorly. The anal fin terminates at a short distance from the caudal, which is deeply forked, with pointed lobes. The pectoral spine is stronger than that of the dorsal fin, and terminates at some distance from the root of the ventral; it is finely serrated along its inner edge. A large blackish blotch on the origin of the lateral line.

Schilbe dispila, Gthr.

D. 1/6. A. 56. P. 1/11. V. 6.

The height of the body is contained four times in the total length (without caudal), the length of the head four times and two-thirds; the greatest width of the head equals its length without snout. The lower jaw is the longer; the cleft of the mouth twice as broad as long. Nasal barbels shorter than those of the maxillaries, which extend to the end of the head; the posterior mandibulary barbels are much longer than the anterior, and are as long as those of the maxillaries. The diameter of the eye is two-ninths of the length of the head. The origin of the dorsal fin is somewhat in advance of that of the ventral, the width of its base being equal to that of the latter; its height is less than the length of the head; its spine is slender, shorter than the first ray, and equal in length to the head without snout; it is finely serrated posteriorly. The anal fin terminates close by the caudal, but is not united with it. Caudal fin forked, with the lobes rounded; the length of the lower lobe is nearly one-seventh of the total. (Pectoral spines broken off, rather strong at the base.) Pectoral fin as long as the dorsal is high. The length of the ventral is one-half of that of the head. Brownish above, silvery on the sides and on the belly; a round black spot on the lateral line between the dorsal and pectoral fins.

Found at Gondokoro; it occurs also in the river Niger.

Schilbe hasselquistii, C. & V.

D. 1/5. A. 63—64. P. $\frac{1}{9-10}$. V. 6.

The upper jaw is longer, or not shorter, than the lower. The length of the head is contained six times and a half in the total; its width is three-fifths of its length. Maxillary barbels half as long as the head.

This species is known to me from Valenciennes' description only.

Eutropius.

Very similar to *Schilbe*. A very small adipose fin; a short dorsal fin with a pungent spine; anal fin long, terminating at some distance from the caudal, which is forked. Barbels eight: one to each maxillary, one to each posterior nostril, and two to each mandible; the mandibulary barbels are placed one behind the other. The palatine teeth are present, and form, together with those of the vomer, a horseshoe-like band. Nostrils open, not prolonged into tubes, situated at some distance from each other. Head covered with skin. The upper jaw is the longer. Ventral with six rays.

Eutropius niloticus, Rüpp. (*Schilbe*.)

D. 1/6.   A. 58—60.   P. 1/9.   V. 6.

The height of the body is contained nearly four times in the total length (without caudal), the length of the head five times and a half. The greatest width of the head equals its length without snout. The upper jaw is the longer: cleft of the mouth twice as broad as deep. Nasal and anterior mandibulary barbels short; maxillary barbels much longer than the posterior of the mandibles, not extending to the base of the pectoral. The diameter of the eye is one-fifth or one-sixth of the length of the head. The dorsal fin is situated entirely before the ventral, the width of its base being equal to that of the latter. Its height equals the length of the head; spine slender, serrated posteriorly. The anal fin terminates at some distance from the caudal. Caudal deeply forked, with the lobes pointed. Pectoral spine rather broad, strongly serrated, terminating at a rather considerable distance from the ventral. A blackish spot at the origin of the lateral line. Common in all parts of the river; grows to a length of twelve inches; bad eating.

SILURANODON.

Similar in form to *Schilbe*. One short dorsal fin without pungent spine; no adipose fin; the anal fin terminates close by the caudal, which is forked. Barbels eight: one at the nostrils, one to each maxillary, and four behind the chin, the roots of the latter being nearly in the same transverse series. No teeth in the jaws or on the palate. Eyes behind and below the angle of the mouth. Neck not elevated. Ventral composed of six rays.

Siluranodon auritus, Geoff.

D. 5.   A. 80.   P. 1/9.   V. 6.

The nasal and maxillary barbels are shorter than those on the chin, which are one-third or one-fourth longer than the head. Pectoral spine rather strong, serrated, and nearly as long as the first ray. Silvery.

This fish must be very scarce, as I have not been able to obtain an example. Geoffroy St. Hilaire says that it is called by the Arabs *Schilbe oudney,* the latter word being spelt *oued denne* by Valenciennes.

Bagrus.

Body scaleless; elongate. Adipose fin long; a short dorsal with a pungent spine and with nine or ten soft rays; anal fin short, with less than twenty rays. Barbels eight. Teeth on the palate in a continuous band. The upper jaw is the longer. Eyes with a free orbital margin. Caudal forked; ventral with six rays, situated far behind the pectorals.

Bagrus bayad, Forsk. (*Bayad.*)

D. 1/10. A. 13—14. P. 1/9. V. 6.

The length of the head is contained thrice and three-fourths in the total. Head broader than high, its greatest width being not quite one-half of its length. Snout spatulate, its length being one-third of that of the head; the upper jaw is slightly the longer. The maxillary barbels very long, extending to the middle of the adipose fin. Dorsal spine of moderate strength, half as long as the head, not serrated. The adipose fin commences immediately behind the dorsal, and is twice as long as the latter, and nearly as high as the hinder part of the tail. Caudal deeply forked. Pectoral spine as long and strong as that of the dorsal fin, serrated at the inner side of its extremity; the pectoral fin extends to the vertical from the first soft dorsal ray; ventral inserted below the end of the dorsal fin.

Very common; grows to a length of three feet; and commonly sold as food. This is the fish figured and noticed by Sir S. Baker in the "Tributaries of the Nile," p. 213.

Bagrus docmac, Forsk. (*Docmac.*)

D. 1/9.   A. 13.   P. 1/10—11.   V. 6.

The length of the head is contained thrice and three-fourths in the total. Head broader than high, its greatest width being two-thirds or three-quarters of its length. Snout spatulate, one-third of the length of the head. The upper jaw is slightly the longer. The maxillary barbel very long, extending to the origin or to the middle of the adipose fin. Head and nape covered with soft skin. Dorsal spine not serrated, of moderate strength, its length being two-fifths of that of the head. The adipose fin commences at a short distance from the dorsal, and is nearly twice as long as the latter, and lower than the hinder part of the tail. Caudal deeply forked. Pectoral spine denticulated along its inner side, as strong as, but rather shorter than, the dorsal spine. The pectoral fin extends to the vertical from the first or second soft dorsal ray; ventral inserted immediately behind the dorsal fin.

Probably not inferior in size to the *Bayad*.

Chrysichthys.

Body scaleless: similar in form to the *Bayad*. An adipose fin of moderate length; a short dorsal fin with a pungent spine and with six soft rays; anal fin short, with less than twenty rays.

Barbels eight. Teeth on the palate in two lateral portions, those on the vomer being confluent with the palatine teeth of each side. Jaws equal in length, or the upper the longer. Eyes with a free orbital margin. Caudal forked; ventral with six rays, situated far behind the pectoral.

Chrysichthys auratus, Geoffr. (*Schal-Abou-Réal; Zamar; Xaxoug-roumi.*)

D. 1/6. A. 10—11. P. 1/8. V. 6.

The height of the body is two-ninths of the total length (without caudal), the length of the head two-sevenths; head entirely covered with thick soft skin, broader than high, its greatest width being three-fourths of its length. Eye of moderate size, its diameter being one-half of the extent of the snout, and rather less than one-fifth of the length of the head. Snout depressed, very broad, its extent being two-fifths of the length of the head; lips thick, the upper jaw is the longer. Nasal barbels very short, as long as the eye; maxillary barbels longer than those of the mandibles, but shorter than the head. Dorsal spine stout, serrated behind, half as long as the head; the first dorsal ray rather higher than the body. The base of the adipose fin equals in length its distance from the dorsal, and exceeds that of the latter fin. Caudal fin forked. Pectoral spine very strong, longer than that of the dorsal fin, strongly denticulated anteriorly. The teeth on the palate are in a horseshoe-like band, interrupted in the middle anteriorly.

Chrysichthys macrops, Gthr.

D. 1/6. A. 11. P. 1/8. V. 6.

This species is very closely allied to *C. auratus,* but it differs in having the upper side of the head covered with thin skin only, so that portions of the bone are nearly naked and granulated; its eye is considerably larger, the diameter being more than one-fifth of the length of the head. The first dorsal ray and the upper caudal lobe are prolonged into filaments.

It appears to be peculiar to the upper parts of the river, and occurs also in West Africa.

CLAROTES.

Body scaleless. Adipose fin subdivided into rays, and with a strong spine *in old individuals;* a short dorsal fin with a pungent spine and with six soft rays; anal fin short. Barbels eight; branchiostegal membranes scarcely united below the throat. Vomerine teeth in two transverse bands, which are not confluent with the palatine teeth. Eyes with a free orbital margin. Caudal forked; ventral with six rays.

This genus is scarcely different from *Chrysichthys,* the division of the adipose fin into rays being dependent on age. In all other respects, except in the unimportant modification of the arrangement of the palatine teeth, *Clarotes* is identical with *Chrysichthys.*

Clarotes laticeps, Rüpp.   (*Abu Mesaeka*.)

D. 1/6.   A. 12.   P. 1/9.

The height of the body is contained from four times and a half to five times and a half in the total length (without caudal), the length of the head thrice and a fourth. Head much depressed, broad, truncated in front, its greatest width being four-fifths of its length; upper jaw overlapping the lower. Nasal barbels slender, not so long as the snout; the maxillary barbels extend to the end of the pectoral, the outer ones of the mandible to the root of the pectoral. The teeth on the palate form four narrow bands of nearly equal length, the vomerine band being interrupted in the middle and not continuous with the palatine band. The upper surface of the head coarsely granulated, the granules being arranged in striæ. Occipital process not much larger than, and similar in shape to, the triangular basal bone of the dorsal spine. Dorsal spine strong, slightly serrated along both edges, more than half as long as the head. Adipose fin short, subdivided into rays only along its upper margin in young individuals; in old specimens the division into rays extends to the base of the fin, and the first ray is changed into a hard, pungent spine. Caudal forked; both lobes equal in length, or the lower rather longer. Pectoral spine as long as, but stronger than, that of the dorsal fin, serrated along both edges, slightly exteriorly and strongly interiorly. Ventral rather shorter than pectoral. Dark grey above, white below; a blackish blotch behind the gill-opening; a broad blackish band along each caudal lobe.

The species appears to be peculiar to the Upper Nile, although single specimens, like that described by Rüppell, may be carried down towards the mouth of the river.

AUCHENASPIS.

Body scaleless. Adipose fin rather long; dorsal short, with a pungent spine and with seven rays; anal short. Snout produced, pointed, with narrow mouth; barbels six. The teeth of each jaw form a pair of small elliptic patches, which are longer than broad; palate edentulous. Nostrils distant from each other; eyes of moderate size. Gill membrane scarcely notched at the throat. Ventral with six rays, situated far behind the pectorals.

Auchenaspis biscutatus, Geoffr. (*Karafchi.*)

D. 1/7.   A. 11—12.   P. 1/9.

Head coarsely granulated above; occipital process very broad, with the lateral margins convex, joining the very large saddle-shaped dorsal plate. Snout produced, pointed, with broad lips and with a narrow mouth. Barbels cylindrical, shorter than the head, the outer ones of the mandible being shorter than those of the maxillaries. Dorsal and pectoral spines strong, nearly equal in length, rather more than half as long as the head. The length of the adipose fin is two-sevenths or one-fourth of the total (without caudal); it is very high in adult examples. Anal fin much higher than long. Caudal subtruncated. Brownish; fins with rounded dark spots.

SYNODONTIS. (*Schal.*)

Body scaleless. Adipose fin of moderate length, or rather long; dorsal with a strong spine and with seven soft rays; anal rather short. Teeth in the lower jaw movable, very thin at the base, and with a slightly dilated, pointed brown apex; palate edentulous. Mouth small, mandibles short. Barbels six, more or less fringed with a membrane or with filaments. Eyes of moderate size. Neck with broad dermal bones. The gill-openings are of moderate width. Ventrals with seven rays, inserted behind the dorsal.

These fishes can easily inflict wounds with their strong serrated pectoral spines, which are said to be poisonous. Hasselquist states that he has been eye-witness of such a wound proving fatal.

Synodontis sorex, Gthr. (Plate I., Fig. B.)

D. 1/7. A. 12. P. 1/9. V. 7.

The gill-opening extends downwards to or before the root of the pectoral fin; snout produced, pointed; mandibulary teeth very long and slender, as long as the eye, from six to eight in number. Maxillary barbels half as long as the head, lined interiorly with a narrow white membrane; the outer mandibulary barbels two-thirds as long as those of the maxillæ, provided with filaments. The height of the body is rather less than one-fourth of the total length (without caudal), the length of the head two-sevenths. Dorsal and pectoral spines slightly crenulated along their outer margins; humeral process as high as long. The first ray of the dorsal and pectoral fins produced. The adipose fin commences at a short distance from the dorsal, its length being contained thrice and a third in the total (without caudal). Caudal fin deeply forked, both lobes being prolonged: the upper is the longer, one-third, or more than one-third, of the total length. Coloration uniform: a black band along each caudal lobe; a blackish spot at the base of the hinder half of the dorsal fin.

This species has been discovered by Mr. Petherick at Khartoum.

Synodontis macrodon. (*Scheilan.*)

D. 1/7.   A. 13.   P. 1/8.   V. 7.

The gill-opening extends downwards to before the root of the pectoral fin; mandibulary teeth very long and slender, nearly as long as the eye. Maxillary barbels about as long as the head, provided with long fringes. Dorsal and pectoral spines serrated along both edges; humeral process not much longer than high.

Synodontis serratus, Rüpp.

D. 1/7.   A. 12—13.   P. 1/9.   V. 7.

The gill-opening extends downwards to before the root of the pectoral fin; mandibulary teeth rather numerous, much shorter than the eye, in a narrow band. Maxillary barbels longer than the head, lined with a narrow membrane interiorly. Dorsal spine longer than the head (in adult specimens), serrated along both edges. Humeral process longer than high, pointed behind. Dorsal and pectoral spines and the upper caudal lobe produced into filaments. Uniformly coloured; young dotted with brown.

Synodontis schal, Bl. Schn.

D. 1/7. A. 12—13. P. 1/8. V. 7.

The gill-opening extends downwards to before the root of the pectoral fin; mandibulary teeth rather numerous, much shorter than the eye, in a narrow band. Maxillary barbels longer than the head, not fringed. Pectoral spine stronger and rather longer than that of the dorsal fin, the latter being not serrated in front, and not much longer than the head. Humeral process much longer than high, pointed behind. The distance between dorsal and adipose fins is much less than the length of the base of the former. Old and half-grown specimens of uniform coloration, young ones irregularly spotted and banded with brown.

The largest specimen I have seen had a weight of about ten pounds; but this fish probably attains to a much larger size.

Synodontis humeratus, Cuv. & Val.

Maxillary barbels not fringed. Dorsal spine serrated in front.

The humeral process is exceedingly long, extending further backwards than the nuchal cuirass.

This has been described by Valenciennes from a figure, but no example has since been found.

Synodontis membranaceus, Geoffr.   (*Schal baten soda.*)

D. 1/7.   A. 12.   P. 1/9.   V. 7.

The gill-opening extends downwards nearly to the middle of the throat; mandibulary teeth very short and small, forming a minute patch. Maxillary barbels shorter than the head, lined with a very broad black membrane. Dorsal spine not serrated in front; humeral process as long as high. The adipose fin commences immediately behind the dorsal. Belly black.

Upper Nile. Specimens, twenty inches long, have been collected by Mr. Petherick.

RHINOGLANIS.

Body scaleless. Two dorsal fins, both composed of rays, the first with a strong spine; anal rather short. Teeth in both jaws minute; palate edentulous; mouth transverse, of moderate width, mandibles well developed. Barbels six, not compressed. Eyes free, of moderate size; anterior and posterior nostrils close together; the posterior nostril very large, open. Neck with broad dermal bones.

Gill-openings rather narrow, not extending downwards beyond the root of the pectoral. Ventrals with seven rays, inserted below the posterior rays of the first dorsal fin.

Rhinoglanis typus, Gthr.

D. $\frac{1}{8}$ | 9.   A. 10.   P. 1/6.   V. 7.

The head is nearly as broad as high, and its length is somewhat more than the height of the body, two-ninths of the total (without caudal); it is entirely osseous above, with a deep and broad longitudinal groove on the forehead. The snout is obtusely rounded in

front, and rather longer than the diameter of the eye, which is two-sevenths of the length of the head, and equal to the width of the interorbital space. The maxillary barbel extends nearly to the origin of the second dorsal; the mandibulary barbels are inserted close to the anterior margin of the mandible, the outer ones extending to the root of the ventrals, the inner ones being somewhat shorter, and provided with two or three additional filaments. The entire neck is cuirassed, the cuirass being composed of three transverse pieces; the lateral margins of the nuchal cuirass are nearly parallel. Humerus with a long, slender process, which extends nearly as far backwards as the nuchal shield. Dorsal spine slightly serrated in front and as long as the head; the pectoral spine is strongly serrated interiorly, stronger and longer than that of the dorsal fin, and extends beyond the root of the ventral. The second dorsal fin has a rounded upper margin, commencing before and terminating behind the anal. Caudal forked. Body immaculate.

The single specimen of this most interesting new genus of Siluroids is only an inch and a half long; it was sent by Mr. Petherick from Gondokoro.

Mochocus.

Body scaleless. Two dorsal fins, both composed of rays; the first with a strong spine; anal short. Teeth in the upper jaw only, in a single series. Mouth of moderate width; barbels, six, thin. Eyes of moderate size. Neck covered with soft skin. Gill-openings rather narrow. Ventrals six-rayed, inserted immediately behind the dorsal.

This genus, which appears to be closely allied to *Rhinoglanis*, has been discovered by M. de Joannis. Unfortunately Valenciennes has not taken any notice of it, so that we are obliged to give an abstract from the notes published by the collector.

Mochocus niloticus, Joannis.

D. ⅛ | 10.   A. 8.   P. 1/3.   V. 6.

The length of the head is two-ninths of the total (without caudal). Barbels subequal in length, scarcely longer than the head. Dorsal spine longer than the head, but only two-thirds as long as the spine of the pectoral fin, which is exceedingly strong. Head, body, the second dorsal, and the caudal with brownish-black spots.

Nile, near Thebes. Only eighteen lines long.

MALAPTERURUS.

Body scaleless, thick, subcylindrical. Only one dorsal fin, which is adipose and situated before the caudal; anal of moderate length, or short; caudal rounded; ventrals six-rayed, inserted somewhat behind the middle of the body; pectorals without pungent spine. Barbels six: one to each maxillary, and two on each side of the mandible. Both jaws with bands of villiform teeth; palate edentulous. The entire head and body covered with soft skin. Eyes small. Gill-opening very narrow, reduced to a slit before the pectoral. An electric organ extends over the whole body, and is situated between two aponeurotic membranes below the external integument.

Malapterurus electricus, L. *(Raad* or *Raasch.)*

The *electric Silurus* is spread over the whole of tropical Africa, but evidently more numerous in the upper part of the Nile than below the cataracts.

CHARACINIDÆ.

CITHARINUS.

Body compressed, covered with scales. Dorsal fin rather short, without spine, placed nearly in the middle of the length of the body; a small adipose fin behind the dorsal; anal rather long; ventrals below the dorsal. Body elevated, covered with small scales; belly rounded in front of the ventrals. Cleft of the mouth transverse, with very thin lips, each lip with a single series of minute, ciliiform, moveable teeth; palate toothless. Intestinal tract with numerous circumvolutions.

Citharinus geoffroyi, Cuv.

D. 19.　A. 28—30.　V. 11.　L. lat. 80—86.

The height of the body is more than one-half of the total length (without caudal); basal half of the adipose fin scaly. Generally uniform silvery, with the back greenish; sometimes the whole back and the tail brownish black.

Citharinus latus, Müll. & Trosch.

D. 22.   A. 26.   V. 11.   L. lat. 68.

Adipose fin larger than in the preceding species.

Alestes.

Body compressed, covered with large scales. The dorsal fin is short, without spine, and placed in the middle of the length of the body; a small adipose fin behind the dorsal; anal fin rather long. Body oblong, covered with scales of moderate or large size; belly rounded. Cleft of the mouth rather small. Maxillary teeth none; intermaxillary teeth in two series; those of the front series more or less compressed, more or less distinctly tricuspid; the teeth of the hinder series are broad, molar-like, each armed with several pointed tubercles. Teeth in the lower jaw in two series: those in the front series laterally compressed, broader behind than in front; the hinder series is composed of two conical teeth. All the teeth are strong, few in number. Nostrils close together, separated by a valve only. Gill-opening wide, the gill membranes being united for a short space only, and not grown to the isthmus.

Small carnivorous fishes, (with the exception of *A. macrolepidotus*) scarcely exceeding twelve inches in length.

Alestes dente, Hasselq. (*Raches.*)

D. 10.   A. 23—24.   V. 10.   L. lat. 45.   L. transv. 9/3½.

The height of the body is a little more than one-fourth of the total length, the length of the head one-fifth. Teeth of moderate strength, not coloured. Body silvery.

Alestes kotschyi, Heck.

D. 10.   A. 26—28.   V. 10.   L. lat. 46.   L. transv. 9½/3½.

The height of the body is two-ninths of the total length (without caudal), the length of the head rather less than one-fifth. Teeth not coloured. The pectoral fin terminates at some distance from the root of the ventral. Body silvery.

Alestes macrolepidotus, C. & V.

D. 10.   A. 16.   V. 10.   L. lat. 23.   L. transv. 4/2.

Teeth of the lower jaw with three or four points. The length of the head is one-fourth or somewhat less than one-fourth of the total (without caudal). Silvery, each scale with a darker base; sometimes a blackish spot behind the gill-opening, above the lateral line.

Alestes nurse, Rüpp.

D. 10.   A. 16.   L. lat. 29.   L. transv. $\frac{5\frac{1}{2}}{2\frac{1}{2}}$.

The height of the body is one-third, or somewhat less than one-third, of the total length (without caudal), the length of the head a little more than one-fourth. The origin of the dorsal fin is only a little behind that of the ventral; the pectoral terminates at some distance from the ventral. Bright silvery, with a very indistinct blackish spot above the lateral line, behind the gill-opening; sometimes another large blackish blotch at the base of the caudal fin. Iris light yellow.

Alestes rüppellii, Gthr.

D. 10.   A. 17.   L. lat. 30.   L. transv. $\frac{5\frac{1}{2}}{2\frac{1}{2}}$.

The height of the body is one-third, or a little less than one-third, of the total length (without caudal), the length of the head one-fourth, or, in younger examples, somewhat more than one-fourth. The origin of the dorsal fin is a little behind that of the ventral, midway between the extremity of the snout and the root of the caudal. The pectoral terminates close to the ventral. Bright silvery, with a very indistinct blackish humeral spot; caudal spot absent or very indistinct. Iris golden, with a broad black ring; sometimes entirely black in specimens preserved in spirits.

Upper Nile.

HYDROCYON. *(Kelb el bahr; Kelb el moyeh. Raschal.)*

Body compressed, covered with large scales. The dorsal fin is in the middle of the length of the body, above the ventrals; a small adipose fin behind the dorsal; anal of moderate length. Body oblong, compressed, covered with scales of moderate size; belly rounded. Cleft of the mouth wide, without lips; the intermaxillaries and mandibles are armed with strong pointed teeth, widely set and few in number; they are received in notches of the opposite jaw, and visible externally, when the mouth is closed. Palate toothless. Cheeks covered with the enlarged suborbital bones. Nostrils close together, situated in the same cavity. Orbit with an anterior and posterior adipose eyelid. Gill-opening wide, the gill membranes being united quite in front of the throat. Intestinal tract short.

The strong dentition of these fishes indicate their rapacious character; this is also expressed by the Arabic name, which signifies "dog of the water."

Hydrocyon forskalii, Cuv.

D. 10.   A. 15—16.   V. 10.   L. lat. 45—48.   L. transv. $\frac{8=9}{6}$.

The height of the body is contained four times and a half or four times and two-thirds in the total length (without caudal), the length of the head four times and one-fourth or four times and two-thirds. There are *two* series of scales between the lateral line and the elongate scale at the root of the ventral fin. The upper jaw with five or six teeth on each side, the lower with four. Silvery, generally a blackish streak along each series of scales above the lateral line.

I have seen heads of individuals which must have weighed twelve pounds at least.

Hydrocyon brevis, Gthr. (Plate III., Fig. A.)

D. 10. A. 16. V. 10. L. lat. 49—50. L. transv. 9/5.

Very similar to *H. forskalii*, but with a shorter body, and with more scales below the lateral line.

The height of the body is contained thrice and a half or thrice and two-thirds in the total length (without caudal), the length of the head four times or thrice and four-fifths. There are *three* series of scales between the lateral line and the elongate scale at the root of the ventral fin. The upper jaw with five or six teeth on each side, the lower with four. Silvery, each series of scales above the lateral line with a very faint darker longitudinal streak.

Upper Nile.

———

DISTICHODUS. *(Nefasch.)*

Body compressed, covered with small scales. Dorsal fin rather long, placed in the middle of the length of the body, above the ventrals; a small adipose fin behind the dorsal; anal of moderate length; caudal and adipose fins covered with small scales. Body oblong, covered with small scales. Belly rounded. Cleft of the mouth transverse, small; intermaxillary and mandible with a series of flattish bicuspid incisors; there is generally another series of smaller similar teeth behind the front series; palate toothless. Nostrils close together, with a valve between them, overlapping the posterior. Gill-openings of moderate width, the gill membranes being attached to the isthmus, having a free hinder edge nearly along their entire extent.

Distichodus niloticus, Hasselq.

D. 24—26.   A. 14—15.   V. 11.   L. lat. 103—105.
L. transv. 20/19.

The height of the body is two-fifths or less than two-fifths of the total length (without caudal) in mature specimens, and only one-third in young ones. The length of the head is contained four times and two-thirds or four times and three-fourths in that of the body in mature specimens, but it is one-fourth of it in young ones. Snout obtuse; interorbital space broad, depressed, not very convex. The lower jaw with about thirty-six teeth in the front series; young individuals have less. The anal fin extends backwards to, or nearly to, the root of the caudal, if laid backwards. Silvery, back greenish; dorsal fin with short, oblique, narrow blackish streaks on the inter-radial membrane. Young specimens with a blackish spot behind the head, between the lateral line and the gill-opening, and with several indistinct transverse blackish blotches on the body.

Attains to a weight of nearly 100 pounds, and is very good eating.

Distichodus rostratus, Gthr.   (Plate III., Fig. B.)

D. 23—25.   A. 14.   V. 11.   L. lat. 89—98.   L. transv. 16/16.

The height of the body is contained thrice and one-fourth in the total length (without caudal), the length of the head four times and three-fourths. Snout rather pointed: in a specimen fourteen inches long it is more than twice as long as the eye; interorbital space broad, convex, its width being contained twice and one-third in the length of the head. The lower jaw with about twenty-eight teeth. The anal fin extends somewhat beyond the root of the caudal, if laid backwards. Silvery, back greenish, sides clouded with blackish; dorsal fin with small blackish spots.

Distichodus engycephalus, Gthr.

D. 24. A. 13. V. 11. L. lat. 80. L. transv. 14/13.

The height of the body is contained thrice, or twice and three-fourths, in the total length (without caudal), the length of the head four times and one-third or four times and one-fourth. Snout pointed, compressed; head compressed; the interorbital space is very convex, its width being contained twice and two-thirds in the length of the head. The lower jaw with about twenty teeth. The anal fin does not extend to the root of the caudal, if laid backwards. Silvery, sides with four irregular series of round blackish spots, each as large as, or smaller than, the eye. Dorsal fin with very indistinct spots, which are partly confluent.

This species will be easily recognized by its compressed head.
Upper Nile.

Distichodus brevipinnis, Gthr. (Plate III., Fig. C.)

D. 2o. A. 15. V. 11. L. lat. 90. L. transv. 17/23.

The height of the body is contained twice and two-thirds in the total length (without caudal), the length of the head thrice and three-fourths. Snout as broad as, or even broader than, long, obtuse in front; lips thick; interorbital space very convex, its width being contained twice and one-fifth in the length of the head. The lower jaw with twenty or twenty-two teeth. The length of the base of the dorsal fin is only three-fourths of that of the head; the distance between the two dorsal fins equals the length of the base of the adipose fin. The anal extends to the root of the caudal, if laid backwards. Body with large rounded blackish spots, each being twice as large as the eye. Dorsal fin with subquadrangular blackish spots, irregularly arranged.

Upper Nile.

Ichthyborus.

Dorsal fin somewhat behind the middle of the length of the body, with fourteen or seventeen rays; anal of moderate length; ventrals a little in advance of the dorsal; caudal scaly, forked. Body compressed, elongate, covered with small scales; lateral line complete. Cheeks naked. Cleft of the mouth wide: the intermaxillaries of both sides coalesce, forming a very moveable flattish bone, which is armed with a pair of canine teeth anteriorly, and with a series of compressed triangular teeth laterally; its inner surface, which forms the anterior part of the roof of the mouth, is covered with minute pointed teeth. The dentaries of the mandible also are coalescent into a single bone, without median suture; their dentition is the same as that of the upper jaw, but there are three canine teeth, the central tooth standing in front of the jaw, and fitting between the upper canines. The maxillary is very small, attached to the extremity of the intermaxillary. Palate toothless. Nostrils in front of the eye, close together, the posterior wide, open. Gill-openings wide, the gill membranes being separate; gill-rakers short, lanceolate.

For our first acquaintance with the fishes of this genus we are indebted to Joannis, who gives a description and figure which do not leave any doubt as to the generic affinity of the fishes found by him, and rediscovered by Mr. Petherick on the Upper Nile. I have long hesitated to separate them specifically, but as Joannis says that there are only fifteen scales in a transverse row, and as he represents in the figure the scales of a corresponding size, it appears probable that the Nile is inhabited by two distinct species. They must be very scarce, as Joannis and Petherick are the only travellers who had the good fortune of meeting with them. It is also worthy of notice that only two examples were in the extensive collections made by Mr. Petherick, which appears to confirm the remark made by Joannis, that these fishes are always found in pairs.

Ichthyborus microlepis, Gthr. (Plate II., Fig. A.)

D. 15—17. A. 14—15. P. 14—15. V. 10. L. lat. 100. L. transv. 12/14.

The height of the body is contained four times and three-fourths or five times and one-fourth in the total length (without caudal), the length of the head thrice and one-fourth or thrice and two-thirds; the diameter of the eye is somewhat less than the width of the interorbital space, one-half of the length of the snout, and two-fifths of that of the postorbital portion of the head. Intermaxillary with nineteen, mandible with fourteen, teeth on each side. Cheek quite naked, the suborbital ring being narrow. Operculum with radiating striæ, twice as high as long. The origin of the dorsal fin is nearer to the root of the caudal than to the extremity of the snout; it is higher than long; anal fin somewhat longer than high; caudal with the lobes rounded, two-thirds as long as the head; the pectoral as long as the ventral, rather more than half as long as the head; the ventral terminates at a great distance from the vent. Uniform silvery; dorsal rays with some faint dots; caudal with five or six rather irregular transverse series of round black spots.

The two specimens are six and a half inches long.

Ichthyborus bessé, Joannis. (*Bessé*.)

As we have mentioned above, this species appears to have much larger scales. Joannis found his specimens at Thebes, and the species has not been rediscovered since his time.

Coregonus niloticus, Joannis.

I take this opportunity of directing the attention of travellers to a small fish, which is evidently distinct from all the other known species of tropical Africa. I am not aware that it exists in any collection, and to ensure its rediscovery I add here a copy of the figure and description given by its discoverer.

The head of this pretty little species is almost equal to one-fifth the length of the body. Mouth small, and slightly proboscidiform; its cleft very small; the upper lip a little longer than the lower. The head is of a conical form; teeth none; ear-opening well marked; the eye reaches almost to the summit of the head. Body fusiform, flesh transparent; the curvature of the back is very slight, and the longitudinal line of the lower surface is quite straight as far as the opercular opening, beneath which it takes a curve, and ascends along the lower profile of the head. The proportion of the greatest height of the body to its length is as $1:6$; the anus is almost median in the length of the body, and about equally distant from the ventrals and from the anal. Scales very fine. Ventral with nine rays, the third being the longest, placed beneath the belly and opposite to the first dorsal. First dorsal with thirteen rays, the third being the longest. This fin is triangular, transparent, and inserted at rather more than one-third of the total length from the tip of the snout. Anal with ten rays, the third and fourth equal, and the longest placed at a distance from the anus equal to that which separates the anus from the ventrals. Colour of the body, yellowish grey; belly and cheeks, silvery; commencement and upper surface of the head, tawny red. There are ten greenish patches placed saddlewise on the back, and six quadrilateral spots of the same colour along the middle of each side and from the dorsal to the end of the caudal. This little fish, which is said to be delicious eating—of which we are unable to judge on account of its small size—is taken along the shores with the other small species. It is not very common. I procured it at Thebes: it is caught principally in the winter, and the Arabs nam it *Samak-el-maleh*.

The length of the specimen described is two inches.

MORMYRIDÆ.

Mormyrus. (*Kisch-oue, Caschive.*)

Body and tail scaly; head scaleless; barbels none. The margin of the upper jaw is formed in the middle by the intermaxillaries, which coalesce into a single bone, and laterally by the maxillaries. Pectoral and ventral fins; no adipose fin. Mouth very small; small teeth in the jaws, or on the palate, or on the tongue. A series of pores along the base of the dorsal and anal fins. Gill-opening reduced to a short slit.

Not esteemed as food.

Mormyrus caschive, Hasselq. (*Chasm el Binât.*)

D. 81—87.   A. 18—20.   V. 6.

Scales very small. Snout conical, much produced, slightly bent downwards, the pupil of the eye being exactly in the middle of the length of the head. Lower lip somewhat projecting beyond the upper; teeth very small, slightly dilated, the crown with a shallow notch. The height of the body is nearly equal to the length of the head, which is two-ninths of the total (without caudal).

Attains to a length of three feet.

Mormyrus oxyrhynchus, Geoffr.

D. 58—66.   A. 18—20.   V. 6.   L. lat. ca. 130.

Snout conical, much produced, slightly bent downwards, the pupil of the eye being scarcely nearer to the end of opercle than to the extremity of the snout. Lower lip somewhat projecting beyond the upper; teeth not very small, slightly dilated, the crown with a shallow notch. The height of the body is nearly equal to the length of the head, which is two-ninths, or a little more than two-ninths, of the total (without caudal).

Mormyrus geoffroyi, C. & V.

D. 74—77.   A. 17—19.   V. 6.

Scales very small. Snout conical, much produced, with its longitudinal axis nearly in the same line as the axis of the body; eye almost in the middle of the length of the head. Lower lip somewhat projecting beyond the upper. Teeth very small, slightly dilated, the crown with a shallow notch. The height of the body is nearly equal to the length of the head, which is two-ninths of the total (without caudal).

Mormyrus hasselquistii, C. & V.

D. 70. A. 18. L. lat. 115.

Snout rather thick and obtuse, with the upper jaw somewhat projecting beyond the lower. Eye situated in the anterior third of the length of the head, which is one-fourth of the total (without caudal). Teeth very small, with their crown slightly emarginate.

Mormyrus cyprinoides, L.

D. 26—28. A. 32—35. V. 6. L. lat. 85.

Snout obtuse, of moderate length, with the lower jaw prominent, and with a very short, skinny flap at the chin. Eye rather small, situated before the middle of the length of the head. Teeth minute, pointed, few in number. Pectoral extending beyond the root of the ventrals. The height of the body is one-fourth or two-sevenths of the total length (without caudal), the length of the head one-fifth, or somewhat less than one-fifth.

Mormyrus bane, Lacép.

D. 30—32. A. 33—36. V. 6. L. lat. 42—45.

Snout obtuse, compressed, very short, elevated, obliquely truncated in front, with the cleft of the mouth at its lower side, below the eye, which is of moderate size. Teeth very small, dilated, and notched, forming a complete series round the entire edge of both jaws. Pectoral extending beyond the root of the ventral, which is short, half as long as the pectoral. The height of the body is contained from twice and one-half to three times and one-quarter in the total length (without caudal), the length of the head four times, or four times and a third.

Mormyrus discorhynchus, Ptrs.

D. 30—36. A. 24—27. L. lat. 70.

Snout obtuse, rounded, compressed, as long as the eye, which is of moderate size; cleft of the mouth at the lower side of the snout, before the vertical from the front margin of the orbit. Teeth very small, dilated, and notched, few in number. The pectoral extends somewhat beyond the middle of the ventral, which is more than half as long as the pectoral. The height of the body is one-third of the total length (without caudal), the length of the head one-fifth. Back and upper parts of the side irregularly marbled with brown.

Mormyrus bovei, C. & V.

D. 20—23. A. 31—33.

Form of the snout as in *M. bane*, the cleft of the mouth being below the middle of the orbit. The height of the body is nearly one-fourth of the total length, the caudal fin included.

Mormyrus isidori, C. & V.

D. 19—20.   A. 24.   L. lat. 55.

Snout obtuse, rounded, compressed, short, but longer than the eye, which is rather small; cleft of the mouth at the lower side of the snout, below the front margin of the orbit. Teeth small, dilated and notched, forming an arched series round the margin of both jaws. Pectoral extending to or somewhat beyond the middle of the ventral, which is not quite half as long as the pectoral. The height of the body is contained from twice and three-fourths to three times and one-third in the total length (without caudal), the length of the head four times and one-half.

Mormyrus dorsalis, Geoffr.

D. 13—16.   A. 56—62.   V. 6.   L. lat. ca. 110.

Snout obtuse, rather short, rounded, with the jaws equal anteriorly, and without labial appendage. Eye small, situated far before the middle of the length of the head. Teeth not very small, fixed, dilated, notched. Pectoral extending beyond the root of the ventral, which is short, but more than half as long as the pectoral. The height of the body is contained from three times and three-fourths to five times in the total length (without caudal), the length of the head five times and one-half. The distance of the origin of the dorsal fin from the root of the caudal is one-half of its distance from the gill-opening.

Mormyrus petersii, Gthr.

Easily distinguished by the prolongation of the lower jaw into a long cylindrical appendage. Originally described from West African specimens, it was rediscovered by Captain Speke on the White Nile; he did not bring specimens, but I have seen a sketch of this fish in a collection of MS. drawings, made by him at Urundogani.

Mormyrus anguilloides, L. *(Erse.)*

D. 26—28. A. 39—42. V. 6. L. lat. 95.

Head nearly twice as long as high; snout subtetrahedral, of moderate length, rounded in front, with the upper jaw a little longer than the lower. Eye very small, situated in the anterior third of the length of the head. Teeth not very small, fixed, forming a curved series in both jaws, slightly notched at the apex. Dorsal fin more than half as long as the anal. The height of the body is contained from five times and a half to six times and a half in the total length (without caudal), the length of the head four times.

Not very common.

GYMNARCHUS.

This genus differs from *Mormyrus* in the fins, the caudal, anal, and ventral fins being absent, whilst the dorsal fin extends nearly over the entire length of the back. Each jaw with a single series of incisors.

Gymnarchus niloticus, Cuv. (*Jerfar*; *Ashoua Kamoura* in Cairo.)

Rare; more common in the Upper Nile and West Africa. Attains to a length of more than five feet.

CYPRINODONTIDÆ.

HAPLOCHILUS.

Snout flat, both jaws being much depressed. Barbels none. Bones of the mandible firmly united; upper jaw protractile; both jaws with a narrow band of villiform teeth. Body oblong, depressed anteriorly, compressed posteriorly. Dorsal fin short, commencing behind the origin of the anal, which is more or less elongate. No adipose fin. Intestinal tract but slightly convoluted; air-bladder present.

Haplochilus fasciolatus, Gthr.

D. 11. A. 18. V. 6—7. L. lat. 28. L. transv. 9—10.

The height of the body is a little less than the length of the head, and one-fourth of the total (without caudal). Head rather elongate, much depressed anteriorly, the snout being longer than the eye, the diameter of which is somewhat more than one-fourth of the length of the head, and one-half of the width of the interorbital space. Lower jaw a little longer than upper. Origin of the dorsal fin midway between the extremity of the caudal and the eye, corresponding to the seventeenth scale of the lateral line, and being rather before the middle of the anal. Pectoral fin extending somewhat beyond the root of the ventral, which reaches the vent. Brownish, each scale with a red spot at the base, disappearing in preserved specimens; the lower part of the sides of the abdomen and tail with eight or nine oblique narrow brownish-black streaks, descending from the middle of the side forwards.

Upper Nile. The largest specimen known is only three in. long.

CYPRINIDÆ.

Labeo.

Scales of moderate or small size. Dorsal fin without osseous ray, with more than nine branched rays, commencing somewhat in advance of the ventrals. Snout obtusely rounded, the skin of the maxillary region being more or less thickened, forming a projection beyond the mouth. Teeth none in the jaws. Mouth transverse, inferior, with the lips thickened, each or one of them being provided with an inner transverse fold, which is covered with a deciduous horny substance forming a sharp edge, which, however, does not rest upon the bone as base, but is soft and moveable. Barbels very small, two or four, the maxillary barbels more or less hidden in a groove behind the angle of the mouth. Anal fin very short. Snout generally more or less covered with hollow tubercles.

Labeo niloticus, Forsk. (*Lebis*; *Lebse*.)

D. 16—19. A. 8. L. lat. 40—43. L. transv. $\frac{l=8}{6=8}$.

Mouth rather broad. Lips thin, fringed, with an inner fold in their entire circumference, more distinct on the upper lip than on the lower. Snout obtuse, moderately projecting, with a very indistinct lobe on each side; maxillary barbel minute, hidden in a lateral groove. Eye of moderate size, not much smaller than a scale, situated before, or, in old examples, in the middle of the length of the head. There are four or five longitudinal series of scales between the lateral line and the ventral fin. Upper margin of the dorsal fin concave, the third and fourth rays being the longest. Body, and especially the tail, compressed, oblong, its depth being contained thrice and two-thirds or four times in the total length (without caudal). Coloration uniform.

Very common in all parts of the river; eaten by the Arabs; attains to a length of eighteen inches.

Labeo coubie, Rüpp. (*Coubie*.)

D. 14—16.   A. 8.   L. lat. 35—37.   L. transv. 6½/6.

Mouth of moderate width. Lips moderately thick, with a distinct inner fold in their entire circumference; lower lip sometimes indistinctly fringed. Snout rather produced, obtuse in front, moderately projecting beyond the lower jaw, with a distinct lobe on each side; maxillary barbel very small, hidden in a deep lateral groove. Eye rather small, as large as a scale in middle-sized specimens, though comparatively smaller in large ones; *it is situated behind the middle of the length of the head in adult examples*, and *in the middle in younger ones*. There are four or five longitudinal series of scales between the lateral line and the ventral fin. Upper margin of the dorsal fin convex, the middle rays being the longest, and certain (male?) specimens having this fin considerably elevated. Body, and especially the tail, compressed and elevated, the greatest depth of the body being contained thrice and one-third or thrice and one-fourth in the total (without caudal). Coloration uniform. Snout of certain specimens with small concave tubercles.

Attains to a length of twelve inches.

Labeo forskalii, Rüpp.

D. 13.   A. 8.   L. lat. 39—40.   L. transv. 6/6.

Mouth broad. Lips very thick, with a distinct inner fold in

their entire circumference; lower lip generally fringed. Snout obtuse, projecting, with a broad distinct lobe on each side; maxillary barbel minute, hidden in a deep groove. Eye small, situated in the posterior half of the head (at least in mature examples), much smaller than a scale. There are four series of scales between the lateral line and the ventral fin. Upper margin of the dorsal fin concave, the third and fourth rays being the longest. Body elongate, its greatest depth being one-fourth of the total length, or even less. Sometimes an indistinct dark band along the side of the body. Snout generally with hollow tubercles.

BARBUS. (Barbels.)

Scales of small, moderate, or large size. Dorsal fin generally with the (third) longest simple ray ossified, enlarged, and frequently serrated; never with more than nine branched rays, commencing opposite, or nearly opposite, the root of the ventral fin. No adipose fin. Anal fin very short, but frequently very high. Mouth arched, without inner folds, inferior or anterior; lips without horny covering and without teeth. Barbels short, four (in the Nile species).

Barbus bynni, Forsk. (*Bynni.*)

D. 13. A. 8. L. lat. 35. L. transv. 7/5.

The osseous dorsal ray is exceedingly strong, normally longer than, but frequently only as long as, the head, not serrated behind.

There are three series of scales between the lateral line and the root of the ventral fin. *Upper and lower lip sometimes with a well developed lobe, nearly as long as the eye, sometimes without a trace of it.* Body strongly compressed, back elevated below the origin of the dorsal fin, where the height of the body is one-third of the total length (without caudal). The length of the head is contained four times and one-third in the same length. Snout somewhat pointed, with thick lips; mouth inferior. Caudal deeply forked.

Very common in all parts of the river, and eaten by the Arabs. Attains to a length of two feet.

Barbus perince, Rüpp. (*Perince.*)

D. 11. A. 7. L. lat. 30. L. transv. $5\frac{1}{2}/4$.

The osseous dorsal ray is rather feeble, smooth. There are three series of scales between the lateral line and the root of the ventral fin. Body compressed and somewhat elevated, as in the roach, its depth being one-third of the total length (without caudal); head small, its length being rather less than one-fourth of the total (without caudal); its depth equals its length (without snout). Eye rather large, equal to the length of the snout, two-sevenths of that of the head, and two-thirds of the width of the interorbital space, which is convex. Mouth anterior; lips thin, the lower with the transverse fold interrupted in the middle. Dorsal fin rather elevated: its origin is somewhat nearer to the end of the snout than to the root of the caudal. Caudal fin deeply forked. Bright silvery, with a bluish stripe from the scapula to the middle of the caudal, and sometimes with a small blackish spot on the root of the caudal. Very common; does not exceed four inches in length.

BARILIUS.

M. de Joannis has described three small Cyprinoids which appear to belong to this genus. He found them near Thebes, and they

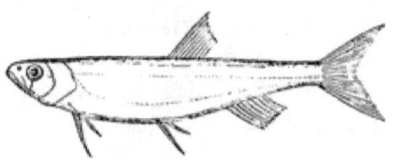

Barilius niloticus.

have not been rediscovered since his time. Copies of the figures

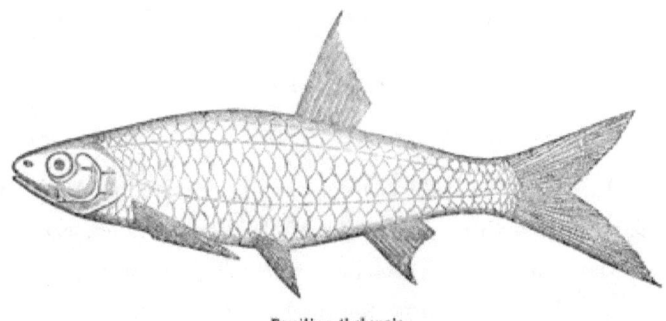

Barilius thebensis.

given by him are here added, in order to direct the attention of travellers to these fishes, specimens of which are much wanted in collections.

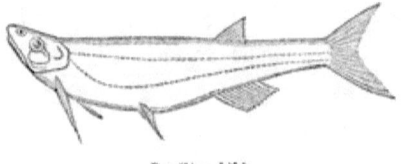

Bavilins bible.

CLUPEIDÆ.

CLUPEA. (Herrings.)

Body compressed, with the abdominal serrature extending forwards into the thoracic region. No barbels. Scales of moderate or large size. Upper jaw not projecting beyond the lower. Cleft of the mouth of moderate width; teeth, if present, rudimentary and deciduous. Anal fin of moderate extent, with less than thirty rays; dorsal fin short, without spine, opposite to the ventrals. Caudal forked. No adipose fin.

Clupea finta, Cuv. (The Shad; *Sabuga.*)

D. 18—20. A. 20—24. V. 9. L. lat. 60—75.

The height of the body is more than the length of the head, which is one-fourth or two-ninths of the total (without caudal). Lower jaw but slightly prominent; maxillary extending to, or nearly to, the vertical from the hind margin of the orbit. No teeth on the palate or the tongue. Gill-rakers stout, osseous, from twenty-one to twenty-seven on the horizontal part of the outer branchial arch. Ventral fins inserted behind the origin of the dorsal, which is nearer to the end of the snout than to the root of the caudal. Basal half of the caudal fin covered with small scales. There are from fifteen to sixteen abdominal scutes behind the base of the ventral fins. Operculum with irregular radiating striæ descending towards the suboperculum. A large blackish blotch in the scapulary region, sometimes followed by a series of four to six similar blotches.

The shad, which enters the Nile from the Mediterranean in the months of December and January, is identical with the British Twaite-shad; it has been described by Hasselquist as *Clupea alosa;* and Geoffroy St. Hilaire has given to it a distinct name, *Clupea nilotica* ("Descr. Eg.," p. 286, pl. 10, fig. 1.)

OSTEOGLOSSIDÆ.

Heterotis.

Body rather elongate, compressed, covered with large hard scales; head compressed, scaleless, bony; abdomen rounded; cleft of the mouth rather small, with the jaws subequal; barbels none. A single series of small teeth in the jaws; pterygoids and hyoid with a patch of small conical teeth; none on the vomer or palatine bones. Gill membranes separate, with eight branchiostegals; the fourth branchial arch with a spiral accessory organ. Air-bladder cellular. Dorsal fin long, opposite to the anal fin, close to the anal fin, without spines. Ventral fins far behind the pectorals.

Heterotis niloticus, Cuv.   (*Gischer, Saide.*)

D. 33—34.   A. 35—36.   L. lat. 35—36.

Attains to a length of four feet, and is more common in the Upper than in the Lower Nile. Bad eating. Not common in European collections.

ANGUILLIDÆ.

ANGUILLA.   (Eels.)

Dorsal, anal, and caudal fins united; pectoral fins present; ventral fins none. Scales minute, hidden in the skin.

Anguilla vulgaris, Cuv.   (*Sumak al hayyāt.*)

The eel is common in the lower Nile; it generally has the snout somewhat more pointed than European examples, but individuals frequently occur which cannot be distinguished from our common eel. This species is easily recognized by the forward position of the dorsal fin, the distance between its commencement and that of the anal fin being equal to, or even more than, the length of the head.

Anguilla latirostris, Cuv.   (The broad-snouted eel.)

Rifaud gives various figures of eels: one was evidently taken from an example of this species, which is distinguished by the backward position of the dorsal fin, the distance between its commencement and that of the anal fin being less than the length of the head.

GYMNODONTIDÆ.

Tetrodon.

Jaws trenchant, without teeth, with a median longitudinal groove; body extensible, covered with a rough spiny skin. The oesophagus can be filled with air, so that these fishes can float on the surface of the water, belly upwards.

Tetrodon lineatus, Forsk. (*Fah-haka.*)

Back and sides with brownish-black longitudinal bands; abdomen without bands.

GANOIDEI.

Polypterus.

Body elongate, covered with hard, smooth, rhombic scales. Jaws with a series of conical teeth, behind which are bands of smalle teeth. Along the back a series of separate spines, each of which bears an articulated finlet.

Polypterus bichir, Geoff.

With about sixteen dorsal finlets.

Common. The flesh is white and good eating, but the fish is not brought to market, as the common people have a prejudice against it.

Polypterus senegalensis, Cuv.

With twelve or thirteen, or even less, finlets.
Common in the Upper Nile and in West Africa.

DIPNOI.

LEPIDOSIREN.

Body eel-shaped, scaly. Two pairs of simple cord-like limbs. Lungs and gills present.

Lepidosiren annectens, Owen.

The discovery of Lepidosiren in the system of the Nile is due to Sir S. Baker, who figured an example from Lake Nyanza, in "The Albert Nyanza," p. 131.

EXPLANATION OF THE PLATES.

PLATE I.	FIG. A.—*Ctenopoma petherici*.
,,	FIG. B.—*Synodontis sorex*.
PLATE II.	FIG. A.—*Ichthyborus microlepis*.
,,	FIG. B.—*Ophiocephalus obscurus*.
PLATE III.	FIG. A.—*Hydrocyon brevis*.
,,	FIG. B.—*Distichodus rostratus*.
,,	FIG. C.—*Distichodus brevipinnis*.

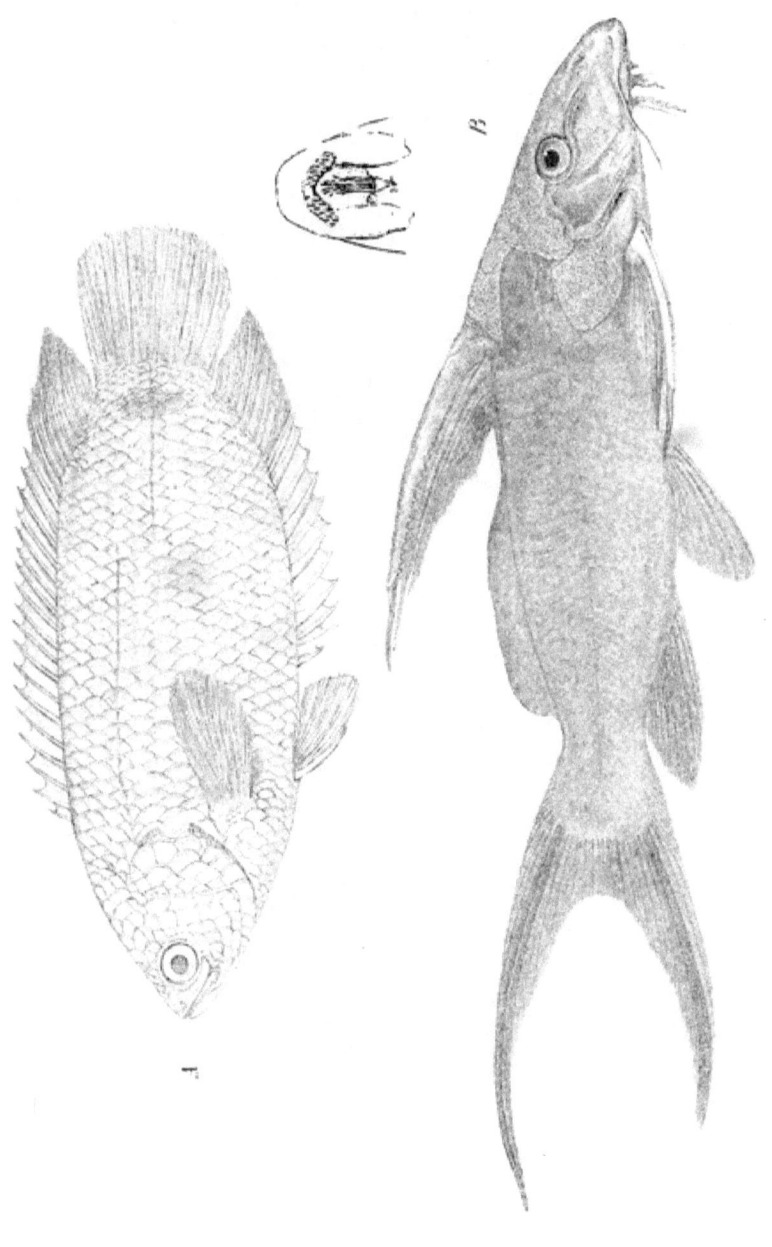

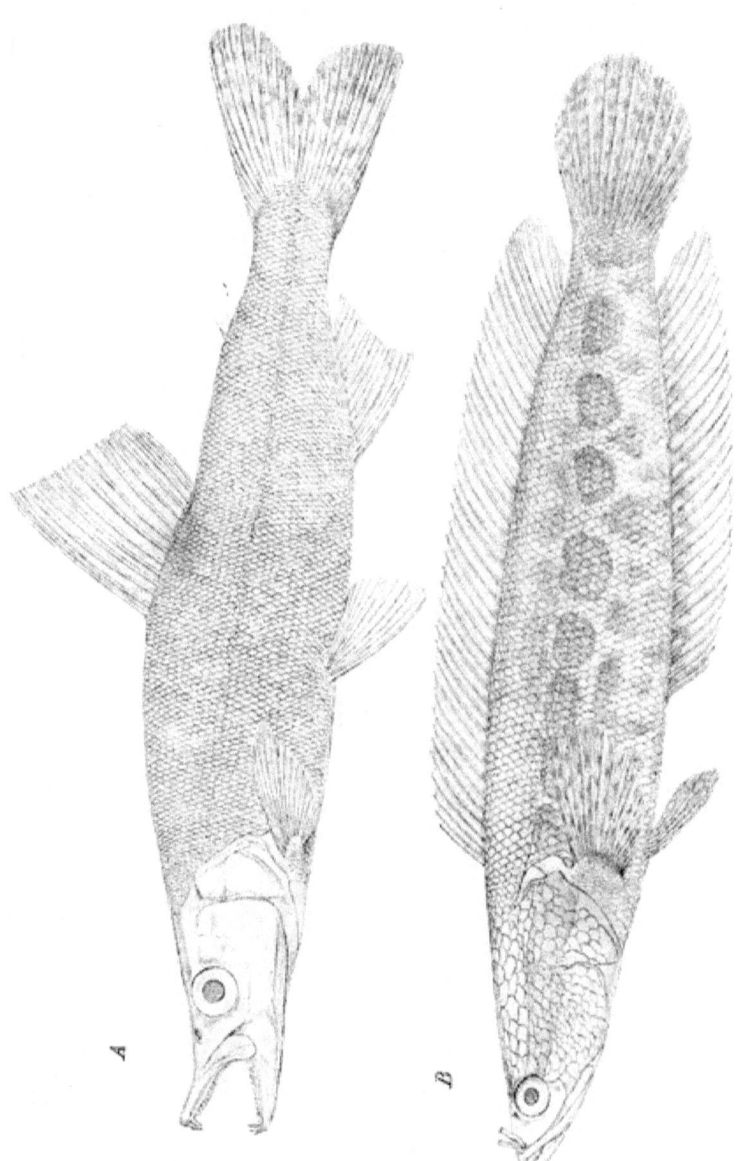

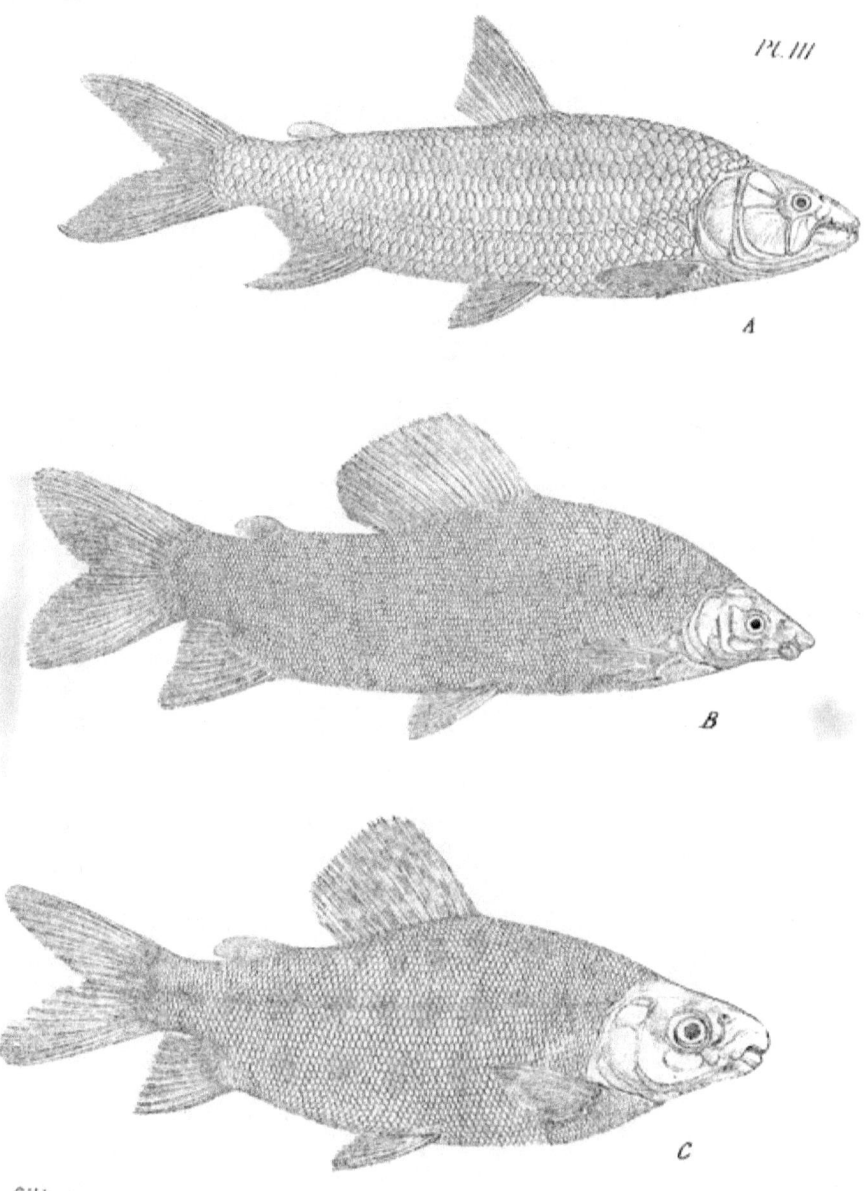

PETHERICK'S OBSERVATIONS.

MR. CONSUL PETHERICK'S

COMPUTED BY EDWIN DUNKIN,

From the Journal of the Royal

Separate Results

Station.	Month and Day.		Star or Planet observed with the Moon.	Resulting Longitude E.					
				Moon E.			Moon W.		
	1862.			°	′	″	°	′	″
KHARTOUM	Feb.	19	Jupiter	32	46	15			
		23	Jupiter	32	36	30			
	Mar.	5	Aldebaran	......			31	50	45
		7	Jupiter	......			32	11	0
		8	Jupiter	......			32	18	45
		13	Jupiter	......			32	43	30
LOLNUN, OR ABU KUKA ...	July	7	Jupiter	30	24	15			
		8	Jupiter	30	53	30			
		16	Sun	......			31	13	0
		16	Sun	......			30	45	45
ADAEL	Sept.	30	Mars	......			30	6	0
	Oct.	4	Mars	......			30	18	0
		4	Mars	......			29	51	45
		5	Antares	29	33	30			
		10	Mars	29	10	45			
		11	Mars	29	24	45			
		12	Sun	......			30	42	30
		14	Sun	......			30	52	15
		15	Sun	......			30	47	0
	Nov.	10	Regulus	......			30	30	0
			Mars	30	6	30			
			Regulus	......			30	13	30
			Mars	30	29	0			
			Regulus	......			30	35	0
			Aldebaran	29	37	45			
			Regulus	......			30	47	45
			Aldebaran	30	12	0			
NEANGARA	Dec.	1	Sun	29	32	30			
		2	Aldebaran Altair?	......			30	41	45
			Aldebaran Altair?	......			30	33	45
			Aldebaran Altair?	......			30	19	45
			Fomalhaut	29	52	0			
			Aldebaran	......			30	4	15
			Fomalhaut	29	42	45			
			Aldebaran	......			30	5	0

OBSERVATIONS,

Esq., GREENWICH OBSERVATORY.

Geographical Society of London for 1865.

for Longitude.

Station.	Month and Day.		Planet or Star observed with the Moon.	Resulting Longitude E.				
				Moon E.			Moon W.	
				°	′	″	°	′	″
NEANGARA	Dec.	2	Fomalhaut	29	40	15			
			Aldebaran	......			30	27	45
		3	Pollux	......			30	22	0
			Mars	29	42	45			
			Pollux	......			30	35	15
			Mars	29	55	0			
			Pollux	......			30	4	0
			Mars	29	52	15			
		13	Sun	......			31	2	0
	1863.								
	Jan.	3	Mars	29	20	45			
			Regulus	......			30	18	30
			Mars	29	34	15			
			Regulus	......			30	59	0
			Mars	29	32	45			
			Regulus	......			30	23	0
			Mars	29	52	0			
		12	Sun	......			30	56	0
		13	Sun	......			30	57	30
WAYO	Feb.	1	Regulus	......			30	30	15
			Mars	30	24	45			
			Regulus	......			30	25	0
			Mars	30	31	0			
			Regulus	......			30	26	30
			Mars	30	18	30			
GONDOKORO	Mar.	25	Venus	31	58	0			
			Regulus	......			32	26	45
MOUTH OF BAHAR IL GAZAL	Apr.	24	Venus	30	4	30			
			Jupiter	......			30	1	0
			Venus	29	25	45			
			Jupiter	......			30	21	30
		25	Venus	30	53	0			
			Jupiter	......			30	31	30
			Venus	30	33	15			
			Jupiter	......			30	39	30
ISLAND OF KYT	Mar.	8	Sun				29	47	45

FINAL RESULT OF Mr. CONSUL PETHERICK'S OBSERVATIONS.

Date	Name of Place	Approximate Position						Reading of Thermometer B.P.	Temperature.	Height.		
		Latitude.			Longitude.					Dunkin.	Error of Instrument.	Result.
		°	′	″	°	′	″	°	°	feet.	+ feet.	feet.
1861.—Aug 11	Korosko	...	...	...	...	...	...	211·0	...	565	40	605
1862.—Mar. 16	Khartoum	15	37	28 N.	32	28	42 E.	210·4	89	913	56	969
May 14	Aliab							210·2	90	1029	104	1133
June 20	Gaba Shambyl							210·1	82	1077	115	1192
July 9	Lolnan, Abu Kuka	6	54	33	30	49	07	210·0	87	1141	121	1262
Oct. 4	Adael, in Agar	6	35	53	30	08	04	210·0	84	1136	141	1277
Dec. 11	Neangara	5	22	41	30	06	26	209·8	88	1831	158	1989
1863.—Feb. 5	Wayo, in Moro	4	46	00	30	26	20	208·1	90	2240	172	2412
Feb. 16	Burra, Neambura							209·0	90	2165	175	2340
Feb. 25	Gondokoro	4	55	00	32	12	24	209·8	99	} 1251	177	1428
								209·8	100			
Apr. 24	Mouth of Bahar il Gazal	8	58	40 ?	30	18	45	209·9	96			
May 8	Island of Kyt	8	27	13	29	47	45					

Consul Petherick was supplied with three boiling-water thermometers, made by Casella; all of them have been returned in good condition.
No. 2534 } was lent to Mr. S. W. Baker at Khartoum in April, 1863; its error on return in Nov. 1863, was 0·60 — from its readings.
No. 2535 } ditto — 0·76 — ditto.
No. 2536 } used by Consul Petherick ditto — 0·86 — ditto.

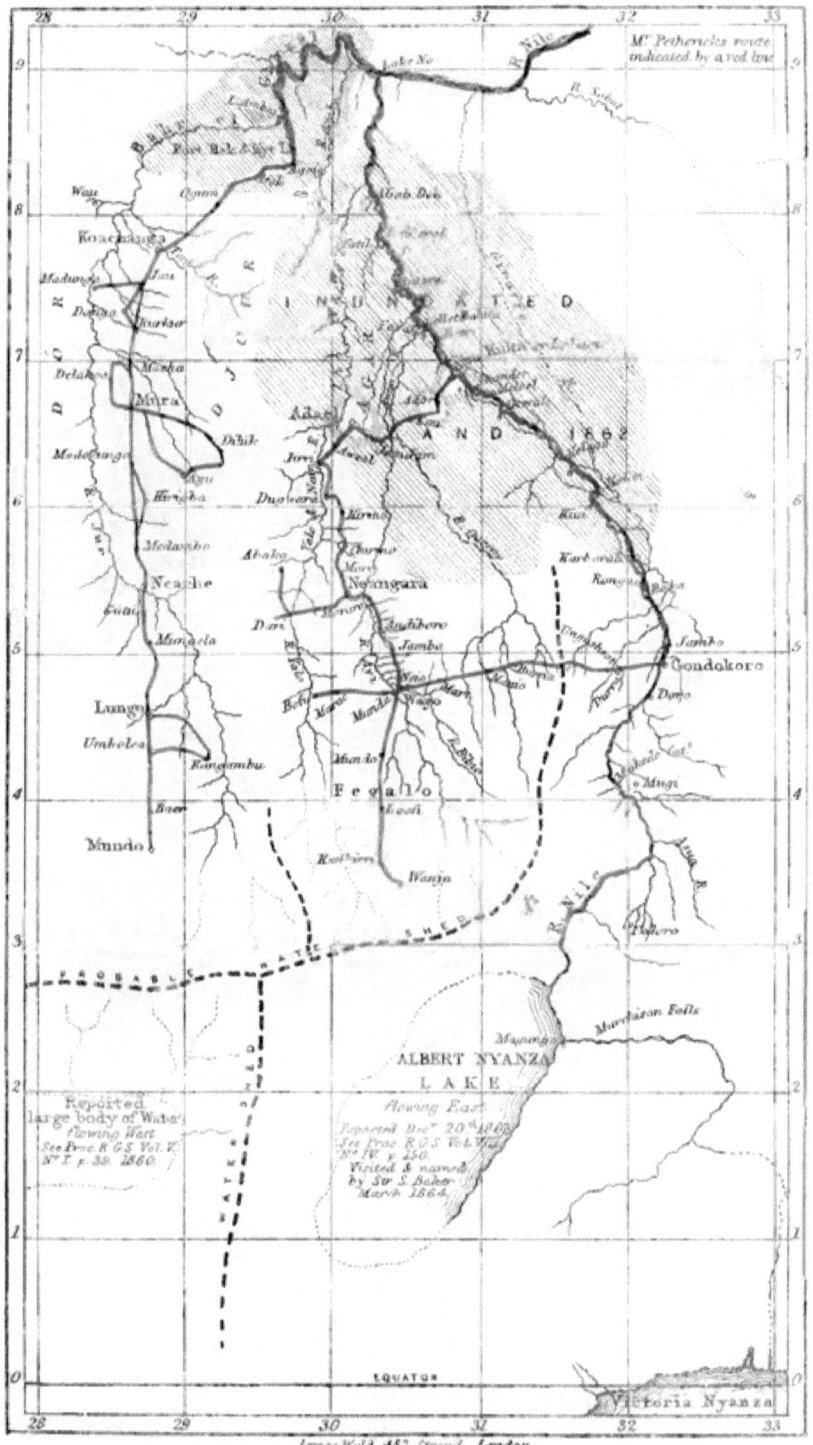

Tinsley Brothers Catalogue.

TINSLEY BROTHERS'
BOOKS OF
TRAVEL, HISTORY, ETC.

A NEW BOOK OF TRAVELS BY CAPT. R. F. BURTON.

Two Volumes, 8vo, with Map and Illustrations, price Thirty Shillings.

EXPLORATIONS
OF THE
HIGHLANDS OF THE BRAZIL:

With a full Account of the Gold and Diamond Mines; also, Canoeing down Fifteen Hundred Miles of the great river, São Francisco, from Sabarà to the Sea.

By CAPTAIN R. F. BURTON, F.R.G.S., &c.

"It is only by driving the reader to the work itself that we can hope to convey a notion of its contents."—*Daily Telegraph.*

"The book is a valuable contribution to science and geography."—*London Review.*

"These two handsome volumes contain prodigious amount of matter, a large portion of which will be quite new to English readers who have little acquaintance with the interior of the country. Captain Burton's narratives have the rare merit of presenting to the eye a picture so realistic in its details, that nothing is left to the mere imagination."—*Morning Star.*

One Volume, 8vo, with Maps and Illustrations.

THE HISTORY
OF THE
PARAGUAYAN WAR.

By CAPTAIN R. F. BURTON, F.R.G.S, &c.

TINSLEY BROTHERS, 18 CATHERINE ST., STRAND.

Two Volumes, post 8vo, Twenty-four Shillings.

FROM WATERLOO
TO THE
PENINSULA.

By GEORGE AUGUSTUS SALA,
Author of "My Diary in America," &c.

One Volume, 8vo, Sixteen Shillings.

ROME AND VENICE,
WITH OTHER WANDERINGS IN ITALY IN 1866-7.

By GEORGE AUGUSTUS SALA,
Author of "My Diary in America," &c.

One Volume, 8vo, Fifteen Shillings.

THE MARCH TO MAGDALA.

By G. A. HENTY,
Special Correspondent to the "Standard."

One Volume, 8vo, Fifteen Shillings.

THE GREAT COUNTRY:
IMPRESSIONS OF AMERICA.

By GEORGE ROSE, M.A. (ARTHUR SKETCHLEY).

One Volume, 8vo, Fifteen Shillings.

A TRIP TO BARBARY
BY A
ROUNDABOUT ROUTE.

By GEORGE AUGUSTUS SALA.

TINSLEY BROTHERS, 18 CATHERINE ST., STRAND.

Two Volumes, with numerous Illustrations, Twenty-five Shillings.

TEN YEARS IN SARAWAK.

By CHARLES BROOKE,
THE "TUANMUDAH" OF SARAWAK.

With an Introduction by H.H. the Rajah Sir JAMES BROOKE.

One Volume, 8vo, Seven Shillings and Sixpence.

THE NILE BASIN.

By CAPTAIN R. F. BURTON,
Author of "A Mission to Dahomey."

One Volume, 8vo, Illustrated, Fifteen Shillings.

A WINTER TOUR IN SPAIN.

By the AUTHOR OF "ALTOGETHER WRONG."

Two Volumes, with Illustrations, Twenty-five Shillings.

A MISSION TO DAHOMEY.

BEING A
THREE MONTHS' RESIDENCE AT THE COURT OF DAHOMEY.

In which are described the Manners and Customs of the Country, including the Human Sacrifice, &c.

By CAPTAIN R. F. BURTON, F.R.G.S., &c.
LATE H.M. COMMISSIONER TO DAHOMEY,
And the Author of "A Pilgrimage to El-Medinah and Meccah," &c.

"He witnessed the grand Customs and the yearly Customs of that grotesquely ceremonious people, including the evolutions of their army of 'Amazons,' and the traces of their cruel human sacrifices, of which he himself, with proper taste, declined to be an actual spectator, and he brought away impressions of the Dahoman proclivities, which are really very curious and instructive, though they were not very satisfactory to himself, nor to be commended to the imitation of the gentle philanthropists who patronise the Dahomans or their congeners under the fallacious impression that they can ever be elevated up to the same level of being as themselves."—*Times.*

TINSLEY BROTHERS, 18 CATHERINE ST., STRAND.

*Two Volumes, with Portrait of the Author, Map and Illustrations,
Twenty-five Shillings.*

ABEOKUTA:
AND AN
EXPLORATION OF THE CAMEROONS MOUNTAINS.

By CAPTAIN R. F. BURTON,
Author of "A Pilgrimage to El-Medinah and Meccah," &c.

Two Volumes, crown 8vo, Twenty-one Shillings.

MY WANDERINGS
IN
WEST AFRICA.

FROM LIVERPOOL TO FERNANDO PO.

By an F.R.G.S.

One Volume, post 8vo, Fourteen Shillings.

FROM CULCUTTA
TO THE
SNOWY RANGE.

By an OLD INDIAN.

With numerous Coloured Illustrations.

One Volume, post 8vo, Ten Shillings and Sixpence.

TODLEBEN'S
DEFENCE OF SEBASTOPOL.

Being a Review of General Todleben's Narrative, 1854-5.

By WILLIAM HOWARD RUSSELL, LL.D.,
Special Correspondent of the "Times" during the Crimean War.

TINSLEY BROTHERS, 18 CATHERINE ST., STRAND.

One Volume, post 8vo, Twelve Shillings.

THE BATTLE-FIELDS OF 1866.

By EDWARD DICEY,
Author of "Rome in 1860," &c.

Two Volumes, crown 8vo, Sixteen Shillings.

THE SCHLESWIG-HOLSTEIN WAR.

By EDWARD DICEY,
Author of "Rome in 1860," &c.

Two Volumes, 8vo, Thirty Shillings.

MY DIARY IN AMERICA
IN THE
MIDST OF WAR.

By GEORGE AUGUSTUS SALA.

With numerous Illustrations, One Volume, 8vo, Twenty-one Shillings.

HOG HUNTING IN THE EAST,
AND
OTHER SPORTS.

By CAPTAIN JAMES T. NEWALL,
Author of "The Eastern Hunters."

One Volume, 8vo, Fifteen Shillings.

NOTES AND SKETCHES
OF THE
PARIS EXHIBITION.

By GEORGE AUGUSTUS SALA,
Author of "My Diary in America," &c.

TINSLEY BROTHERS, 18 CATHERINE ST., STRAND.

Two Volumes, crown 8vo, Twenty-one Shillings.

SHOOTING AND FISHING
IN THE
RIVERS, PRAIRIES, AND BACKWOODS OF NORTH AMERICA.

By B. H. REVOIL.

One Volume, 8vo, with numerous Illustrations, Sixteen Shillings.

THE EASTERN HUNTERS.

By CAPTAIN JAMES T. NEWALL.

New and cheaper Edition, with Corrections and Additions, One Volume.

THE PILGRIM AND THE SHRINE;
OR,
PASSAGES FROM THE LIFE AND CORRESPONDENCE OF HERBERT AINSLIE, B.A. Cantab.

"The real interest and chief merit of the book lie in its delineation of certain opinions. These opinions, which are expressed with much force and felicity of language, and with remarkable boldness and unreserve, treat of topics which are of the highest interest and importance to every human being. . . . The sketches of scenery and of the incidents of travel are extremely vivid and picturesque. Indeed, if all the theology and metaphysics were cut bodily out of the book, there would remain a residuum of spirit-stirring adventure, such as any one would be glad to read. . . . . His speculations are nowhere dragged in awkwardly; they are almost always aroused by the scenery and people with whom he is surrounded, or by the incidents in which he is taking part. . . . However much some of our readers may disagree with the conclusions at which he arrives, they will certainly allow that he writes clearly and vigorously. . . . This is a powerful and original book, and no one can rise from its perusal without having obtained valuable food for reflection. It will do no injury to true vital Christianity, but it indicates with merciless accuracy those 'spots in our feasts of charity' which too often render such feasts formal, meaningless, and lifeless. To the younger and more impulsive reader, however, we would give a caution. He may be troubled with Herbert Ainslie's doubts, but he is not likely to obtain Herbert Ainslie's opportunities. It is not given to every youth who hesitates, from scruples of conscience, to enter the ministry of the Church, to taste the delightful perils of semi-savage life, and then to find consolation and repose in the arms of such a lovely and sympathetic woman as Mary Travers is depicted."—*Times, December* 30, 1868.

TINSLEY BROTHERS, 18 CATHERINE ST., STRAND.

New and Enlarged Edition.
One Volume, crown 8vo, Seven Shillings and Sixpence.

THE NIGHT SIDE OF LONDON.

By JAMES EWING RITCHIE,
Author of "About London," &c.

"There is a matter-of-fact reality about the sketches, but they are chiefly remarkable for the moral tone of their reflections. Generally speaking, painters of these subjects rather throw a purple light over the actual scenes, and say nothing of the consequences to which they lead. Mr. Ritchie is ever stripping off the mask of the mock gaiety before him, and pointing the end to which it must finally come."—*Spectator.*

One Volume, fcap. 8vo, Five Shillings.

ABOUT LONDON.

By J. EWING RITCHIE,
Author of "The Night Side of London."

Two Volumes, 8vo, with Portraits, Thirty-six Shillings.

THE LIFE OF DAVID GARRICK.
FROM ORIGINAL FAMILY PAPERS, AND NUMEROUS PUBLISHED AND UNPUBLISHED SOURCES.

By PERCY FITZGERALD, M.A.

"Once taken up, it will not be easily laid down. Unquestionably, it is the most satisfactory biography that has yet appeared of our English Roscius."—*Examiner.*

"Mr. Fitzgerald is fairly entitled to be considered the only writer who has yet given us a 'Life of Garrick' worthy to be so called."—*Reader.*

"Pleasant reading in itself, and does credit to Mr. Fitzgerald's industry. We may recommend these volumes to the lovers of biography, and especially to lovers of the lives of actors."—*Athenæum.*

"These volumes are full to overflowing of interesting details which cannot fail to amuse the reader. . . We have found it vastly more entertaining than a sensational novel. . . The book is not merely readable, but highly amusing."—*Spectator.*

"A couple of handsomely-printed volumes, pleasantly written, rich in illustrations of the history of the stage, in pictures of social life, and in characteristic anecdotes of the notabilities with whom the great actor associated."—*Notes and Queries.*

TINSLEY BROTHERS, 18 CATHERINE ST., STRAND.

Two Volumes, 8vo, Thirty Shillings.

THE LIFE OF EDMUND KEAN.

FROM

VARIOUS PUBLISHED AND ORIGINAL SOURCES.

By F. W. HAWKINS.

"In all romance, in all literature, there is nothing more melancholy, nothing more utterly tragic, than the story of the career of Edmund Kean. So bitter and weary a struggle for a chance, so splendid and bewildering a success, so sad a waste of genius and fortune, so lamentable a fall, can hardly be found among all the records of the follies and sins and misfortunes of genius."—*Morning Star.*

Three Volumes, 8vo, £2 2s. Second Edition.

MEMOIRS OF THE LIFE

AND

REIGN OF GEORGE III.

WITH ORIGINAL LETTERS OF THE KING, AND OTHER UNPUBLISHED MSS.

By J. HENEAGE JESSE,

Author of "The Court of England under the Stuarts," &c.

"The very nature of his subject has given these volumes peculiar interest."—*Times.*

"Here, however, we must part with Mr. Jesse, not without renewed thanks for the amusement which he has given us."—*Quarterly Review.*

"Mr. Jesse's volumes are brimful of amusement and interest."—*Spectator.*

"Mr. Jesse's book is one to be eagerly read, and enjoyed to a degree rarely experienced in the perusal of English memoirs."—*Morning Post.*

"Nor do we hesitate to recommend the result of his labours to general even more than to studious readers, satisfied that whilst unconsciously imbibing instructive information, they will be carried along from chapter to chapter by a keen sense of intense and unflagging amusement."—*Daily Telegraph.*

TINSLEY BROTHERS, 18 CATHERINE ST., STRAND.

Two Volumes, 8vo, Thirty Shillings.

THE MARRIED LIFE OF ANNE OF AUSTRIA,

QUEEN OF FRANCE, MOTHER OF LOUIS XIV.;

AND THE

HISTORY OF DON SEBASTIAN,

KING OF PORTUGAL.

HISTORICAL STUDIES. FROM NUMEROUS UNPUBLISHED SOURCES.

By MARTHA WALKER FREER.

"The married life of Anne of Austria as the Queen of Louis XIII., and her subsequent life as his widow and Regent of France, constitute one of the most important phases in French history, and certainly one of the best topics that a writer, up in the curious revelations of the French memoirs relating thereto, could select to make an amusing and even fascinating book. We have here a book entertaining in a high degree, and authentic as far as it goes; discriminating even in special transactions—full of choice materials well combined."—*Times.*

Four Volumes, 8vo, Sixty Shillings.

HISTORY OF FRANCE UNDER THE BOURBONS, 1589-1830.

By CHARLES DUKE YONGE,

Regius Professor, Queen's College, Belfast.

Volumes I. and II. contain the Reigns of Henry IV., Louis XIII. and XIV.; Volumes III. and IV. contain the Reigns of Louis XV. and XVI.

Two Volumes, 8vo, Thirty Shillings.

THE REGENCY OF ANNE OF AUSTRIA,

QUEEN OF FRANCE, MOTHER OF LOUIS XIV.

FROM PUBLISHED AND UNPUBLISHED SOURCES. WITH PORTRAIT.

By MISS FREER.

TINSLEY BROTHERS, 18 CATHERINE ST., STRAND.

Two Volumes, post 8vo, Twenty-five Shillings.

THE STORY OF THE DIAMOND NECKLACE,

Told in detail for the first time, chiefly by the aid of Original Letters, Official and other Documents, and Contemporary Memoirs recently made public; and comprising a

SKETCH OF THE LIFE OF THE COUNTESS DE LA MOTTE
(Pretended Confidante of Marie Antoinette),

And Particulars of the Careers of the other Actors in this remarkable Drama.

By HENRY VIZETELLY.

Illustrated with an exact representation of the Diamond Necklace, and a Portrait of the Countess de la Motte, engraved on steel.

"We can, without fear of contradiction, describe the 'Story of the Diamond Necklace' as a book of thrilling interest."—*Standard.*

"Mr. Vizetelly has performed his work admirably. His two volumes are absorbing in their interest, and after a perusal of them the best novels are dull."—*Daily Telegraph.*

Two Volumes, 8vo.

THE LIFE AND TIMES OF MARGARET OF ANJOU.

By MRS. HOOKHAM.

Two Volumes, Twenty-one Shillings.

MORNINGS OF THE RECESS IN 1861-4.

Being a Series of Literary and Biographical Papers, reprinted and revised from the "Times," by permission, by the Author.

TINSLEY BROTHERS, 18 CATHERINE ST., STRAND.

Two Volumes, post 8vo, Twenty-one Shillings.

BIOGRAPHIES AND PORTRAITS
OF SOME
CELEBRATED PEOPLE.

By ALPHONSE DE LAMARTINE.

Two volumes, crown 8vo, Twenty-five Shillings.

JOHNNY ROBINSON:
THE STORY OF THE CHILDHOOD AND SCHOOLDAYS OF AN "INTELLIGENT ARTISAN."

By the AUTHOR OF "SOME HABITS AND CUSTOMS OF THE WORKING CLASSES."

Two Volumes, crown 8vo, Twenty-one Shillings.

AFTER BREAKFAST.

By GEORGE AUGUSTUS SALA.

DANTE'S DIVINA COMMEDIA. Translated into English in the Metre and Triple Rhyme of the Original. By Mrs. RAMSAY. 3 vols. 18s.

WIT AND WISDOM FROM WEST AFRICA; or, a Book of Proverbial Philosophy, Idioms, Enigmas, and Laconisms. Compiled by RICHARD F. BURTON, Author of "A Mission to Dahomey," "A Pilgrimage to El-Medinah and Meccah," &c. 12s. 6d.

CON AMORE; OR, CRITICAL CHAPTERS. By JUSTIN M'CARTHY, Author of "The Waterdale Neighbours." Post 8vo, 12s.

THE SAVAGE CLUB PAPERS. A Volume of Literary and Artistic Contributions, by numerous Authors and Artists of eminence. 12s. Also the Second Series, for 1868. 12s.

THREE HUNDRED YEARS OF A NORMAN HOUSE. With Genealogical Miscellanies. By JAMES HANNAY, Author of "A Course of English Literature," "Satire and Satirists," &c. 12s.

TINSLEY BROTHERS, 18 CATHERINE ST., STRAND.

ENGLISH PHOTOGRAPHS. By An American. 8vo, 12s.

THE HISTORY OF MONACO. By H. Pemberton. 8vo, 12s.

BRITISH SENATORS; or, Political Sketches, Past and Present. By J. Ewing Ritchie. Post 8vo, 10s. 6d.

MASANIELLO OF NAPLES. By Mrs. Horace St. John. Crown 8vo, 10s. 6d.

BORDER AND BASTILLE. By the Author of "Guy Livingstone," "Barren Honour," &c. 8vo, 10s. 6d.

A SAXON'S REMEDY FOR IRISH DISCONTENT. Crown 8vo, 9s.

THE PUBLIC LIFE OF LORD MACAULAY. By Frederick Arnold, B.A. of Christ Church, Oxford. Post 8vo, 7s. 6d.

CHATEAU FRISSAC; or, HOME SCENES IN FRANCE. By the Author of "Photographs of Paris Life." Crown 8vo, 7s. 6d.

THE LAW: WHAT I HAVE SEEN, WHAT I HAVE HEARD, AND WHAT I HAVE KNOWN. By Cyrus Jay. Post 8vo, 7s. 6d.

A BUNDLE OF BALLADS. Edited by the Author of "Guy Livingstone." Small 4to, 6s. 6d.

FISH HATCHING, AND THE ARTIFICIAL CULTURE OF FISH. By Frank Buckland. With five Illustrations. Crown 8vo, 5s.

DUTCH PICTURES. With some Sketches in the Flemish Manner. By George Augustus Sala. Crown 8vo, 5s.

TINSLEY BROTHERS'
NEW NOVELS.

THE CRUST AND THE CAKE. By the Author of "Occupations of a Retired Life." 3 vols.

A COUNTY FAMILY. A Novel. By the Author of "Lost Sir Massingberd," &c. 3 vols.

TINSLEY BROTHERS, 18 CATHERINE ST,, STRAND.

THE WYVERN MYSTERY. A Novel. By J. S. LE FANU, Author of "Uncle Silas," "Guy Deverell," "Haunted Lives," &c. 3 vols.

THE BUCKHURST VOLUNTEERS. By J. M. CAPES, M.A., Author of "The Mosaic-Worker's Daughter." 3 vols.

UP AND DOWN THE WORLD. By the Author of "Never—for Ever." 3 vols.

LOST FOOTSTEPS. A Novel. By JOSEPH VEREY. 3 vols.

THE GAGE OF HONOUR. By Captain J. T. NEWALL. 3 vols.

MARTHA PLANEBARKE. A Novel. 3 vols.

DAISIE'S DREAM. By the Author of "Recommended to Mercy," &c. 3 vols.

WEE WIFIE. By ROSA NOUCHETTE CAREY, Author of "Nellie's Memories." 3 vols.

OBERON'S SPELL. A Novel. 3 vols.

SIMPLE AS A DOVE. By the Author of "Olive Varcoe." Second Edition. 3 vols.

NETHERTON-ON-SEA. A Story. 3 vols.

STRETTON. By HENRY KINGSLEY, Author of "Geoffry Hamlyn," &c. 3 vols.

FALSE COLOURS. By ANNIE THOMAS (Mrs. PENDER CUD-LIP), Author of "Denis Donne." 3 vols.

MY ENEMY'S DAUGHTER. A Novel. By JUSTIN M'CAR-THY, Author of "The Waterdale Neighbours," "Paul Massie," &c. 3 vols.

"We do not pretend to have made any great discovery in the novel before us, Mr. M'Carthy being already well known to all lovers of pure and wholesome fiction; but none the less are we of opinion that a novel which has a purpose and a character so distinct from the ordinary run of stories should be instantly distinguished and warmly commended. . . . . It is given to few of our living writers of fiction to create such an interest in their imaginary personages as Mr. M'Carthy has done in his touching story of Christina Braun. It is a sad story, as we say, but it is a very real and a very true one. The vividness of the characters, the subdued and artistic fashion in which the narrative of their lives is told, the fine interpretation of every-day moods and feelings, and the dramatic descriptions of more powerful passions, evidence in every page of the book the hand of a master. The novel is worthy of the author who gave us the 'Waterdale Neighbours.'"—*Examiner.*

TINSLEY BROTHERS, 18 CATHERINE ST., STRAND.

BREAKING A BUTTERFLY; OR, BLANCHE ELLERSLIE'S ENDING. By the Author of "Guy Livingstone," &c. 3 vols.

THE GIRL HE MARRIED. By JAMES GRANT, Author of "The Romance of War," "First Love and Last Love," &c. 3 vols.

IN SILK ATTIRE. By WILLIAM BLACK, Author of "Love or Marriage." 3 vols. Second Edition.

ALL BUT LOST. By G. A. HENTY, Author of "The March to Magdala." 3 vols.

A LONDON ROMANCE. By CHARLES H. ROSS. 3 vols.

NEVERMORE; OR, BURNT BUTTERFLIES. By JOHN GAUNT. 2 vols.

FATAL ZERO. By the Author of "Polly," &c. 2 vols.

HOME FROM INDIA. By JOHN POMEROY. 2 vols.

THE TOWN TALK OF CLYDA. By the Author of "One Foot in the Grave." 2 vols.

ONLY A WOMAN'S LOVE. By the EARL OF DESART. 2 vols.

TWICE REFUSED. By CHARLES E. STIRLING. 2 vols.

FOUND DEAD. By the Author of "Lost Sir Massingberd." 1 vol.

A PERFECT TREASURE. A Novel. 1 vol.

TINSLEY BROTHERS' POPULAR NOVELS.

Published at 10s. 6d. per Volume.

EQUAL TO EITHER FORTUNE. A Novel. By the Author of "A Man of Mark," &c. 3 vols.

UNDER LOCK AND KEY. A Novel. By THOMAS SPEIGHT, Author of "Brought to Light," &c. 3 vols.

TINSLEY BROTHERS, 18 CATHERINE ST., STRAND.

MAD: A STORY OF DUST AND ASHES. By GEORGE MANVILLE FENN, Author of "Bent, not Broken." 3 vols.

STRANGE WORK. By THOMAS ARCHER. 3 vols.

NELLIE'S MEMORIES: A DOMESTIC STORY. By ROSA NOUCHETTE CAREY. 3 vols.

CLARISSA. A Novel. By SAMUEL RICHARDSON. Edited by E. S. DALLAS, Author of "The Gay Science," &c. 3 vols.

HAUNTED LIVES. By J. S. LE FANU. 3 vols.

ANNE HEREFORD. By Mrs. HENRY WOOD, Author of "East Lynne," &c. 3 vols.

LOVE, OR MARRIAGE? By WILLIAM BLACK. 3 vols.

JOHN HALLER'S NIECE. By the Author of "Never—for Ever." 3 vols.

NEIGHBOURS AND FRIENDS. By the Hon. Mrs. HENRY WEYLAND CHETWYND, Author of "Three Hundred a Year." 3 vols.

MARTYRS TO FASHION. By JOSEPH VEREY. 3 vols.

A HOUSE OF CARDS. By Mrs. CASHEL HOEY. 3 vols.

THE MOONSTONE. By WILKIE COLLINS, Author of "The Woman in White." 3 vols. Second Edition.

OUT OF THE MESHES. A Story in 3 vols.

DIANA GAY. By PERCY FITZGERALD. 3 vols.

THE RED COURT FARM. By Mrs. HENRY WOOD, Author of "East Lynne," "Trevelyn Hold," &c. 3 vols.

THE TWO RUBIES. By the Author of "Recommended to Mercy," &c. 3 vols.

WILD AS A HAWK. By Mrs. MACQUOID, Author of "Hester Kirton," &c. 3 vols.

THE SEABOARD PARISH. By GEORGE MAC DONALD, Author of "Alec Forbes of Howglen," &c. 3 vols.

THE OCCUPATIONS OF A RETIRED LIFE. By EDWARD GARRET. 3 vols.

THE LOST LINK. By TOM HOOD, Author of "A Golden Heart," &c. 3 vols.

TINSLEY BROTHERS, 18 CATHERINE ST., STRAND.

FRANCESCA'S LOVE. By Mrs. EDWARD PULLEYNE. 3 vols.

THE DEAR GIRL. By PERCY FITZGERALD, Author of "Never Forgotten," "Seventy-five Brooke Street," &c. 3 vols.

SINK OR SWIM? By the Author of "Recommended to Mercy," &c. 3 vols.

HIGH STAKES. By ANNIE THOMAS (Mrs. PENDER CUDLIP), Author of "Called to Account." 3 vols.

ONLY TO BE MARRIED. By Mrs. FLORENCE WILLIAMSON, Author of "Frederick Rivers," &c. 3 vols.

CHARLOTTE BURNEY. By KATHERINE S. MACQUOID, Author of "Hester Kirton," "By the Sea," &c. 3 vols.

GIANT DESPAIR. By MORLEY FARROW. 3 vols.

THE TENANTS OF MALORY. By J. S. LE FANU, Author of "Uncle Silas," "The House by the Churchyard," &c., &c. 3 vols.

A SEARCH FOR A SECRET. By G. A. HENTY. 3 vols.

A GOLDEN HEART. By TOM HOOD. 3 vols.

SOWING THE WIND. By Mrs. E. LYNN LINTON, Author of "Lizzie Lorton of Greyrigg," &c. 3 vols.

THE DOCTOR OF BEAUWEIR. By WILLIAM GILBERT, Author of "Shirley Hall Asylum," "Dr. Austin's Guests," &c., &c. 2 vols.

THE GOVERNOR'S DAUGHTER. By HENRY SUTHERLAND EDWARDS, Author of "The Three Louisas," &c. 2 vols.

POLLY: A VILLAGE PORTRAIT. 2 vols.

CAPTAIN JACK; OR, THE GREAT VAN BROEK PROPERTY. By JAMES A. MAITLAND. 2 vols.

JOHN TWILLER: A ROMANCE OF THE HEART. By D. STARKEY, LL.D. 1 vol.

BURIED ALONE. A Story. By a New Writer. 1 vol.

TINSLEY BROTHERS, 18 CATHERINE ST., STRAND.

THREE HUNDRED A YEAR. By the Hon. Mrs. HENRY WEYLAND CHETWYND. 2 vols.

CALLED TO ACCOUNT. By ANNIE THOMAS, Author of "Dennis Donne," "Sir Victor's Choice," &c. 3 vols.

THE TALLANTS OF BARTON. By JOSEPH HATTON, Author of "Bitter Sweets," &c. 3 vols.

WEBS IN THE WAY. By GEORGE MANVILLE FENN, Author of "Bent, not Broken," &c. 3 vols.

HIDDEN FIRE. 3 vols.

TAKEN UPON TRUST. By the Author of "Recommended to Mercy," &c. 3 vols.

THE SECOND MRS. TILLOTSON. By PERCY FITZGERALD, Author of "Bella Donna," "Jenny Bell," &c. 3 vols.

THE OLD LEDGER. By G. L. M. STRAUSS. 3 vols.

WHAT MONEY CAN'T DO. By the Author of "Altogether Wrong." 3 vols.

ONE AGAINST THE WORLD. By the Author of "Abel Drake's Wife," &c. 3 vols.

BITTER SWEETS. A Love Story. By JOSEPH HATTON. 3 vols.

WEIGHED IN THE BALANCE. By JAMES A. ST. JOHN. 3 vols.

A WOMAN'S WAY. By the Author of "The Field of Life." 3 vols.

GUY WATERMAN. By the Author of "Abel Drake's Wife." 3 vols.

THE LOVE THAT KILLS. By W. G. WILLS, Author of "The Wife's Evidence." 3 vols.

DACIA SINGLETON. By the Author of "What Money can't Do," "Altogether Wrong," &c. 3 vols.

BENT, NOT BROKEN. By GEORGE MANVILLE FENN. 3 vols.

TINSLEY BROTHERS, 18 CATHERINE ST., STRAND.

PAUL MASSIE. A Romance. 3 vols.

CARLETON GRANGE. By the Author of "Abbot's Cleve." 3 vols.

ALTOGETHER WRONG. By the Author of "The World's Furniture." 3 vols.

EMILY FOINDER. By F. Devonshire. 3 vols.

HAZEL COMBE; or, the Golden Rule. By the Author of "Recommended to Mercy," "Taken upon Trust," &c. 3 vols.

SOWING THE WIND. By Mrs. E. Lynn Linton, Author of "Lizzie Lorton of Greyrigg," &c. 3 vols.

SEVENTY-FIVE BROOKE STREET. By Percy Fitzgerald, Author of "The Second Mrs. Tillotson." 3 vols.

THE FORLORN HOPE. By Edmund Yates, Author of "Black Sheep," "Kissing the Rod," &c. 3 vols.

THE CLIVES OF BURCOT. By Hesba Stretton, Author of "The Travelling Post-Office" in "Mugby Junction." 3 vols.

ADA MOORE'S STORY. 3 vols.

MORE THAN A MATCH. By the Author of "Recommended to Mercy," &c. 3 vols.

JESSIE'S EXPIATION. By Oswald Boyle. 3 vols.

IRKDALE: A Lancashire Story. By Benjamin Brierley. 2 vols.

JOHN NEVILLE: Soldier, Sportsman, and Gentleman. By Captain J. T. Newall. 2 vols.

TINSLEY BROTHERS, 18 *CATHERINE ST., STRAND.*

TINSLEY BROTHERS'

SERIES OF

SEVEN-AND-SIXPENNY WORKS.

Handsomely bound in bevelled boards.

❖

MAXIMS BY A MAN OF THE WORLD. By the Author of "Lost Sir Massingberd."

THE ADVENTURES OF A BRIC-A-BRAC HUNTER. By Major BYNG HALL.

TOWN AND COUNTRY SKETCHES. By ANDREW HALLIDAY, Author of "Sunnyside Papers."

A COURSE OF ENGLISH LITERATURE. By JAMES HANNAY. Suitable for Students and Schools.

MODERN CHARACTERISTICS: A SERIES OF ESSAYS FROM THE "SATURDAY REVIEW." Revised by the Author.

SUNNYSIDE PAPERS. By ANDREW HALLIDAY, Author of "Everyday Papers," &c.

ESSAYS IN DEFENCE OF WOMEN. Crown 8vo, handsomely bound in cloth, gilt, bevelled boards.

New Edition, revised, of " Everyday Papers."

EVERYDAY PAPERS. Reprinted from "All the Year Round," and adapted for Evening Reading at Mechanics' Institutes, Penny Reading Clubs, &c. By ANDREW HALLIDAY. 5s.

TINSLEY BROTHERS, 18 CATHERINE ST., STRAND.

A NEW WORK BY "THE JOURNEYMAN ENGINEER."

One Volume, Seven and Sixpence.

THE GREAT UNWASHED.

By "The Journeyman Engineer,"
Author of "Some Habits and Customs of the Working Classes."

"When we say we wish his book could be largely read among his own class, we do not mean to say that it is only suited to them. It is, as we think we have shown, a book that everybody ought to read; for everybody must be anxious to know what sort of folks 'our future masters' really are."—*Imperial Review.*

"For the second part, which may be regarded as padding introduced to bring up the publication to the size of an honest volume, we can say no more than that its light and rather 'scrappy' papers are amusing, and in no way below the average standard of magazine literature. But much higher praise is due to the new articles."—*Athenæum.*

"It deals with the working classes, to quote the author, 'in their public relations, and with the phases of the inner,' or, rather, their domestic, 'life.' Their relations to the Church and to politics are among the subjects treated under the first head; their club-houses, pay-days, Saturday trading, night-work, and cheap literature, come under the last."—*Star.*

"The work is full of valuable information, a considerable portion of which will be new to those who have not heretofore duly estimated the importance of acquiring a thorough acquaintance with the habits and feelings of the majority of their fellow-countrymen."—*The Observer.*

TINSLEY BROTHERS, 18 CATHERINE ST., STRAND.

*By the same Author, uniform with "The Great Unwashed,"
One Volume, Seven and Sixpence.*

SOME HABITS AND CUSTOMS
OF THE
WORKING CLASSES.

———◆———

"Readers who care to know what a spokesman of the working classes has to say for his order will find this a capital book. The writer is a clever fellow; but he is more than that."—*Athenæum.*

"The book is written in a plain, straightforward style, with an entire absence of humbug. It sets before us a very intelligible picture, and one which we may assume to be substantially correct, of the manners and habits of the classes whom he wishes to describe."—*Saturday Review.*

"We are distinctly of opinion that a more just representation of the working man himself has never appeared in print."—*Pall Mall Gazette.*

"We have here, in a book lately published, a monograph of the working classes, by one of themselves, which speaks with clear utterance, neither exaggerating nor extenuating."—*All the Year Round.*

"Professing only to describe some modern characteristics of the working classes, it fastens on all the most important, and is likely to throw some useful light on the subject."—*Examiner.*

TINSLEY BROTHERS, 18 *CATHERINE ST., STRAND.*

TINSLEY BROTHERS'
CHEAP EDITIONS OF POPULAR NOVELS.

By Mrs. J. RIDDELL, Author of "George Geith," &c.

FAR ABOVE RUBIES. 6s.	PHEMIE KELLER. 6s.
RACE FOR WEALTH. 6s.	MAXWELL DREWITT. 6s.
GEORGE GEITH. 6s.	TOO MUCH ALONE. 6s.
THE RICH HUSBAND. 6s.	CITY AND SUBURB. 6s.

By Mrs. HENRY WOOD, Author of "East Lynne," &c.

ELSTER'S FOLLY. 6s.	MILDRED ARKELL. 6s.
ST. MARTIN'S EVE. 6s.	TREVLYN HOLD. 6s.

By the Author of "Guy Livingstone."

SWORD AND GOWN. 4s. 6d.	MAURICE DERING. 6s.
BARREN HONOUR. 6s.	GUY LIVINGSTONE. 5s.
BRAKESPEARE. 6s.	SANS MERCI. 6s.

Also, now ready, uniform with the above.

THE ROCK AHEAD. By EDMUND YATES. 6s.

THE ADVENTURES OF DR. BRADY. By W. H. RUSSELL, LL.D. 6s.

BLACK SHEEP. By EDMUND YATES, Author of "The Rock Ahead," &c.

NOT WISELY, BUT TOO WELL. By the Author of "Cometh up as a Flower." 6s.

LIZZIE LORTON OF GREYRIGG. By Mrs. LYNN LINTON, Author of "Sowing the Wind," &c. 6s.

ARCHIE LOVELL. By the Author of "The Morals of Mayfair," &c. 6s.

MISS FORRESTER. By the Author of "Archie Lovell," &c. 6s.

RECOMMENDED TO MERCY. By the Author of "Sink or Swim?" 6s.

TINSLEY BROTHERS, 18 CATHERINE ST., STRAND.

TINSLEY BROTHERS'
TWO-SHILLING VOLUMES.

Uniformly bound in Illustrated Wrappers.

To be had at every Railway Stall and of every Bookseller in the Kingdom.

THE ADVENTURES OF DR. BRADY. By W. H. Russell, LL.D.

NOT WISELY, BUT TOO WELL. By the Author of "Cometh up as a Flower."

SANS MERCI. By the Author of "Guy Livingstone."

RECOMMENDED TO MERCY. By the Author of "Sink or Swim?"

THE ROCK AHEAD. By Edmund Yates, Author of "Black Sheep," &c.

MAURICE DERING. By the Author of "Guy Livingstone," &c.

THE WATERDALE NEIGHBOURS. By Justin M'Carthy, Author of "Paul Massie," &c.

THE PRETTY WIDOW. By Charles H. Ross.

MISS FORRESTER. By the Author of "Archie Lovell."

BLACK SHEEP. By Edmund Yates.

BARREN HONOUR. By the Author of "Guy Livingstone."

SWORD AND GOWN. By the same Author.

THE DOWER-HOUSE. By Annie Thomas (Mrs. Pender Cudlip), Author of "Denis Donne," &c.

THE SAVAGE CLUB PAPERS (1867). With all the Original Illustrations; also the Second Series for 1868.

TINSLEY BROTHERS, 18 *CATHERINE ST., STRAND.*

Now ready, in One Volume, price Two Shillings, the Cheap Edition of

NOT WISELY, BUT TOO WELL.

By the AUTHOR OF "COMETH UP AS A FLOWER."

"We could select many powerful and eloquent passages from this book, but we will leave our readers to find them out for themselves. The novel is decidedly clever, and belongs to a much higher category than the mass of tame, colourless nonentities which every season sends forth."—*Times.*

"The description of Kate's delight when she first discovers that her hero loves her, is very different from what we are accustomed to find in ordinary novels, and so is the account of her state of mind when she has entirely given herself up to the luxury of loving him. . . . . As the study of the effects of a great passion on such a mind as hers, the record of her unwise love is decidedly interesting, and its merits are greatly enhanced by the fact of its being written in a bold, vigorous style."—*Saturday Review.*

"The author expresses through fiction an emotion, a doubt, a sentiment—call it what you will—which has rarely been expressed except in poetry, but which surges up now and again in the mind of every human being with a mind at all, beaten back by the pious, indulged by the pleasure-loving—a feeling not only that all is Vanity, but that all ought not to be, that there is some mistake, some misarrangement, some failure in the grand scheme."—*Spectator.*

Also, now ready, price Two Shillings, uniform with the above,

THE ADVENTURES OF DR. BRADY.

By W. H. RUSSELL, LL.D.

"The novel is one which succeeds in holding the attention in an unusual degree. . . . . We can remember few stories so rich in incident and adventure, or so full of change and variety, as that which Dr. Brady relates of himself and his acquaintance. . . . . It is not a novel of the ordinary type; but it is everywhere full of interest of the purest kind; and we know of few recent books which we could recommend with greater confidence to the general reader."—*Times.*

"As might be expected, Dr. Russell has written a powerful and interesting work. The characters are lifelike and attractive, and, what is far more in these days, original; and this alone would distinguish it from the ordinary novels of the day."—*Athenæum.*

"'The Adventures of Dr. Brady' is a very clever, a very interesting, and a most instructive work, and cannot fail to raise even to a higher level the well-earned reputation of the author."—*Morning Post.*

TINSLEY BROTHERS, 18 CATHERINE ST., STRAND.

TINSLEYS' MAGAZINE:

An Illustrated Monthly.

PRICE ONE SHILLING.

OPINIONS OF THE PRESS.

"*Tinsley* is fast making head into the first ranks of the shilling monthlies; both as regards matter and illustrations it is running hard all other competitors. Mrs. Henry Wood's story, 'George Canterbury's Will,' is one of the best she has written."—*Cambridge Chronicle.*

"Well edited, well written, well illustrated, and produced in a neat and handsome style, it can hardly fail to achieve success."—*Daily Telegraph.*

"'The Adventures of Dr. Brady' open with all the dash, spirit, and descriptive power which are naturally to be looked for from their author, and are pervaded also by a keen, easy, racy humour, which, if it be necessary to institute any comparison for so good a thing, will remind the reader of Theodore Hook, in the best style of his best days. Since Cuthbert Gurney came home from India, and carried surprise and desolation into the bosom of his family, no 'Exile of Ind' has appeared to compare with the trio composed of Master Brady, Mohun, and Jacko."—*Morning Post.*

"This enterprise of Dr. Russell's in a new field seems likely to bring him fresh laurels. The story so far keeps to the soil of Ireland, and the style is something like that of Charles Lever suddenly endowed with depth and strength, and a gleam of bright imagination."—*Star.*

"Right well does it look, and right well does it read. Its contributors are men of mark; and they have not merely given their names, but their brains. Dr. William Russell opens with a capital beginning of

---

TINSLEY BROTHERS, 18 *CATHERINE ST., STRAND.*

such a story as it is a thousand wonders and pities he has not penned before. . . . . . It is illustrated with a neatly-coloured fashion-plate, which is quite an innovation in a high-class periodical publication, but an innovation that will not be unwelcome to the sex which chiefly reads magazines."—*Standard.*

"The wit is genial, and the satire pungent without the least cynicism. There is one feature, however, that must not be unmentioned, inasmuch as it is wholly a novelty in the serial literature of the day—a clever and thoroughly reliable description of the latest Parisian fashions, which must commend itself to hosts of ladies, both young and old, and secure their favourable consideration."—*Bell's Weekly Messenger.*

"The new magazine—which, we ought to say, is very handsomely appointed in typographic and exterior matters—is ably illustrated; and one of its features is an elaborate notice of the Paris fashions, with coloured and other illustrations—a bait, and not a bad one, for lady readers."—*Westmoreland Gazette and Kendal Advertiser.*

"The article, which is very elaborate, going into all the details of costume from bonnet to boots, is written with much care, and yet with a pleasant dash. Altogether *Tinsleys' Magazine* is a magazine for the day. There is great freshness in the articles—not only in their treatment, but in their subjects. The magazine is very readable. We may add that it is beautifully illustrated with engravings on wood, and that it is admirably printed."—*Arbroath Guide.*

"A novel feature is presented in the devotion of an article to a subject which cannot fail to enlist the sympathies of the ladies—and that is, 'Paris Fashions.' The fair sex, married or single, have only to ask for *Tinsleys' Magazine* and they will get to know all about the latest designs in bathing dresses, *toilettes de campagne* or *soirée*, or the most recent discoveries in chignons."—*Dewsbury Chronicle.*

"The general style of the publication is excellent: good paper, attractive type, well drawn and carefully engraved illustrations, and, above all, the readable nature of the contents, serve at once to give it a high position in the ranks of periodical literature."—*Carmarthen Journal.*

"It is a splendid shilling's worth—even as shilling's worths in magazines now go."—*Birmingham Daily Gazette*

"Here is another wonderful shilling's worth—wonderful not so much for the amount of matter contained in one hundred and twenty-eight beautifully printed double-column pages, as for the eminence and well-

---

TINSLEY BROTHERS, 18 CATHERINE ST., STRAND.

known worth of its writers, the diversity of its subjects, and the beauty of its illustrations. . . . . The number opens with 'The Adventures of Dr. Brady,' an Irish story of great promise, by Dr. Russell. The scenes are drawn with that graphic power and force for which Dr. Russell has no living rival."—*Aberystwith Observer.*

"*Tinsleys'* has made its appearance, and looks as though it would make its way. Paper, print, illustrations, editor, and contributors, all look well."—*Bookseller.*

"The new magazine bids fair to take a high place among English literature."—*Kentish Gazette.*

"There is much sparkle of fun, glow of sentiment, and rare descriptive power in Dr. Russell's chapters."—*Whitehaven Herald.*

"*Tinsleys' Magazine* promises to be in every way a success."—*Aberdeen Herald.*

"The contributions to the opening number of this new literary candidate for public favour are all of a high mark."—*Star of Gwent.*

"In outward appearance it is chaste and elegant, and the interior is a nice specimen of the typographical art."—*Merioneth Standard.*

"The getting-up of the magazine is highly credible to the publishers, editor, and authors alike."—*Swansea Journal.*

Tinsley never appears without a sterling article of interest either to sportsmen or naturalists."—*Land and Water.*

"A landscape illustrative to a poem, 'The Shortest Way Home,' is the prettiest picture in any illustrated magazine of the present month." —*Glasgow Free Press.*

"This new monthly is richly embellished, and is very cheap at a shilling."—*Staffordshire Sentinel.*

"The illustrations are superior, especially a landscape to accompany a poetical sketch drawn by a practised hand with a good eye for perspective and a capital finger for finish."—*Dover Telegraph.*

"If continued in the style in which it has been commenced it cannot fail to insure an extensive circulation."—*Gravesend Free Press.*

"A marvellous shilling's worth."—*Fifeshire Journal.*

TINSLEY BROTHERS, 18 CATHERINE ST., STRAND.

"Exteriorly it has an attractive appearance, and interiorly it is well got up, printed with excellent type in the antique style, and the illustrations are first class."—*Wrexham Advertiser.*

"The woodcut illustrating the pretty little poem called 'The Shortest Way Home,' is a perfect gem."—*Essex and West Suffolk Gazette.*

"'Dr. Brady's Adventures' gives great promise of Irish nature and character above the written average."—*Auckland Chronicle.*

"Dr. Russell's account of 'The Adventures of Dr. Brady' will turn out a first-rate Irish novel."—*London Scotsman.*

"Printed on good paper, with excellent type, and contains articles to suit all tastes."—*Buckingham Express.*

"Handsomely printed and illustrated, with double-column pages, and specially caters for the ladies by giving a coloured fashion-plate and an article upon the fashions."—*Northern Daily Express.*

"The latest Paris fashions are most elegantly drawn, and an accurate description given of the new modes of dressing the hair."—*Bucks Herald.*

"A new candidate for public favour, and we are bound to say, after an attentive perusal of its contents, that it well deserves it."—*Preston Herald.*

"'The Adventures of Dr. Brady,' by W. H. Russell, LL.D., certainly gives proof of becoming a first class serial tale."—*Barrow Times.*

"In addition to the usual literary topics *Tinsleys' Magazine* contains a new feature—Paris fashions well written and well illustrated."—*Halesworth Times.*

"Destined, we think, to win early a good place in public favour."—*Bath Chronicle.*

"Is beautifully printed in good clear type, is tastefully illustrated, and in every way well got up."—*Northampton Herald.*

"It is lively, clever, and interesting."—*Coventry Standard.*

"Very much better than the average."—*Andover Advertiser.*

TINSLEY BROTHERS, 18 *CATHERINE ST., STRAND.*

"It is neatly got up, is well printed on good paper, with a new, neat, and clear type, and there are five or six clever illustrations."—*Alloa Advertiser.*

"Must rapidly become a favourite with those who appreciate first-class productions."—*Blandford Express.*

"Paper, print, illustrations, editor, contributors, all look well."—*Derbyshire Courier.*

"Calculated to become highly popular, more especially among the ladies."—*Border Advertiser.*

TINSLEY BROTHERS, 18 CATHERINE ST., STRAND.

www.ingramcontent.com/pod-product-compliance
Lightning Source LLC
Chambersburg PA
CBHW030729230426
43667CB00007B/647